The Bahamas

WORLD BIBLIOGRAPHICAL SERIES

General Editors:
Robert G. Neville (Executive Editor)
John J. Horton   Ian Wallace
Hans H. Wellisch   Ralph Lee Woodward, Jr.

John J. Horton is Deputy Librarian of the University of Bradford and currently Chairman of its Academic Board of Studies in Social Sciences. He has maintained a longstanding interest in the discipline of area studies and its associated bibliographical problems, with special reference to European Studies. In particular he has published in the field of Icelandic and of Yugoslav studies, including the two relevant volumes in the World Bibliographical Series.

Ian Wallace is Professor of Modern Languages at Loughborough University of Technology. A graduate of Oxford in French and German, he also studied in Tübingen, Heidelberg and Lausanne before taking teaching posts at universities in the USA, Scotland and England. He specializes in East German affairs, especially literature and culture, on which he has published numerous articles and books. In 1979 he founded the journal *GDR Monitor*, which he continues to edit.

Hans H. Wellisch is Professor emeritus at the College of Library and Information Services, University of Maryland. He was President of the American Society of Indexers and was a member of the International Federation for Documentation. He is the author of numerous articles and several books on indexing and abstracting, and has published *The Conversion of Scripts* and *Indexing and Abstracting: an International Bibliography*. He also contributes frequently to *Journal of the American Society for Information Science, The Indexer* and other professional journals.

Ralph Lee Woodward, Jr. is Chairman of the Department of History at Tulane University, New Orleans, where he has been Professor of History since 1970. He is the author of *Central America, a Nation Divided*, 2nd ed. (1985), as well as several monographs and more than sixty scholarly articles on modern Latin America. He has also compiled volumes in the World Bibliographical Series on *Belize* (1980), *Nicaragua* (1983), and *El Salvador* (1988). Dr. Woodward edited the Central American section of the *Research Guide to Central America and the Caribbean* (1985) and is currently editor of the Central American history section of the *Handbook of Latin American Studies*.

VOLUME 108

The Bahamas

Paul G. Boultbee

Compiler

CLIO PRESS

OXFORD, ENGLAND · SANTA BARBARA, CALIFORNIA
DENVER, COLORADO

British Library Cataloguing in Publication Data

Boultbee, Paul G.
Bahamas. — (World bibliographical series, 108).
1. Bahamas – Bibliographies
I. Title   II. Series
016.97296

ISBN 1–85109–102–5

Clio Press Ltd.,
55 St. Thomas' Street,
Oxford OX1 1JG, England.

ABC-CLIO,
130 Cremona Drive,
Santa Barbara,
CA 93117, USA.

Designed by Bernard Crossland.
Typeset by Columns Design and Production Services, Reading, England.
Printed and bound in Great Britain by
Billing and Sons Ltd., Worcester.

THE WORLD BIBLIOGRAPHICAL SERIES

This series, which is principally designed for the English speaker, will eventually cover every country in the world, each in a separate volume comprising annotated entries on works dealing with its history, geography, economy and politics; and with its people, their culture, customs, religion and social organization. Attention will also be paid to current living conditions – housing, education, newspapers, clothing, etc. – that are all too often ignored in standard bibliographies; and to those particular aspects relevant to individual countries. Each volume seeks to achieve, by use of careful selectivity and critical assessment of the literature, an expression of the country and an appreciation of its nature and national aspirations, to guide the reader towards an understanding of its importance. The keynote of the series is to provide, in a uniform format, an interpretation of each country that will express its culture, its place in the world, and the qualities and background that make it unique. The views expressed in individual volumes, however, are not necessarily those of the publisher.

VOLUMES IN THE SERIES

1 *Yugoslavia*, John J. Horton
2 *Lebanon*, Shereen Khairallah
3 *Lesotho*, Shelagh M. Willet and David Ambrose
4 *Rhodesia/Zimbabwe*, Oliver B. Pollack and Karen Pollack
5 *Saudi Arabia*, Frank A. Clements
6 *USSR*, Anthony Thompson
7 *South Africa*, Reuben Musiker
8 *Malawi*, Robert B. Boeder
9 *Guatemala*, Woodman B. Franklin
11 *Uganda*, Robert L. Collison
12 *Malaysia*, Ian Brown and Rajeswary Ampalavanar
13 *France*, Frances Chambers
14 *Panama*, Eleanor DeSelms Langstaff
15 *Hungary*, Thomas Kabdebo
16 *USA*, Sheila R. Herstein and Naomi Robbins
17 *Greece*, Richard Clogg and Mary Jo Clogg
18 *New Zealand*, R. F. Grover
19 *Algeria*, Richard I. Lawless
20 *Sri Lanka*, Vijaya Samaraweera
21 *Belize*, Ralph Lee Woodward, Jr.
23 *Luxembourg*, Carlo Hury and Jul Christophory
24 *Swaziland*, Balam Nyeko
25 *Kenya*, Robert L. Collison
26 *India*, Brijen K. Gupta and Datta S. Kharbas
27 *Turkey*, Merel Güçlü
28 *Cyprus*, P. M. Kitromilides and M. L. Evriviades
29 *Oman*, Frank A. Clements
31 *Finland*, J. E. O. Screen
32 *Poland*, Richard C. Lewański
33 *Tunisia*, Allan M. Findlay, Anne M. Findlay and Richard I. Lawless
34 *Scotland*, Eric G. Grant
35 *China*, Peter Cheng
36 *Qatar*, P. T. H. Unwin
37 *Iceland*, John J. Horton
39 *Haiti*, Frances Chambers
40 *Sudan*, M. W. Daly
41 *Vatican City State*, Michael J. Walsh
42 *Iraq*, A. J. Abdulrahman
43 *United Arab Emirates*, Frank A. Clements
44 *Nicaragua*, Ralph Lee Woodward, Jr.
45 *Jamaica*, K. E. Ingram
46 *Australia*, I. Kepars

47 *Morocco*, Anne M. Findlay, Allan M. Findlay and Richard I. Lawless
48 *Mexico*, Naomi Robbins
49 *Bahrain*, P. T. H. Unwin
50 *The Yemens*, G. Rex Smith
51 *Zambia*, Anne M. Bliss and J. A. Rigg
52 *Puerto Rico*, Elena E. Cevallos
53 *Namibia*, Stanley Schoeman and Elna Schoeman
54 *Tanzania*, Colin Darch
55 *Jordan*, Ian J. Seccombe
56 *Kuwait*, Frank A. Clements
57 *Brazil*, Solena V. Bryant
58 *Israel*, Esther M. Snyder (preliminary compilation E. Kreiner)
59 *Romania*, Andrea Deletant and Dennis Deletant
60 *Spain*, Graham J. Shields
61 *Atlantic Ocean*, H. G. R. King
63 *Cameroon*, Mark W. DeLancey and Peter J. Schraeder
64 *Malta*, John Richard Thackrah
65 *Thailand*, Michael Watts
66 *Austria*, Denys Salt with the assistance of Arthur Farrand Radley
67 *Norway*, Leland B. Sather
68 *Czechoslovakia*, David Short
69 *Irish Republic*, Michael Owen Shannon
70 *Pacific Basin and Oceania*, Gerald W. Fry and Rufino Mauricio
71 *Portugal*, P. T. H. Unwin
72 *West Germany*, Donald S. Detwiler and Ilse E. Detwiler
73 *Syria*, Ian J. Seccombe
74 *Trinidad and Tobago*, Frances Chambers
76 *Barbados*, Robert B. Potter and Graham M. S. Dann
77 *East Germany*, Ian Wallace
78 *Mozambique*, Colin Darch
79 *Libya*, Richard I. Lawless

80 *Sweden*, Leland B. Sather and Alan Swanson
81 *Iran*, Reza Navabpour
82 *Dominica*, Robert A. Myers
83 *Denmark*, Kenneth E. Miller
84 *Paraguay*, R. Andrew Nickson
85 *Indian Ocean*, Julia J. Gotthold with the assistance of Donald W. Gotthold
86 *Egypt*, Ragai, N. Makar
87 *Gibraltar*, Graham J. Shields
88 *The Netherlands*, Peter King and Michael Wintle
89 *Bolivia*, Gertrude M. Yeager
90 *Papua New Guinea*, Fraiser McConnell
91 *The Gambia*, David P. Gamble
92 *Somalia*, Mark W. DeLancey, Sheila L. Elliott, December Green, Kenneth J. Menkhaus, Mohammad Haji Moqtar, Peter J. Schraeder
93 *Brunei*, Sylvia C. Engelen Krausse, Gerald H. Krausse
94 *Albania*, William B. Bland
95 *Singapore*, Stella R. Quah, Jon S. T. Quah
96 *Guyana*, Frances Chambers
97 *Chile*, Harold Blakemore
98 *El Salvador*, Ralph Lee Woodward, Jr.
99 *The Arctic*, H.G.R. King
100 *Nigeria*, Robert A. Myers
101 *Ecuador*, David Corkhill
102 *Uruguay*, Henry Finch with the assistance of Alicia Casas de Barrán
103 *Japan*, Frank Joseph Shulman
104 *Belgium*, R.C. Riley
105 *Macau*, Richard Louis Edmonds
106 *Philippines*, Jim Richardson
107 *Bulgaria*, Richard J. Crampton
108 *The Bahamas*, Paul G. Boultbee

For Glynis,
with all my love

Contents

INTRODUCTION xiii

THE COUNTRY AND ITS PEOPLE 1

GEOGRAPHY 5
    General 5
    Blue holes 6
    Maps and atlases 7

GEOLOGY 8

TRAVEL GUIDES 15
    General 15
    Individual islands 20
        Exuma 20
        Grand Bahama 20
        New Providence 20

TRAVELLERS' ACCOUNTS 22

TOURISM 27

FLORA AND FAUNA 29
    General 29
    Vegetation 32
    Marine life 36
    Birds 41
    Insects 46
    Mammals 46
    Molluscs 47
    Reptiles 48

PREHISTORY AND ARCHAEOLOGY 50
    The Lucayans 50
    Archaeology 52

Contents

HISTORY 55
    History of the Caribbean/West Indies   55
    General history of the Bahamas   56
    Columbus' first landfall in the New World   62
    The first settlers, 1629–84   68
    Buccaneers, 1684–1717   68
    The eighteenth century, 1717–1815   69
      The American Revolution   69
      The Loyalists   70
      The Seminole Negroes   72
    The nineteenth century, 1815–1914   73
    The twentieth century to independence, 1914–73   75
    The twentieth century after independence, 1973– .   78
    Individual islands   79
      Abaco   79
      Eleuthera   80
      Exuma   81
      Grand Bahama   81
      New Providence   82
      Paradise Island   83
      San Salvador   83

SLAVERY 84

POPULATION 88
    General   88
    Internal migration   89
    Minorities   90
    Overseas population   91

FOLKLORE 92

RELIGION 96

OBEAH 100

SOCIAL CONDITIONS 102

DRUG TRADE 109

HEALTH AND BUSH MEDICINE 112
    Health   112
    Bush medicine   113

POLITICS AND GOVERNMENT 115

CONSTITUTION AND LEGAL SYSTEM 120
    Constitution   120
    Legal system   122

Contents

ECONOMY 123

FINANCE AND BANKING 127

INDUSTRY, TRADE AND LABOUR 130
General 130
Specific industries 132

AGRICULTURE 135

POSTAL SYSTEM 136

ENVIRONMENT 137

STATISTICS 139

EDUCATION 141

LANGUAGES AND DIALECTS 143
General 143
Dictionaries 144

LITERATURE 145
Anthologies 145
Individual writers 146
Foreign literature set in the Bahamas 151

THE ARTS 155
Visual arts 155
Music 156
Festivals – Junkanoo 157
Architecture 157

FOOD AND DRINK 159

LIBRARIES AND ARCHIVES 160
Libraries 160
Archives 161

MASS MEDIA 163
Journalism 163
Newspapers 164

PERIODICALS 165

DIRECTORIES 166

BIBLIOGRAPHIES 167

Contents

INDEX OF AUTHORS, TITLES AND SUBJECTS 169

MAP OF THE BAHAMAS 197

Introduction

The Commonwealth of the Bahamas is an archipelago of some 700 islands and 2,400 cays, stretching from fifty miles off the southeast coast of Florida to fifty miles off the northwest coast of Cuba. The name comes from the Spanish *bajamar*, which means shallow sea. Only thirty of the islands are inhabited. According to the last census, conducted in 1980, the population is 209,505. Of this number, eighty-five per cent are black, most being the descendants of former slaves. Bahamian residents, and visitors, enjoy a tropical marine climate, moderated by the warm Gulf Stream. The islands themselves are long, flat, coral limestone formations with low rounded hills. The highest point in the country, 206 feet, is found on Cat Island.

Prior to the arrival of Columbus in the New World, the Bahamas were inhabited by a group of people who have come to be known as the Lucayans, which means 'island people'. Although little is known about these people, some information has been pieced together over the years. They came originally from South America but were driven north through the Caribbean by the Carib Indians. The gentle Lucayans were no match for the highly warlike, sometimes cannibalistic, Caribs. They fled, therefore, to the Bahama islands, where they had a rather idyllic, if somewhat meagre, existence until the arrival of Christopher Columbus in 1492.

Historians generally agree that Christopher Columbus first set foot in the New World somewhere in the Bahamas on 12 October, 1492. According to his *Journal*, or *Log* (q.v.), he landed on an island called Guanahani, renamed it San Salvador and claimed it for Spain. So San Salvador Island in the Bahamas, for a period called Watlings (or sometimes Watling) Island, is said to be the first landfall of Columbus. However, this has been disputed since at least 1625 and nine different islands have been proposed. The exact site of Columbus' first landfall may never be determined, but the fact that he made it in the Bahamas has rarely been in question.

Despite Columbus' discovery, the Spanish never colonized the Bahamas, being more concerned to find the treasures of the East for which Columbus had been searching. The only 'treasures' found by the Spanish were the Lucayans, who were carried off to Cuba and Hispaniola (now divided between Haiti and the Dominican Republic) to work in the gold mines. By 1520, there were no Lucayans left and the islands remained uninhabited until the English arrived, over a century later. The only other Spaniard of note to explore the Bahamas was Ponce de León who, in 1513, was sent to settle the island of Bimini where there was, it was alleged, a 'fountain of youth'. It was not found and no settlement was established.

The English, who eventually controlled the Bahamas until independence in 1973, did not begin to take an interest in the islands until 1629, when Charles I granted proprietary rights to Sir Robert Heath. Sir Robert held the land as the King's tenant and never colonized the area. His lack of interest was such that, in 1633, Cardinal Richelieu, with or without proper authority, granted five of the islands to prominent Frenchmen. Like the English, the French paid little attention to the Bahamas, and the rights granted by the Cardinal meant nothing in practice.

It was not until 1648 that a permanent, post-Columbian settlement was created in the Bahamas. Captain William Sayle and a group of English Puritans from Bermuda, calling themselves The Company of Adventurers for the Plantation of the Islands of Eleutheria, established a colony at Governor's Harbour on what they named the Island of Eleuthera. One of the first tasks undertaken by this group of settlers, now known in the Bahamas as the Eleutherian Adventurers, was the drawing up of a document entitled 'Articles and Orders', by which they would be governed. This became known as the 'First Constitution' of the Bahamas. Within twenty years, the Island of New Providence had been settled by Bermudian seamen and farmers and, in 1670, the Bahamas officially became a British colony.

The proprietary rights to the Bahamas and parts of the southern United States, originally given to Sir Robert Heath, were granted by Charles II to the Duke of Albemarle and five others, in 1670. These six Proprietors drafted a document, 'Fundamental Constitutions', a semi-feudal instrument which was to serve as a model constitution for those lands in America which were under their control. The inhabitants of the Bahamas considered the Proprietors to be merely absentee landlords and ignored both them and their 'model constitution'. In response to this, and to the neglect of the islands by the Proprietors, the Bahamas 'Second Constitution', Royal Instructions to Proprietors, was drawn up, in 1671, under the order of Charles II; under this, the Crown was forced to take a more active part in the development of the islands, and to listen to the wishes of the inhabitants.

Despite attempts to create a civilized society in the islands, all was not well during the colony's first eighty years. Convoys of Spanish treasure ships sailing from the Caribbean moved through and around the Bahamas on their way to Europe. These tempting prizes quickly attracted pirates and privateers who preyed on the laden galleons. By 1697, Nassau, with its protected harbour and easy access to the treasure shipping lanes, had become a pirate base, and buccaneer rule was the order of the day. As a result, Proprietary government ended, for all practical purposes, in 1703, though the Proprietors' heirs did not relinquish their claims until 1787.

Eventually, Britain was compelled to do something about the pirates and buccaneers who had come to control Nassau and the Bahamas. In 1717, the islands became a Crown Colony, and the following year Woodes Rogers, the first Royal Governor, arrived to assume his post. As a former privateer, Rogers was more than capable of dealing with the pirates who controlled the Colony: he quickly expelled them from the Bahamas and restored order. The Bahamian motto 'Expulsis Piratis, Restituta Commercia' (With the Expulsion of the Pirates, Trade Has Been Revived) first appeared on a public seal approved in 1723 to commemorate Rogers' successful efforts.

The re-establishment of order in the Bahamas led to the 'Third Constitution' for the Colony, a document composed of the Royal Instructions of 1718 and an Order in Council of 1728. It allowed for an Assembly to be called for the purpose of governing the Colony. This Assembly, of twenty-four members, first met on September 29, 1729.

The next half century passed relatively uneventfully for the Bahamians, until the American Revolution of 1775 brought both benefits and hardship. In order to strike back at Great Britain and to obtain necessary war supplies, American forces attacked and captured the Bahamas twice during the Revolution. The Spanish also seized the opportunity, offered by America's war with Great Britain, to take the Bahamas in 1781. Two years later the islands were retrieved by Lt. Col. Andrew Deveaux, a Loyalist from South Carolina. Under the 1873 Treaty of Versailles, the islands were formally restored to Great Britain.

These attacks, though painful, did not provide the lasting legacy of the American Revolution. The greatest impact on the Bahamas resulted from the influx of Loyalists from the United States between 1783 and 1785. The exact number of Loyalists who fled to the Bahamas with their slaves is not known, but it is estimated that between 5,000 and 7,000 individuals moved to the islands. Initially, the Loyalists tried to establish the lifestyle to which they were accustomed and, within five years, 128 large cotton plantations had been established. By 1800, because of pests and poor soil, all of these large plantations had disappeared. However, the Loyalists did influence the Bahamas in ways which are still evident today, especially in the areas of politics, culture, economics, education and architecture.

The Loyalists were not the first to bring slaves to the Bahamas. Although the Eleutherian Adventurers were opposed to slavery and the first blacks on the islands were free ·men and women from Bermuda, there were just under 1,000 slaves in the Bahamas prior to the early 1780s. With the coming of the Loyalists, the slave population rose dramatically, as over 4,000 slaves fled the American Revolution with their masters.

By 1804, no more slaves were needed, and so their importation into the Bahamas ended. Within three years, the slave trade ceased throughout the British Empire. However, slaves were still being imported into the United States – providing these slave ships could evade the British Royal Navy. Between 1808 and 1838, approximately 3,000 would-be slaves were captured by the Royal Navy from such ships, and landed on the Bahamas. These 'recaptives' established several of the better-known black villages on the Island of New Providence. The 1834 Emancipation Act freed all slaves in the Bahamas, though it did allow for a period of apprenticeship from 1834 to 1838 to allow them a time of transition between slavery and freedom.

The Bahamian economy, never strong, lagged severely through the first half of the nineteenth century. Agriculture had not been well established and the only profitable industry was wrecking. Bahamians had been wreckers since the 1660s and, by 1856, one-half of all able-bodied men in the Colony were engaged in what the Bahamians called 'this noble second profession'.

The American Civil War (1861–65) provided a tremendous, if temporary, boost to the Bahamian economy. Because of its geographical location, Nassau became an ideal centre for blockade-running. The Union government established a blockade in order to prevent the Confederacy from exporting cotton and importing goods and war materials from abroad. About 1,650 ships were able to break this blockade and around 8,000 trips were made, back and forth, between the United States and Nassau. The economic boom which resulted was unlike anything seen before in the Bahamas. Unfortunately, as swiftly as it began, it ended, with the cessation of hostilities: once again, the Bahamian economy was struggling.

By 1870, there was some respite because the sponging industry had begun to grow in importance, as had the agricultural crops of pineapple, citrus fruit and sisal. However, as so often happened in the Bahamas, these industries did not fare well, and eventually failed because of high American import duties and increased competition from abroad. The sponging industry lasted until 1938, when a microscopic fungoid killed ninety per cent of the sponges and caused its collapse.

The twentieth century has proved to be more profitable for the Bahamas. There have been problems, but in general the country has done well, particularly from the tourist industry. As early as the mid 1700s, Nassau was seen as a health resort. Boarding homes for visitors were available by the 1840s, and at the turn of the century increasing numbers of people were coming for extended stays during the winter months. Today, tourism is the economic mainstay of the Bahamas, employing about two-thirds of the labour force. The industry provides two-thirds of the government's revenue and one-half of the country's foreign exchange.

The Bahamas has also begun to attract other industries. The largest, next to tourism, is the international finance and banking business. The Bahamas was one of the first offshore tax havens, and is among the largest. A small agricultural industry is also being actively promoted by the government. Finally, natural resources such as aragonite, limestone and salt are being exploited for their commercial value. Among the country's chief exports are rum, petroleum and its products, chemicals, salt, crawfish and aragonite. Imports include foodstuffs, manufactured articles, vehicles and machinery.

Other events during the twentieth century have affected the Bahamas and its place in the global community. In 1919, the Congress of the United States passed the Volstead Act which provided for the enforcement of the prohibition of alcoholic beverages under the 18th Amendment to the Constitution. This period of prohibition, which lasted until 1933, led to great prosperity because of the rum-running from the Bahamas to the US coast, leading to a situation not unlike that of the blockade-running of the American Civil War.

In 1940, the Duke of Windsor, formerly King Edward VIII of Great Britain, was appointed Governor. The British Government took this step to ensure that the Duke was as far removed from Europe and the Second World War as possible. He did much to try to improve the lot of Bahamians, especially the blacks, but his efforts were overshadowed by more spectacular events.

Two such events were particularly damaging. Soon after his arrival, the Duke persuaded the United States to construct two air fields on the Island of New Providence. 'The Project', as it was called, brought added wages to the country; it also brought a riot in 1942, to protest at the discrepancy between wages offered by the Bahamian Government and those paid by the American contractors. One year later, in the summer of 1943, multi-millionaire industrialist Sir Harry Oakes was brutally murdered in his Bahamian home. The Duke of Windsor took control of the highly publicized and politicized murder investigation. He handled it poorly and has often been blamed for the fact that the murder remains unsolved.

The twentieth century has seen great forward strides in the politics and government of the Bahamas. Prior to the 1950s, the representatives in the House of Assembly all came from the white merchant class of Nassau, locally known as the 'Bay Street Boys'. In 1953, the Bahamas' first political party was organized. This, the Progressive Liberal Party (PLP), was formed by the black majority. It was soon followed by the Bahamas Democratic League (BDL), a multi-racial party formed in 1955, and the United Bahamian Party (UBP), organized by the Bay Street Boys in 1958. The PLP, which has been in power since 1967 under the leadership of Sir Lynden Oscar Pindling, is the only one of these original political parties to have survived.

The PLP's original philosophy was one of majority rule, as Party members could not tolerate a country with a black majority being governed by a white minority. Eventually, the Party sought independence. Complete internal self-government was achieved in 1964 and the Commonwealth of the Bahamas was declared independent on 10 July, 1973.

One of the worst problems facing the Bahamas in the twentieth century is drug trafficking. Because the nation is made up of hundreds of small, uninhabited islands and cays, it is a natural stopping-off point for drug dealers from South America smuggling drugs into the United States. In 1983, a Royal Commission was charged with the responsibility of investigating connections between drug trafficking and officials in the Bahamian government. Following the delivery of the Commission's report in 1984, three government Ministers and one Senator resigned, while two other Ministers were dismissed. The problem of drug trafficking has not been resolved and may even be increasing.

The Bahamas has made great attempts, particularly since independence, to overcome the boom-bust cycles that have characterized its history. Progress has been made in the fields of education, industry and agriculture, allowing the country and its citizens to become increasingly self-sufficient. More and more, the country is involving itself in the affairs of the Caribbean region and venturing onto the world stage. The Bahamas is not a large or highly populated country, but its citizens realize that they do have contributions to make and are striving to make them.

The bibliography

Although selective, this bibliography is the first to list Bahamian and related items in a variety of subject areas: other bibliographies which are available are restricted to one subject area. The 703 entries have been grouped into thirty-five categories, with subcategories, which are similar to those found in other volumes of the *World Bibliographical Series*, though some headings have been added because of special Bahamian circumstances. There are, for example, separate sections for: slavery; obeah, a form of voodoo; bush medicine; and Junkanoo, a Bahamian festival. The section on travel guides provides citations for guides both to the country as a whole and to individual islands. Similarly, the history section includes items about the country and the individual islands. Although the Turks and Caicos Islands to the southeast are, geographically, a part of the Bahamas, politically, there is no connection. This island group, therefore, has not been considered.

With two exceptions, all sections are arranged with the most recent items listed first. Historical items are arranged chronologically; the literature entries by a single author are arranged alphabetically by the author's last name. Books and journal articles have been listed along with a few government documents. Theses and dissertations have not been included.

Acknowledgements

I would like to express my thanks to all those who have helped me in the compilation of this bibliography. I was able to see a great deal of the material at the University of Florida in Gainesville. The librarians and library staff members of the Latin American Collection, the Department of Rare Books and Manuscripts and the P.K. Yonge Library of Florida History were particularly helpful. I would also like to thank the staff members of both the Library of Congress Social Science Reading Room and the Nettie Lee Benson Latin American Collection at the University of Texas at Austin.

Dr. Gail Saunders, Chief Archivist of the Bahamas, was most enthusiastic about this project. I appreciate her encouragement and am most grateful for the time she spent in reading the manuscript and suggesting items with which I was unfamiliar. Dr. Dean Collinwood of Weber State College in Ogden, Utah, a Director of the Bahamas Research Institute, lent his moral support and his Bahamian collection, and for that I am grateful. I would also like to thank another Director of the Bahamas Research Institute, Dr. Steve Dodge of Millikin University in Decatur, Illinois, for taking time to share his Bahamian collection with me.

Thanks must go also to the Interlibrary Loan staff of the National Library of Canada for providing me with locations for over 500 items, and to Joanne Bowrey, Supervisor of Circulation Services at the Red Deer College Learning Resources Centre in Red Deer, Alberta, for assisting me with my loan requests.

I am grateful to other members of Red Deer College, including the Learning Resources Centre staff who assisted and supported me while I was on sabbatical. My thanks go to both the College-Wide Professional Development Committee which recommended that I should be given a sabbatical to compile the bibliography and to the College's Board of Governors which approved the Committee's recommendation. In particular, I thank Joanne Bucklee, Dean of Educational Resources, who encouraged me in this project and supported me throughout.

I would also like to thank *WBS* Senior Assistant Editor, Rachel Houghton, whose thoughtful questions and suggested revisions were invaluable.

Special thanks go to Jackie and Jim Rinder of Annapolis, Maryland who opened their home to me and my wife, thus assuring that my research in Washington, DC went very smoothly.

Finally, I thank my wife, Glynis, who has always been such a tower of strength and support. She has never failed to offer me her encouragement and I particularly appreciate her valuable suggestions and sound advice throughout this project.

Paul G. Boultbee
June 1989

The Country and Its People

1 **Bahamas.**
Patricia E. McCulla. New York: Chelsea House, 1988. 104p. map.
(Places and People of the World Series).
This work, designed for teenage readers, surveys the history, topography, people and
culture of the Bahamas, with an emphasis on the country's current economy, industry
and place in the political world. It includes 'Facts at a glance' for quick reference to
vital statistics and 'History at a glance' covering all major events.

2 **Bahamas.**
Edited by Sara Whittier. Singapore: APA Productions, 1986. 305p.
10 maps. (Insight Guide Series, vol. 40).
This item is an excellent guide and overview to the Bahamas. The articles, which are
written by well-known Bahamian authors, cover history, the people and their culture,
all of the islands and settlements, undersea life, fishing, superstition and folkore. The
colour photographs which accompany the text arguably provide the highlight of the
work.

3 **Bahamas: a special *Caribbean Chronicle* survey.**
Larry Smith. *Caribbean and West Indies Chronicle*, vol. 100
(April/May 1985), p. 15–22.
This economic, political and historical survey includes an interview with the Prime
Minister, Sir Lynden Pindling.

4 **The Bahamas reference annual.**
Cyril St. John Stevenson. Nassau: Interpress Public Relations
Consultants, 1985- . annual.
A comprehensive handbook to the Bahamas, this reference work is similar to the
Bahamas handbook and businessman's annual (q.v.). It provides, in the first edition, a
wealth of information on the land and its people; the Family Islands; constitutional

1

development; religion; civic, social and charitable organizations; and government. It does not, however, contain feature articles highlighting various topics within the country. It remains to be seen whether the publication will continue.

5 **The Bahamas.**
Dean W. Collinwood. In: *Latin American and Caribbean contemporary record.* Edited by Jack W. Hopkins. New York: Holmes & Meier, 1983– . annual.

In this annual profile, Collinwood discusses political affairs, both domestic and foreign, education and culture, the economy and business, health and social conditions, and any special highlights of the preceding year. He also includes a chart which gives a statistical overview of the country.

6 **The Bahamas: a decade of independence.**
Thad Martin. *Ebony*, vol. 38, no. 6 (April 1983), p. 117–18, 120, 123.

This article, praising the accomplishments of the Bahamas, examines the country ten years after independence. Martin describes what is good about the country and puts little emphasis on what is not.

7 **The Bahamas: boom times and buccaneering.**
Peter Benchley. *National Geographic Magazine*, vol. 162, no. 3 (Sept. 1982), p. 364–95.

Benchley examines the links between early history and present-day events. His article also touches on Haitian immigrants, drugs, tourism and the economy.

8 **The Bahamas: a social studies course for secondary schools.**
John Berryman. London: Macmillan Caribbean, 1980. 100p. 12 maps. bibliog.

Berryman has brought together information from a number of secondary sources in order to produce a textbook to meet the needs of candidates, twelve to fourteen year olds, for the Bahamas Junior Certificate Examination in Social Studies. Contents include the environment, land use and economy, history, culture and life style and the government. The work is not exhaustive, nor is it meant to be, but it does provide a very good introduction to the country. The author has included exercises for teachers who use this work in the classroom.

9 **Out Island portraits: Bahamas, 1946–1956.**
Ruth Rodriguez. New York: Out Island, 1978. 150p. map.

This is a pictorial work with photographs from Man-O-War Cay, Harbour Island, Upper Bogue, Eleuthera and Spanish Wells. Of particular interest are the photographs of boatbuilding for which Man-O-War Cay is famous. It is a unique volume, not a picture book depicting the tourist side of the country but rather a presentation of the people and their everyday lives.

10 **Caribbean year book.**
Toronto: Caribook, 1977/78– . annual.

This annual reference book was first published in 1926/27 under the title, *West Indies and Caribbean year book*. It is a very good quick-reference book for the Bahamas as well as for all other countries in the Caribbean area. It includes information on history, climate, population, languages, religion, government, social services, public utilities, communications, natural resources, industry, finance, trade and commerce, diplomatic and consular offices, travel and tourism, newspapers and periodicals. There is also a business directory for Nassau and Freeport.

11   **The Bahamas.**
George Hunte.   London: Batsford, 1975. 200p. map. bibliog.
This general description of the Bahamas, written for the prospective traveller, is not just a tourist guide. It is also as much a history as it is a geography or travel book. All the inhabited islands are described, including the Turks and Caicos Islands. Also included are a general information section and a chronology, listing events from 1492 to 1973. It was first published in the United States (North Pomfret, Vermont: 1974. 224p.).

12   **The Bahama Islands: in full colour.**
Hans W. Hannau.   London: Hale, 1970. 125p. 12 maps.
This is a large pictorial volume about the Bahamas which contains outstanding colour photographs. The text provides a brief overview of Bahamian history and chapters describe fourteen of the inhabited islands. Each of these chapters includes a map of the island with all major settlements indicated. The book has also been published under the title *Islands of the Bahamas in full colour* (New York: Hastings House, 1971. 136p.). It is suitable for the 'armchair traveller'.

13   **Bahamas.**
John H. Bounds.   *Focus*, vol. 19, no. 9 (May 1969), p. 1–7.
A brief, general description of the country, which covers geography, history, economic development and industry.

14   **Bahamas.**
Edward John Long.   Garden City, New York: Nelson Doubleday, 1969. 64p. 6 maps. (Around the World Program).
This little booklet, prepared with the cooperation of the American Geographical Society, provides a brief overview of Bahamian history and culture. It is well illustrated and designed for the younger reader. A chronology of important dates up to 1967 is appended to the text.

15   **More of sea than of land: the Bahamas.**
Carleton Mitchell.   *National Geographic Magazine*, vol. 131, no. 2 (Feb. 1967), p. 218–67.
This is an update of his 1958 article, 'The Bahamas: isles of the blue-green sea' (q.v.). This article and the 1958 one together provide information on almost a decade of change. The photographs are also very useful.

16   **Bahamas handbook and businessman's annual.**
Nassau: E. Dupuch, Jr., Publications, 1960– . annual.
This important and valuable publication about the Bahamas should be a part of every

Bahamian collection, large or small. Each edition contains a selection of feature articles on various aspects of the Bahamas, such as the Nassau Public Library, the Gulf Stream, Bahamian family reunions, the *lignum vitae* (the Bahamian national tree), Bahamian life styles and regional cooking. These are followed by articles on tourism, the Family Islands and business and finance. The blue pages which constitute about a quarter of each edition provide a wealth of information on the Bahamas, a compendium of everything one may want to know about the country. A third section outlines the current Bahamian government – Ministers, Members of the Senate, Members of the House of Assembly, other public and government officials, representatives of the Bahamas abroad and foreign representatives in the Bahamas.

17 **The Bahamas, isles of the blue-green sea.**
Carleton Mitchell. *National Geographic Magazine*, vol. 113, no. 2 (Feb. 1958), p. 147–203.

Mitchell provides a general description of and introduction to the Bahamas. Although his references to the government and the economy are now dated, his observations of the people and the land are still valid. There is an emphasis on white Bahamians and tourism.

18 **Bahama holiday.**
Frederick Simpich. *National Geographic Magazine*, vol. 69, no. 2 (Feb. 1936), p. 219–45.

This general introduction and description should be compared and contrasted with Mitchell's 'The Bahamas: isles of the blue-green sea' (q.v.) and 'More of sea than of land: the Bahamas' (q.v.). By doing so, one gets a very good view of the Bahamas as seen by outsiders in the mid twentieth century.

19 **The Bahamas handbook.**
Mary Moseley. Nassau: Nassau Guardian, 1926. 237p. 4 maps.

Moseley's handbook provides excellent descriptions of New Providence and the Out Islands, the government, flora and fauna, industries, trade and manufacturing, sports, religion and education. It brings together a wealth of information about the Bahamas in general and in the 1920s in particular. Much of the factual information is now out of date but this book remains the foundation of all work about the Bahamas and is the starting point for any researcher intent on writing about the country.

Geography

General

20 **Bahamian landscapes: an introduction to the geography of the Bahamas.**
Neil E. Sealey.   London: Collins Caribbean, 1985. 96p. 18 maps.
bibliog.
Sealey has attempted to collate a considerable amount of material which has been
produced, particularly over the last twenty-five years, by a number of noted geologists.
The result is both a geological history and a geographical inventory. It is the first study
of the physical geography of the Bahamas and is particularly suitable for secondary
school students as well as the informed layperson. Topics covered include the origin
and structure of the Bahamas Platform, the sedimentary banks, the ocean canyons,
geological history of the islands, the landscapes and landforms of the islands and
natural resources.

21 **The climate of the Bahamas.**
Michael Halkitis, Stephen Smith, Karen Rigg.   Nassau: Bahamas
Geographical Association, 1980. 30p. 4 maps.
This is primarily a teacher's reference book which includes charts and tables for
rainfall, temperature and wind.

22 **The Bahamas.**
F.C. Evans, R.N. Young.   Cambridge, England: Cambridge University
Press, 1976. 64p. 9 maps.
This work is primarily intended as a geography book for Bahamian school children but
can be equally useful to non-Bahamians. The demographic information is now obsolete
but the book is still useful for the basics of Bahamian geography such as geology, soils
and vegetation. As well as dealing with the Bahamas as a whole, Evans and Young
provide individual chapters on the inhabited islands.

23 **A historical geography of the British colonies.**
Charles Prestwood Lucas.   Oxford: Clarendon, 1887–1920.
7 vols. in 12.
Volume two (1905) of this set contains information on the Bahamas. Lucas provides a brief history and discusses topography, sponges and agriculture. There are excellent footnotes.

Blue holes

24 **In the lair of the Lusca.**
Robert Palmer.   *Natural History*, vol. 96, no. 1 (Jan. 1987), p. 42–47.
Palmer describes the origins of the complex cave system which links individual blue holes and marine holes with inland holes. He also describes the fauna of the marine and inland blue holes. The Lusca of the title is a legendary sea creature, half octopus and half shark. According to Bahamians, the creature inhabits the blue holes and draws fishermen and their boats down as it inhales and then exhales the indigestible flotsam. Actually, the phenomenon is a result of tides pouring into a deep hole in the sea floor and creating whirlpools at the surface which are often strong enough to pull in floating debris or unwary swimmers.

25 **The blue holes of the Bahamas.**
Robert Palmer.   Salem, New Hampshire: Merrimack Pubs. Circle, 1986. 184p. 7 maps.
This is an absorbing account of the exploration of the blue holes off Grand Bahama Island and Andros Island conducted as part of the 1981–84 British Blue Hole Expeditions. It was first published in London by Jonathan Cape in 1985. The 1983 film *Deep into the blue holes* chronicles these explorations.

26 **Life in a sunless sea.**
Robert Palmer.   *Sea Frontiers*, vol. 32, no. 4 (July/Aug. 1986), p. 269–77.
Another article by Palmer describing the blue holes of the Bahamas. The author concludes that these ocean holes may link one side of an island to another, allowing the tides to flow back and forth. In turn, these tides carry organic debris into the holes allowing rich marine life to survive. This article is preliminary to Palmer's 'In the lair of the Lusca' (q.v.).

27 **Ecology beneath the Bahama Banks.**
Robert Palmer.   *New Scientist*, vol. 110, no. 1507 (May 8, 1986), p. 44–48.
This is a short explanation of how blue holes are formed and what they contain.

28   **Three adventures: Galapagos, Titicaca, the blue holes.**
Jacques-Yves Cousteau, Philippe Diole, translated from the French by
J.F. Bernard.   Garden City, New York: Doubleday, 1973. 304p.
6 maps. (The Undersea Discoveries of Jacques-Yves Cousteau).
This work includes Cousteau's investigations of blue holes off the coast of British
Honduras (Belize) and Andros Island in the Bahamas. It is a very well illustrated,
interesting and informative account of underwater exploration, which will appeal to the
vicarious swimmer or scuba diver and students interested in oceanography.

29   **Diving into the blue holes of the Bahamas.**
George J. Benjamin.   *National Geographic Magazine*, vol. 138, no. 3
(Sept. 1970), p. 346–63.
Describes the formation of the blue holes off the east coast of Andros and the flora and
fauna present in these underwater caves.

Maps and atlases

30   **Atlas of the Commonwealth of the Bahamas.**
Kingston Publishers.   Nassau: Ministry of Education, 1985. rev. ed.
48p. 38 maps.
This atlas includes thirty-eight maps and forty-five plans of cities, towns and
settlements. Topical maps cover land use, agriculture, population and climate. The
linear scales are varied to enlarge the smaller islands. Depiction of relief is shown on
larger scale insets but is not always given for an entire island. With landscapes as level
as those in the Bahamas, every mound assumes importance and the relief scales used
do not allow for this. However, spot heights are given allowing the user some idea of a
particular island's topography. Because similar scales are used, this collection provides
an interesting historical comparison with *Maps of the Bahama Islands* (q.v.).

31   **Maps of the Bahama Islands.**
London: Stanford's Geographical Establishment, 1926. 23p. 20 maps.
This atlas contains a brief introduction, twenty maps of varying scales and eight pages
of index.

Geology

32 Proceedings of the third symposium on the geology of the Bahamas, June 1986.
Edited by Harold Allen Curran.   Fort Lauderdale, Florida: College Center of the Finger Lakes, Bahamian Field Station, 1987. 250p.

This collection includes the majority of papers presented at the symposium. Topics covered include deep ocean drilling, modern and ancient coral reefs, hydrology, karst topography, sedimentation and stratigraphic theories.

33 Mystery muds of Great Bahama Bank.
Eugene A. Shinn.   *Sea Frontiers*, vol. 31 (Nov./Dec. 1985), p. 337–46.

Shinn describes the huge patches of lime mud, called whitings, that dot the Bahama Bank and discusses the importance of this mud. Lime mud becomes limestone which makes up half of the world's sedimentary rocks. Half of the world's oil can be pumped from limestone, making this type of formation very important to the Bahamian economy. The origin of whitings remains a mystery. Bahamian fishermen explain that this mud has been churned up by huge schools of fish. However, some geologists claim that the whitings are caused by spontaneous precipitation of calcium carbonate from the water column.

34 Geology of Great Exuma Island: field guide for second symposium on the geology of the Bahamas.
Steven Mitchell.   Fort Lauderdale, Florida: College Center of the Finger Lakes, Bahamian Field Station, 1984. 45p.

This guide describes the major geologic features of Great Exuma Island and the nearby smaller cay, Stocking Island.

35   **Geology of New Providence Island, Bahamas.**
     Peter Garrett, Stephen Jay Gould.   *Geological Society of America Bulletin*, vol. 95, no. 2 (Feb. 1984), p. 209–20.

This highly technical description of the geology of New Providence points out that the island consists principally of elevated marine sand-flat and protected lagoon deposits, not eolianite deposits as was commonly thought.

36   **Proceedings of the second symposium on the geology of the Bahamas, June 16–20, 1984.**
     Edited by James W. Teeter.   San Salvador, Bahamas: College Center of the Finger Lakes, Bahamian Field Station, 1984. 296p. 7 maps.

Eighteen papers are presented in this collection. All but two of them deal with the geology of the Island of San Salvador. Topics include living and fossil ostracodes, coral reefs, stromatolites and algae, Pleistocene and post-Pleistocene depositional history, stratigraphy, soils and paleosoils, diagenesis and cave development. The current address for the College Center is Fort Lauderdale, Florida, rather than San Salvador, and all publications can be ordered from the Florida address.

37   **Field guide to the geology of San Salvador.**
     Edited by Donald T. Gerace.   Fort Lauderdale, Florida: College Center of the Finger Lakes, 1983. 3rd ed. 172p.

This guide, for professionals and interested laypeople, describes the various geologic features of San Salvador Island. It includes directions on how to reach sites and lists of the numerous features which can be observed. It also describes in detail various caves and sinkholes, trace fossils, present-day and fossil beaches, coral reefs and the overall stratigraphy of the island. Many of the features discussed are common to all the islands.

38   **Proceedings of the first symposium on the geology of the Bahamas, March 23–25, 1982.**
     San Salvador, Bahamas: College Center of the Finger Lakes, Bahamian Field Station, 1983. 62p. 4 maps.

The nine articles presented in this collection are shortened versions of the papers presented at the symposium. Although the symposium was on the geology of the Bahamas, all of the papers deal with the Island of San Salvador. Topics covered are fossil foraminifera and ostracoda, chronostratigraphy, trace fossils, karst features, Cerion variations and Holocene lithification.

39   **The topographic, hydrographic and sedimentologic setting of Little Lake, San Salvador Island, Bahamas.**
     James W. Teeter.   Fort Lauderdale, Florida: College Center of the Finger Lakes, Bahamian Field Station, 1983. 10p. (Occasional Papers 1983, no. 3).

This booklet reports on the water depth, temperature, pH, dissolved oxygen, salinity, sediment types and distribution and bedrock topography of Little Lake, San Salvador Island.

Geology

40 **Bahamian carbonate platforms: the deep and the past.**
Wolfgang Schlager, Robert N. Ginsburg. *Marine Geology*, vol. 44 (1981), p. 1–24.
A good summary of present knowledge which pays particular attention to the deep water troughs. The authors examine the sediments of the Bahamas Bank which are widely accepted as the standard for the interpretation of comparable ancient deposits. Both authors have written many papers about the Bahamas, all worth reading, and this is an excellent introduction to their work.

41 **Facies anatomy and diagenesis of a Bahamian ooid shoal.**
Paul Mitchell Harris. Miami, Florida: University of Miami, 1979. 163p. map. bibliog. (Sedimenta VII).
Harris describes a thick Holocene shoal north of Andros Island in which oolites, the most common grain type, occur mixed with other non-skeletal grains or lime mud. He documents the characteristics of this sedimentary deposit which is the result of the rising sea level over the last 10,000 years.

42 **Field guide to some carbonate rock environments: Florida Keys and Western Bahamas.**
H. Gray Multer. Dubuque, Iowa: Kendall/Hunt, 1977. 415p. 53 maps. bibliog.
This excellent collection of papers is designed to be used as a guide in the field and as a reference text in the classroom and laboratory. The purpose of the field guide is to serve the students of carbonate rocks by helping them locate, examine and discuss both modern and Pleistocene environments.

43 **Sedimentation on the modern carbonate tidal flats of northwest Andros Island, Bahamas.**
Edited by Lawrence A. Hardie. Baltimore, Maryland: Johns Hopkins University Press, 1977. 202p. 5 maps. bibliog. (Johns Hopkins University. Studies in Geology, 22).
Hardie's introduction best describes the purpose of this work. He writes, 'Our aim was to determine as precisely as possible what information on climate, weather, tides, water chemistry, and indigenous life is recorded in the sediments of this one particular kind of tropical carbonate tidal flat type – the low-energy, high-rainfall, nonevaporitic, totally marine type'. The studies reported here conclude that these particular tidal flat sediments were able to record small differences in environmental conditions.

44 **Guidebook for modern Bahamian platform environments.**
Conrad D. Gebelein. Boulder, Colorado: Geological Society of America, 1974. 2nd ed. 101p. 15 maps. bibliog.
This guidebook was prepared originally for a field trip of the Geological Society of America's annual meeting in 1974. Gebelein provides a very good introduction to the geology of the Bahamas and describes the results of investigations of thirteen geological platform environments which were visited on this particular field trip. He covers such areas as platform sediments, topography, climate and hydrology. There is also an extensive bibliography.

Geology

45   Formation of a deep-water submarine canyon head in the Tongue of the
     Ocean.
     Robert Pryor.   *Bulletin of Marine Science*, vol. 20, no. 4 (Dec. 1970),
     p. 813–29.
Pryor uses sedimentary and structural evidence to investigate the formation of the
Great Bahama Canyon. This submarine canyon is 125 miles long and reaches depths
from 900 fathoms at its head to 2,475 fathoms at its terminus. It is considered to be one
of the longest and deepest submarine canyons in the world.

46   Geotectonic evolution and subsidence of the Bahama Platform.
     Robert S. Dietz.   *Geological Society of America Bulletin*, vol. 81
     (1970), p. 1915–28.
In this highly scientific paper, Dietz contends that the Bahamas is geologically part of
Africa and the island nation was formed by continental drift. This is a sound study of
the geophysical evolution of the Bahamas.

47   Great Bahama Canyon.
     James E. Andrews, Francis P. Shepard, Robert J. Hurley.   *Geological
     Society of America Bulletin*, vol. 81, no. 4 (April 1970), p. 1061–78.
Investigates the origins of the Great Bahama Canyon. The canyon has two main
branches, one following the North West Providence Channel and the other forming the
Tongue of the Ocean. These two branches meet approximately fifteen miles northwest
of the Island of New Providence.

48   Anatomy of a modern carbonate tidal-flat, Andros Island, Bahamas.
     Eugene A. Shinn, R. Michael Lloyd.   *Journal of Sedimentary
     Petrology*, vol. 39, no. 3 (Sept. 1969), p. 1202–28.
The authors have described the three geomorphic areas which compose the carbonate
tidal-flat complex: the adjacent marine belt, the channelled belt and the marsh area.
The three tidal zones which affect sedimentary accumulations in the tidal-flat complex
are also described, these being the subtidal, intertidal and supratidal zones.

49   Coastal landforms of Cat Island, Bahamas: a study of holocene
     accretionary topography and sea-level change.
     Aulis O. Lind.   Chicago: University of Chicago, Department of
     Geography, 1969. 156p. 3 maps. bibliog. (Department of Geography.
     Research Paper, 122).
This study examines the coastal landforms of Cat Island and interprets them within the
perspective of repeated sea-level changes in recent times. Lind's work is a good study
in coastal geomorphology.

50   Environmental atlas of the Tongue of the Ocean, Bahamas.
     United States. Naval Oceanographic Office.   Washington, DC: Naval
     Oceanographic Office, 1967. 74p. bibliog. (US Naval Oceanographic
     Office. Special Publication, SP-94).
This atlas provides a compilation of published and unpublished data concerning the

Geology

oceanographic environment of the Tongue of the Ocean. Data on bottom materials and topology, sound velocity, physical properties of sea water, tides and currents and marine and wave climatology are presented. Coastal and bottom photographs are included in several of the figures. The work is chiefly made up of charts and figures.

51 **Mineralogy of Tongue of the Ocean sediments.**
Orrin H. Pilkey, James B. Rucker. *Journal of Marine Research,* vol. 24, no. 3 (Sept. 1966), p. 276–85.

After examining twenty-five short core samples from the Tongue of the Ocean, the authors conclude that the carbonate mineralogy present in the core samples may reflect Pleistocene sea-level changes. This suggested relationship of mineralogy to sea level may find wide application in the study of carbonate sedimentation in intermediate-depth water near to carbonate banks.

52 **Rare Atlantic atoll.**
John D. Milliman, William M. Stephens. *Sea Frontiers,* vol. 11, no. 6 (Nov./Dec. 1965), p. 342–53.

There are more than 400 atolls in the world, of which ninety per cent are in the Indo-Pacific region. There are only two in the Atlantic Ocean; Hogsty Reef (formerly known as Los Coralles) in the Bahamas is one. This article discusses the origins of atolls in general and Hogsty Reef in particular. There is also a description of the flora and fauna on and around the atoll.

53 **Ecology and oceanography of the coral-reef tract, Abaco Island, Bahamas.**
John F. Storr. New York: Geological Society of America, 1964. 98p. 3 maps. bibliog. (GSA Special Papers, no. 79).

This is an ecological and oceanographic study of the Hopetown Reef located off Elbow Cay, one of a chain of small islands that parallels the coast of the Little and Great Abaco Islands. Storr examines reef structure, ecological zonation, bottom sediments, water temperature, salinity and currents.

54 **The Bahama Banks: a "living" fossil-environment.**
Louis S. Kornicker. *Journal of Geological Education,* vol. 11, no. 1 (March 1963), p. 17–25.

The Bahama Banks represents an environment of carbonate sedimentation which is rare and affords the geologist with an opportunity of learning firsthand about geological processes. Kornicker summarizes information on geography, sediments and ecology and encourages geologists to use information about the Bahamas in the classroom setting.

55 **Submarine geology of the Tongue of the Ocean, Bahamas.**
Roswell F. Busby. Washington, DC: US Naval Oceanographic Office, 1962. 84p. 9 maps. bibliog. (US Naval Oceanographic Office. Technical Report, TR-108).

This report, which includes a review of the literature, discusses the properties and distribution of sediments on the floor of the Tongue of the Ocean.

56 **Geological studies on the Great Bahama Bank.**
Norman D. Newell, J. Keith Rigby. *Bulletin of the Society of Economic Palaeontologists and Mineralogists*, (1957), p. 15–72. (Special Publication, no. 5).

This paper is an introduction to the marine geology and environments of the Great Bahama Bank, paying particular attention to the reefs and lagoons of Andros Island. It is part of a collection of published papers from a symposium entitled *Regional aspects of carbonate deposition*, edited by Rufus J. LeBlanc and Julia G. Breeding (Tulsa, Oklahoma: Society of Economic Palaeontologists and Mineralogists, 1957. 178p.). Newell and Rigby's work is considered to be the classic geological study of the Bahamas.

57 **Bahamian platforms.**
Norman D. Newell. In: *Crust of the earth: a symposium*. Edited by Arie Poldervaart. New York: Geological Society of America, 1955, p. 303–15. (GSA Special Papers, no. 62).

Newell points out that the Bahamian platforms are among the best examples of contemporary limestone sea areas anywhere. In places, the pure carbonate deposits reach to a depth of 14,500 feet with no evidence of folding or faulting. Although the Bahamian platforms resemble Pacific coral atolls, they are relatively new, having only been formed since the last glaciation. The author concludes that these platforms, which were originally coral reefs formed in the late Tertiary period, were nearly exterminated during the Pleistocene epoch and finally formed by blanketing oolite deposits laid down over the original Tertiary reefs.

58 **Landforms of the southeast Bahamas.**
Edwin Doran, Jr. Austin, Texas: Department of Geography, University of Texas, 1955. 38p. 12 maps. bibliog. (University of Texas Publication, 5509).

This report describes and classifies the landforms of the southeast Bahamas, shows their distribution on a series of maps at a scale of one inch per mile and comments on their origin. The southeast Bahamas includes all the islands from Crooked Island to Grand Turk. The Turks and Caicos Islands are part of the Bahamas geomorphically, though not politically, and are therefore included in the report. There are sections on shallow water forms, shoreline forms, plains forms, ridge forms and geomorphic history.

59 **Bahaman calcareous sands.**
Leslie V. Illing. *Bulletin of the American Association of Petroleum Geologists*, vol. 38, no. 1 (Jan. 1954), p. 1–95.

In this major study of Bahamian sediments, Illing investigates the origins of the calcareous sands which cover the Bahama Banks.

60 **Geophysical surveys on the Bahama Banks.**
C.S. Lee. *Journal of the Institute of Petroleum*, vol. 37, no. 334 (Oct. 1951), p. 633–57.

Previous geophysical and geological surveys are reviewed and compared to mid-twentieth century work conducted in Abaco, Eleuthera and Ragged Island. This article

Geology

presents findings concerning structural build up and the processes of sedimentation. There are also discussions of the methods used for gravity surveys and seismic and magnetometer surveys.

61 **Shoal-water geology and environments, Eastern Andros, Bahamas.**
Norman D. Newell (et al). *Bulletin of the American Museum of Natural History*, vol. 97, (June 28, 1951), p. 1–29.

This article emphasizes the geology of the Bahama Banks. There is a detailed discussion of the principal habitats and sedimentary environments of shore areas, estuaries and lagoons, barrier reefs, off-shore geologic platforms and the Tongue of the Ocean.

62 **The Great Bahama Bank.**
C. Lavett Smith. *Journal of Marine Research*, vol. 3, no. 2 (1940), p. 147–89.

This article is divided into two major sections: general hydrographic and chemical features, and calcium carbonate precipitation. In the first section, Smith provides information on wind-controlled water movements and temperature and salinity as well as other hydrographic data. In section two, he discusses the precipitation of calcium carbonates and the seasonal variations in this precipitation.

63 **Geology of the Bahamas.**
Richard M. Field. *Bulletin of the Geological Society of America*, vol. 42 (Sept. 1931), p. 759–84.

Field has included sections on the history of previous investigations, gravity data, oceanology, marine ecology and the character of marine sediments, microbiology, the stratigraphy of Andros Island and structural geology.

64 **Subterranean water ways in the Bahama Islands.**
Charles Johnson Maynard. *Contributions to Science*, vol. 2 (Dec. 1894), p. 182–91.

Discusses the geological development of the Bahamas with particular emphasis on coral reef growth, and investigates the blue holes off the coast of Andros.

65 **On the geology of the Bahamas and on coral formations generally.**
Richard Nelson. *Quarterly Journal of the Geological Society of London*, vol. 9 (1853), p. 200–15.

This is an early, general investigation of Bahamian geology. It is still useful, especially for historical purposes.

Travel Guides

General

66 The Bahamas: a family of islands.
D. Gail Saunders.   London: Macmillan Caribbean, 1989. 189p.
15 maps. bibliog. (Macmillan Caribbean Guides).
This is a comprehensive guide to the Bahamas, written by the nation's Chief Archivist.
There is a general introduction to the Bahamas and its people, along with a brief
history of the country. Saunders also provides information on flora and fauna,
underwater life, agriculture, sports and walking tours of Nassau. Her coverage of the
Bahamas is extensive and well-written. The colour photographs which accompany the
text are excellent.

67 Islands in the stream.
Gregg Loomis.   *Flying*, vol. 115 (Dec. 1988), p. 62–68.
Loomis provides good, detailed information on piloting personal aircraft into, through
and out of the Bahamas.

68 Cruising the Bahamas: an insider's guide.
Randall Peffer.   *Sail*, (Sept. 1988), p. 54–62.
This is an excellent article giving a concise overview of cruising in the Bahamas.
'Cruising' refers to individuals or families sailing their own vessels rather than those
holidaying on a cruise ship. There are short sections on what types of people undertake
these cruises, types of boats and gear needed, passage routes, weather, navigation,
anchorages, where to buy supplies and highlights of some of the Out Islands. The
article is useful – though anyone contemplating a cruise would need a great deal more
information. For this purpose, Randall recommends Wilensky's *Cruising guide to the
Abacos and the northern Bahamas* (q.v) and *Yachtsman's guide to the Bahamas* (q.v).

69   **Diver's almanac: guide to the Bahamas and Caribbean.**
      Edited by Stephen F. Guettermann.   Costa Mesa, California: HDL
      Communications; Medford, Oregon: Sports Almanacs, 1987. 202p.
      26 maps.
This profusely illustrated and glossy book provides a wealth of information for the
diver interested in the Bahamas and the Caribbean. For each Bahamian island the
editor provides historical and topographic information, land-based attractions, dive
services, dive site descriptions and transportation information concerning how to get to
and around the island. There are also articles on diving equipment and education, the
medical and safety aspects of diving and weather. Approximately one-quarter of the
book is devoted to the Bahamas.

70   **Fodor's Bahamas.**
      New York: Fodor's Travel Guides, 1986– . annual.
Eugene Fodor started the Fodor's Travel Guides series in 1936. This annual began
publication in 1960 under the title *Fodor's guide to the Caribbean, Bahamas, and
Bermuda*. The publication subsequently became *Fodor's Caribbean, Bahamas, and
Bermuda* and then in 1980, *Fodor's Caribbean and the Bahamas*. The publishers began
to treat the Bahamas as a separate entity in 1986. This very useful guide provides a
great deal of practical information about all of the islands most likely to be visited as
well as extended sections on New Providence Island and Grand Bahama Island. The
publication is compiled, researched and edited by an international team of travel
writers, field correspondents and editors.

71   **Frommer's dollarwise guide to Bermuda and the Bahamas, 1986–87– .**
      Darwin Porter.   New York: Frommer/Pasmantier, 1986– . biennial.
This guide is produced for value-conscious tourists and details a wide range of
accommodations and restaurants. There is also information on sightseeing, shopping
and transportation along with sections on Bahamian history, culture and art.

72   **Birnbaum's Caribbean, Bermuda and the Bahamas.**
      Edited by Stephen Birnbaum.   Boston, Massachusetts: Houghton
      Mifflin, 1985– . annual. (A Stephen Birnbaum Travel Guide).
Birnbaum's guide provides the usual information found in such a volume. It covers
dining, accommodation, shopping, nightlife and other activities. This guide includes
the whole of the Caribbean as well as Bermuda and the Bahamas, so that coverage for
the Bahamas is limited. It is useful for those people who are planning a tour of the
region rather than an extended stay in the Bahamas.

73   **Diving and snorkeling guide to the Bahamas: Nassau and New Providence
      Island.**
      Steve Blount.   New York: Pisces Books, 1985. 64p. 2 maps. (Diving
      and Snorkeling Guides Series).
Blount gives detailed descriptions of eleven dive sites off the Island of New
Providence, with details for each on depth range, current conditions, expertise
required and access. There is also information on travel and customs, currency,
shopping and diving safety.

74 **Fodor's fun in the Bahamas.**
Anita Gates. New York: Fodor's Travel Guides, 1985– . annual.
This is a highly selective guide which is quick and easy to use. Gates provides information on hotels, restaurants, sports, shopping and nightlife. It is less expensive than most of the other travel guides and its small physical size allows it to be carried easily in a handbag or pocket.

75 **Cruising handbook.**
Leonard L. Spangler. Vero Beach, Florida: Atlantic Coast Equity, 1984– .
There is no indication as to how many volumes there will be in this series, for which Spangler has produced three titles. Volume one, subtitled *The Abacos*, charts the area to the north and west of Grand Bahama Island. Volume two is entitled *The Florida Keys*, and volume three, *The central Bahamas*. The volumes in this series are to be updated annually with loose-leaf inserts. This may prove to make them some of the most useful of the cruising guides.

76 **The Pelican guide to the Bahamas.**
James E. Moore. Gretna, Louisiana: Pelican, 1984– . biennial.
This is one of the most comprehensive of the travel guides to the Bahamas and the first to treat the Bahamas separately. Moore provides an introduction to the people, customs and history and includes detailed information on hotels, restaurants, shopping and activities.

77 **Fielding's Bermuda and the Bahamas.**
Rachel J. Christmas, Walter Christmas. New York: Fielding Travel Guides, 1983– . annual.
This annual publication provides information on when to go to the Bahamas and how to get there, as well as on sports, shopping, nightlife, tours, dining and accommodation. Hotels are rated and prices given. There is also a section on the Out Islands. This guide is not as extensive as those devoted solely to the Bahamas, as it considers Bermuda in the same volume.

78 **Flying the Bahamas: the weekend pilot's guide.**
Frank Kingston Smith. Blue Ridge Summit, Pennsylvania: TAB Books, 1983. 278p. 72 maps.
This guide can be used by the general public as well as by pilots, since only four of the sixteen chapters are aimed towards private aircraft. Smith provides a great deal of information about the Bahamas but his travel guide is not a formal one like *Fielding's* . . . (q.v.) or *Fodor's* . . . (q.v.) which evaluate accommodation and restaurants.

79 **Bahamas 1983– .**
Dianne Nicholson Lawes, edited by Robert C. Fisher. New York: Fisher Travel Guides, 1982– . annual. (Fisher's World Travel Guides).
This guide begins with a very detailed introduction to the country and presents a great many facts which are of use to the tourist. There are also articles on both Nassau and Grand Bahama. For each, there is information on hotels and restaurants, entertainment and shopping, sports, tours and historic sites. There are similar but briefer sections for

all of the other islands. All hotels and restaurants have been rated from one star to five stars by the author. This is a useful, informal travel guide, one of a series known until 1986 as Fisher Annotated Travel Guides.

80 **Cruising guide to the Abacos and the northern Bahamas.**
    Julius M. Wilensky.   Stamford, Connecticut: Wescott Cove, 1980.
    2nd rev. ed.. 220p. 68 maps.

This guide provides thorough sailing charts for those islands north of 25° latitude: the Abacos, Grand Bahama, Bimini, north Andros, New Providence and north Eleuthera. The detailed text advises on getting from one island to another. Wilensky has produced an excellent sailing guide, although it should, probably, now be updated.

81 **Pilot's Bahamas aviation guide: including the Turks and Caicos Islands and Haiti.**
    Dale Cady, edited by Kelly Dunigan, Donn Pfaff.   Ocala, Florida: Pilot Publications, 1979– . annual.

For each Bahamian island, the editors provide a map, a description, a photograph of and the approach to each airstrip and general remarks and information. This guide, originally written by Dale Cady and first published in 1979, is very detailed in its presentation. For the 1988 tenth edition, Brian Strong replaced Kelly Dunigan as joint editor.

82 **Bahamas diver's guide.**
    Shlomo Cohen.   Tel Aviv: Seapen Books, 1977. 184p. 32 maps.

Provides a guide to twenty-seven dive sites throughout the Bahamas. For each site, the guide gives the latitude and longitude, a map and photograph of the area, and an aerial photograph with a transparent overlay showing bearings, depth and a cross-section of the reef area. There are narratives for each site, giving directions, descriptions and any special notes for the area. It is a useful volume for the diving enthusiast.

83 **Diving guide to the Bahamas: including Turks and Caicos Islands.**
    Gordon Lomer.   New York: Hastings House, 1975. 56p. 25 maps.

Attempts to detail as many specific dive sites as possible and to give descriptive comments as to depths and features of each area. Although this slim volume is not as detailed as other diving guides, it does provide a useful overview for the first-time diver in the Bahamas. It also includes 117 small coloured photographs of marine life, for identification purposes.

84 **Bahama Islands: a boatman's guide to the land and the water.**
    J. Linton Rigg, revised by Harry Kline.   New York: Scribner, 1973.
    4th ed. 292p. 137 maps.

This is one of the first and most important sailing guides to the Bahamas, which includes charts and directions for cruising throughout all the islands. However, as Kline points out in his preface, 'While all information in the text and on the charts is reliable as of the time we obtained it, the Bahamas are noted for being "subject to change"'. It is advisable to use the *Yachtsman's guide to the Bahamas* (q.v.) in conjunction with this text. Rigg's book was first published in 1949.

85 **Sun 'n sixpence: a guide to Nassau and the Bahama Out Islands.**
Michael Craton, edited by S.P. Dupuch. Nassau: E. Dupuch, Jr.,
Publications, 1964. 240p. 16 maps. bibliog.

This is Craton's personal guide to the Bahamas and, as such, it is sprinkled with anecdotes, and is replete with historical information. Each island is described, including the Turks and Caicos Islands, and there are chapters on sailing and fishing in the Bahamas. It is now interesting for historical purposes, as there were no further editions.

86 **The Bahama Islands.**
Egbert T. Smith. Fort Myers, Florida: Egbert T. Smith, 1950.
91p. map.

In this very cheerful tourist guide or travelogue, which is similar to *Fodor's* . . . (q.v.), Smith provides the reader with historical background to the Bahamas. Unfortunately, he glosses over any controversy in the country's history. For instance, he refers to Sir Harry Oakes as a most beloved and respected citizen and, when commenting on the murder trial of Oakes, discusses only what the lawyers and police wore. Smith's book is not useful for current travel but it is interesting when considering the evolution of Bahamian travel guides.

87 **Yachtsman's guide to the Bahamas.**
Edited by Meredith H. Fields. Miami: Tropic Isle, 1950– . annual.

This annual provides thorough descriptions of the waters, reefs and shallows near virtually every island and cay in the Bahamas. It also includes information on the documents required for official entry and coastal inspections, communications and safety. Those who know deem this guide to be indispensible to people sailing Bahamian waters in a yacht.

88 **Bahama harbors: a pilot book for the Great Bahama Bank, British West Indies.**
Arthur Churchill Strong. Annapolis, Maryland: The Author, 1936.
57p. 14 maps.

Strong's guide was printed privately and limited to 112 numbered copies, which are available in major libraries. It is an interesting book that includes general information, sailing directions and a glossary. The fourteen maps or charts are excellent enlargements of some seldom-visited harbours, especially in the Exuma Cays. It is most certainly now out of date but is one of the few chart books available, as well as being valuable as a collectors' item.

89 **The Atlantic islands as resorts of health and pleasure.**
S[amuel] G[reene] W[heeler] Benjamin. New York: Harper &
Brothers, 1878. 274p. 11 maps.

The Bahamas is one of several islands and island groups described in this work. In the Bahamas sections (p. 13–32, 260–61) there are observations on Nassau, the characteristics of 'Negroes', wrecking, sponging, pirates and the American Civil War. The author also describes cruises that can be taken to Harbour Island and Eleuthera, Hopetown and Spanish Wells. The appendix provides information on how to get to the Bahamas ($90 round trip from New York), where to stay ($3.00 per night at the Royal

Victoria Hotel) and the effects of the country and climate on health. This guide should be considered to be primarily a curiosity.

90 **Fishing guide to the Bahamas: including Turks and Caicos Islands.**
George W. Hartwell. Miami: Argos; New York: Hastings House, [n.d.]. 64p. 14 maps.
A guide to the types of gamefish to be found in the waters of the Bahamas as well as to where these fish may be found. For each island he discusses, Hartwell provides a map showing where certain gamefish can usually be found. He also gives general information and tips as well as information on gamefish records.

Individual islands

Exuma

91 **Doing nothing in the Exumas.**
Vanessa Westgate. *Oceans*, vol. 19, no. 6 (Nov./Dec. 1986), p. 44–49, 63.
A general travel article about the Exumas, this is useful for its account of the Family Island Regatta begun in 1954 and held every April.

Grand Bahama

92 **Life in Freeport/Lucaya.**
Hans W. Hannau. Miami: Argos, 1973. 80p.
This picture book of Freeport/Lucaya is similar to those Hannau has published on the Bahamas in general, in that it contains some descriptive text and many, in this case fifty-six, colour plates.

93 **Freeport/Lucaya, Grand Bahama Island.**
Hans W. Hannau. Munich: W. Andermann; Garden City, New York: Doubleday, 1969. 60p. 3 maps. (Panorama Books).
A slight volume, offering a brief introduction to Freeport/Lucaya. The text is accompanied by thirty-four colour plates.

New Providence

94 **The compleat guide to Nassau.**
Steve Dodge. Decatur, Illinois: White Sound, 1987. 116p. 17 maps.
Dodge has produced an excellent guide to the city of Nassau and the island of New

Providence. He has included an informative and detailed walking tour of old Nassau, along with descriptions of all the major areas of the Island of New Providence. There are also articles on gambling; Bahamian history, sociology and politics; goombay, a style of Bahamian music; and the festival Junkanoo, as well as a guide to restaurants and a list of hotels.

95 **Pictorial Nassau: an illustrated guide to Nassau and New Providence Island including Paradise Island and Cable Beach.**
Locust Valley, New York: Pisces Books, 1985. 36p. 2 maps.
This glossy booklet is geared toward the tourist. There are two simple but useful maps and forty-eight excellent colour photographs accompanied by brief captions.

96 **Journey through New Providence.**
Nassau: Arawak Editors, 1971. 62p. 2 maps.
This book has been written primarily for classroom use for eight to twelve year olds. The editors have used the device of a walking tour through Nassau and the Island of New Providence to teach Bahamian school children about their country's history, geography, politics and sociology.

97 **Nassau in the Bahamas.**
Hans W. Hannau.   Munich: Andermann; Garden City, New York: Doubleday, 1962. 59p. 2 maps. (Panorama Books).
A brief introduction to Nassau is accompanied by thirty colour plates. Captions are in German, English and French.

98 **Presenting Nassau.**
Helen Burns Higgs.   Chicago: Pryor, 1936. 96p. 3 maps.
Higgs presents a gentle and general introduction to the Bahamas and, more particularly, Nassau, for the pre-war winter visitor. Contents include such topics as what to wear, what club to belong to and how to rent a house. The work is now of curiosity value and is a source of social history.

99 **Notes on Nassau, the capital of the Bahamas.**
Edgar Mayhew Bacon.   New York: Grand Central Printers, 1927. 113p. map.
Bacon originally began gathering his 'notes' for his own gratification and instruction but eventually felt that others might benefit from his observations. He saw his book as more than a travel guide but that is primarily what it is. Although the book contains a brief history of Nassau, it is more useful as an observation of Nassau in the mid 1920s. An appendix lists land grants given to American Loyalists and there are ten full-page advertisements for Nassau businesses which are of curiosity value.

Travellers' Accounts

100 **The roof of the wind.**
Nelson Taylor Hayes.   Garden City, New York: Doubleday, 1961.
216p. map.
Hayes' account of the cruise of the *Sea Beast* centres on Green Cay, east of southern Andros. It is written in a 'brink-of-disaster' style, as he and his wife found themselves in some tense situations while cruising through this area. In part, the book is sensitively and descriptively written especially when considering the sea and the difficulties this couple encountered.

101 **Islands in the sun.**
Joan Rosita Torr Forbes.   London: Evans Brothers, 1949. 167p.
2 maps.
In this account of her travels through the islands, Forbes provides a lively social commentary on the Bahamas, Nassau, and Eleuthera in the late 1940s.

102 **A unicorn in the Bahamas.**
Joan Rosita Torr Forbes.   New York: Dutton, 1940. 244p. map.
An inveterate traveller, Forbes reads of a buccaneer who sails to the Bahamas on the *Unicorn*. She does the same – the 'unicorn' of the title being a metaphor for her dreams. The work is a social travelogue and a personal account of the Bahamas of the late 1930s. Eventually the author arrives on the island of Eleuthera where a small girl gives her 'a perfect little sea horse with a horn on his forehead'. Forbes has found her unicorn and builds a house on Eleuthera. This work, pleasant to read though superficial in its coverage, provides good illustrations and amusing anecdotes, written in flamboyant prose. The first British edition was published in 1939 (London: H. Jenkins).

103 **The Fortunate Islands, being adventures with the Negro in the Bahamas.**
Amelia Dorothy Defries. London: C. Palmer, 1929. 160p. map.
A rather condescending look at the Bahamas in the 1920s. The author is not afraid to explore her surroundings and to say what she pleases.

104 **A winter in paradise.**
Alan Parsons. London: A.M. Philpot, 1926. 227p. map.
Parsons had no intention of publishing his diary when he first began keeping notes of his trip from England to Cuba, Florida and Nassau, between November 1924 and February 1925, but friends persuaded him otherwise. The bulk of the author's trip and, therefore, the bulk of the book was spent in Nassau. This diary was written when visitors to Nassau only spent time there during 'the season', in the months December to February/March. Parsons provides a very good view of the social life during 'the season' as well as a good description of Junkanoo in the 1920s. His volume can be compared with and read at the same time as McKenna's *By intervention of Providence* (q.v), to best picture Nassau in this period.

105 **By intervention of Providence.**
Stephen McKenna. Boston, Massachusetts: Little, Brown; London: Chapman & Hall, 1923. 298p.
This is a rather self-indulgent travel narrative, focusing on time spent in Barbados, Jamaica, Cuba and the Bahamas. The bulk of the account takes place in Nassau and is, therefore, useful for imagining that city in the 1920s. It does not provide a great many facts; the work's value lies in its evocation of the atmosphere of the city at that time.

106 **In a forgotten colony, being some studies in Nassau and at Grand Bahama during 1916.**
Amelia Dorothy Defries. Nassau: Guardian Office, 1917. 278p.
Defries provides much information about the Bahamas, gathered during her stay. She describes sponge gathering and sisal growing, Junkanoo and bush medicine, religion and music and the social life in Nassau during the winter months, which were then the highlight of the tourist season. She also includes the text of her unpublished play, 'The nameless one' and an outline for a play entitled, 'Progress' which was to present the history of the Bahamas from the Lucayans to the turn of the twentieth century.

107 **Sketches of summerland, giving some account of Nassau and the Bahama Islands.**
George J.H. Northcroft. Nassau: Nassau Guardian, 1900. 309p. 3 maps.
Northcroft presents his impressions of the Bahamas, gained during a number of years spent there chiefly in Nassau, in the late-nineteenth century. He discusses a variety of subjects, including social life in Nassau, folklore and religion, climate and geography and flora and fauna. The forty-eight pages of advertisements appended to this edition are, in themselves, fascinating.

108 **History and guide to the Bahama islands, containing a description of everything on or about the Bahama Islands of which the visitor or resident may desire information, including their history, inhabitants, climate, agriculture, geology, government and resources.**
James Henry Stark.   Boston, Massachusetts: Plimpton, 1891. 243p. 5 maps.

Stark's work is a combined history and travel guide. It includes advertisements for both steamship lines serving the Bahamas and for hotels on the islands, which provide historical information and are of curiosity value. This is, perhaps, the most useful of the travellers' accounts of the late-nineteenth century.

109 **Land of the pink pearl; or, recollections of life in the Bahamas.**
Louis Diston Powles.   London: Sampson Low, Marston, Searle & Rivington, 1888. 321p. map.

Powles was a Circuit Judge in the Bahamas in the late-nineteenth century. He is very observant, speaks frankly about the country and is quite critical of the government. Powles is also extremely critical of the way the justice system treated blacks in the colony. Included in this work is a section entitled 'History of the Lightbourn case', in which Powles outlines his attempts to uphold justice in favour of the blacks. Criticism aroused by his judgment in the case was the cause of his resignation as Circuit Judge.

110 **In the trades, the tropics, and the roaring forties.**
Lady Brassey.   London: Longmans & Green; New York: Holt, 1885. 532p. 9 maps.

Baroness Brassey née Annie Allnutt, offers a description of the Bahamas based on a voyage of four month's duration throughout the Caribbean in 1883. She includes accounts of the sponging and pineapple industries and the flora and fauna. Featured are air and water temperature graphs and charts. This work was also published in two volumes in Leipzig in the same year.

111 **The isles of summer; or, Nassau and the Bahamas.**
Charles Ives.   New Haven, Connecticut: The Author, 1880. 356p. map.

This is a personal account touching on all conceivable aspects of the Bahamas including flora and fauna, geology, climate, health and sanitation. Ives provides excellent descriptions of Nassau; his volume includes fourteen wood engravings and twelve lithographs.

112 **Letters from the Bahama Islands, written in 1823–4.**
Miss Hart (pseud.), edited by Richard Kent.   London: J. Culmer, 1948. 115p.

This collection of twenty letters was first published in Philadelphia in 1827. The letters describe a stay of several months in Nassau and provide a detailed account of life in the city. This epistolary style is a very familiar literary device. The letters were obviously written for publication and Miss Hart (a pseudonym for Adela Del Lorraine) proves to be an entertaining as well as intelligent observer.

113   **A tour through the British West Indies, in the years 1802 and 1803, giving a particular account of the Bahama Islands.**
Daniel McKinnon.   London: Printed for J. White, by S. Woolmer, 1812. 2nd ed. 288p. map.
McKinnon describes Barbados, Dominica, Antigua, Jamaica and the Bahamas. His descriptions of the Bahamas and, in particular, the Out Islands are very good, being amusing and observant accounts of people and activities. Interestingly, he views slavery in a favourable light and pardons the supposed criminality of the slave trade by comparing the slaves' wretched state when first imported with their treatment under good masters. This is arguably the most useful of the travellers' accounts of the early-nineteenth century.

114   **Travels in the Confederation, 1783–1784.**
Johann David Schoepf, translated and edited by Alfred J. Morrison. New York: Burt Franklin, 1968. 2 vols. (Research and Source Works Series, no. 206).
Travels in the Confederation was originally published in German in 1788, while the Morrison translation was first published in 1911 (Philadelphia: W.J. Campbell). Schoepf (1752-1800), a life-long student of medicine and the natural sciences, travelled extensively in Europe and America. In volume two, he provides excellent observations of the Bahamas and comments on the Gulf Stream, sea life and fish, musical instruments, Nassau, the geology of New Providence, agricultural crops, fauna, trees, wrecking and animals. This is one of the earliest accounts of a visit to the Bahamas and is a very useful consideration of the pre-Loyalist era.

115   **Memoirs of Peter Henry Bruce, Esq., a military officer in the services of Prussia, Russia & Great Britain, containing an account of his travels in Germany, Russia, Tartary, Turkey, the West Indies, etc., as also several very interesting private anecdotes of the Czar, Peter I of Russia.**
Peter Henry Bruce.   Dublin: J. and R. Byrn, 1783. 2nd ed. Reprinted, London: F. Cass; New York: Da Capo, 1970. 527p. (Russia Through European Eyes, no. 9).
Peter Henry Bruce (1692-1757) was a military engineer sent out from England in 1740 to fortify the Bahamas against the Spanish. He was in Nassau from November 1740 to April 1741. Books eleven and twelve include a fascinating account of Bruce's time in Nassau. His memoir provides an excellent view of mid-eighteenth century social history. This section was published separately, with a new introduction, in 1949 as *Bahamian interlude* . . . (q.v.), but this edition of the entire memoirs is more easily obtained.

116   **Bahamian interlude: being an account of life at Nassau in the Bahama Islands in the eighteenth century.**
Peter Henry Bruce, introduced by Richard Kent.   London: J. Culmer, 1949. 62p.
This is a reprint of books eleven and twelve from the *Memoirs of Peter Henry Bruce, Esq.* . . . (q.v.). This section of his memoirs describes his trip to Nassau, his time there

Travellers' Accounts

and his trip back to England. Not only does it provide a glimpse of Nassau in the mid-eighteenth century but it also gives a good description of the fortifications erected in defence against the Spanish at the time. The introduction by Kent is particularly useful.

Tourism

117   Tourism in the Caribbean.
Neil E. Sealey.   London: Hodder & Stoughton, 1982. 60p. 10 maps.

This book was written as a social studies text for Caribbean students while the author was a lecturer at the College of the Bahamas. Since the book does not simply describe tourism in the Caribbean but rather explains it, the reader is able to understand the nature of tourism and the impact it has made on the area. The work provides comparative data tables for Jamaica, St. Lucia and the Bahamas. There are also activity suggestions and exercises.

118   The impact of tourism: a case from the Bahama Islands.
Alan G. LaFlamme.   *Annals of Tourism Research*, vol. 6, no. 2 (1979), p. 137–48.

This article discusses the socio-cultural impact of increased tourism on an unnamed small, once isolated island community in the Bahamas. It shows that although material living standards, occupational specializations and race relations have been significantly altered, the community's traditions have, for the most part, been maintained. For a number of reasons, the local people have not taken on the role of 'professional natives'.

119   Tourism in the economy of the Bahamas.
Ramesh F. Ramsaran.   *Caribbean Studies*, vol. 19, no. 1/2 (April/June 1979), p. 75–91.

Discusses the growth of tourism in the Bahamas, the structure of the Bahamian economy, the interaction of government and tourism, and current problems. Ramsaran offers guidelines for policy formulation which are aimed at transforming the framework of the tourist industry.

120 **The Bahamas tourism industry: past, present and future.**

John H. Bounds. *Revista Geográfica*, no. 88 (Dec. 1978), p. 167–219.

This article, which outlines the development of tourism in the Bahamas from the mid 1800s to the mid 1970s, is very useful because it provides statistics and a history of the industry.

121 **Tourism in the Bahamas and Bermuda: two case studies.**

Brian Archer. Bangor, Wales: University of Wales Press, 1977. 87p.

2 maps. (Bangor Occasional Papers in Economics, no. 10).

The principal objective of this paper is to trace the flow of the average tourist dollar through the economy of each of the two countries. Chapter four, which makes up nearly half of the book, deals with the Bahamas. In this chapter, Archer provides geographical and historical background to the Bahamas, information on the present economic situation, a description of the tourist industry and his findings and conclusions.

122 **Tourism.**

Anne Nason Lyons. *Focus*, vol. 19, no. 9 (May 1969), p. 8–11.

Outlines the rise of tourism in the Bahamas and discusses its place on New Providence, the Abacos, Bimini, Andros, Eleuthera, the Exumas and Great Inagua, and in Freeport.

Flora and Fauna

General

123   **A field guide to southeastern and Caribbean seashores: Cape Hatteras, the Gulf Coast, Florida and the Caribbean.**
Eugene Herbert Kaplan.   London: Thomas Allen & Son; Boston, Massachusetts: Houghton Mifflin, 1988. 425p. map. bibliog. (Peterson Field Guide Series).

This work, sponsored by the National Audubon Society and the National Wildlife Federation, describes the ecology and common organisms of seashores from North Carolina through to Florida, the Gulf Coast and the Caribbean. It identifies plants and animals and describes all the common Bahamian seashore environments – sandy beaches, rocky shores, turtle grass beds, mangrove swamps and scrub forests. A glossary is included.

124   **Man and the variable vulnerability of island life: a study of recent vegetation change in the Bahamas.**
Roger Byrne.   Washington, DC: Smithsonian Institution, 1980. 200p. bibliog. (Atoll Research Bulletin, no. 240).

Discusses whether the vegetation of Cat Island was vulnerable to culturally induced disturbances in the same way as the vegetation of remote islands such as the Hawaiian or the Galapagos Islands, and concludes that man's impact has been surprisingly slight.

125   **The ephemeral islands: a natural history of the Bahamas.**
David G. Campbell.   London: Macmillan, 1978. 151p. 2 maps. bibliog.

This work defines the geological, climatic, biological and social conditions that gave rise to the Bahamas of today. Campbell explores those living resources that remain in the islands and points out the stresses to which they are subjected. He also discusses birds, coral, fishes, crustaceans, flora, gastropods, insects, mammals, reptiles and spiders. The work is easy to read and understand and avoids technical jargon.

126 **The vertebrate fauna and the vegetation of East Plana Cay, Bahama Islands.**
Garrett C. Clough, George Fulk. Washington, DC: Smithsonian Institution, 1971. 17p. bibliog. (Atoll Research Bulletin, no. 138).
The authors report on observations and collections of lizards, birds and plants of East Plana Cay and give a general account of the island, with a brief note on West Plana Cay.

127 **Mark Catesby: the colonial Audubon.**
George Frederick Frick, Raymond Phineas Stearns. Urbana, Illinois: University of Illinois Press, 1961. 137p. bibliog.
Mark Catesby (1683–1749) was a pioneer in the field of scientific illustration. His two-volume *The natural history of Carolina, Florida, and the Bahamas* . . . (q.v.) was a landmark work when it was first published in London in 1731–43. In this biography, Frick and Stearns use original sources as well as evaluations of Catesby's work to piece together his life. They also consider his influence on the history of science. The biography includes sixteen black-and-white reproductions from Catesby's *The natural history* . . . (q.v.). This is the only available full-length biography of Catesby.

128 **Bahamian Land-and-Sea Park.**
John E. Randall, Carleton Ray. *Sea Frontiers*, vol. 4, no. 1 (Feb. 1958), p. 72–80.
Outlines a proposal for a land and sea conservation park, which was subsequently established in the Exuma Cays and surrounding waters in the southcentral Bahamas. The authors also describe the flora and fauna of the area.

129 **Twenty years under the sea.**
John Ernest Williamson. Boston, Massachusetts: R.T. Hale, 1944. 320p. map.
This is the record of the labours, adventures and achievements of the inventor of the Williamson submarine tube, known as the photosphere, for taking pictures underwater. Although the writing is amateurish, the work is entertaining and educational. Williamson includes a description of how films were made of Jules Verne's novels *20,000 leagues under the sea* (1916) and *The mysterious island* (1929). All of Williamson's work was carried out in the Bahamas.

130 **Inagua: which is the name of a very lonely and nearly forgotten island.**
Gilbert C. Klingel. New York: Dodd, Mead, 1940. 385p. map.
This is a record of the highlights of two expeditions taken by the author to Inagua. The technical accounts of these expeditions have been published in the *American Museum Novitiates* and the *Bulletin of the Natural History Society of Maryland*. Klingel's account is non-technical and includes those events from the expeditions which have no place in a biological treatise. The book was also published under the title *The ocean island (Inagua)* (New York: Dodd, Mead, 1940. 385p.).

131 **Under the sea with helmet and camera: experiences of an amateur.**
Alexis Felix Du Pont. New York: Dodd, Mead, 1940. 87p.
An amateur underwater photographer offers an account of his introduction to diving in
a helmet in the Bahamas. In the second part of the book, there is a detailed description
of the diving equipment used, of water-tight camera cases and of underwater dangers.

132 **New light on Mark Catesby.**
Elsa G. Allen. *Auk*, vol. 54, no. 3 (July 1937), p. 349–63.
Allen has attempted to deal with some of the undocumented features of the life of
Mark Catesby in this early biographical article. She comments on his family and
parentage, marriage, patrons, publications and death. Frick and Stearns' *Mark
Catesby: the colonial Audubon* (q.v.) is far more complete.

133 **Shipwrecked on Inagua.**
Gilbert C. Klingel. *Natural History*, vol. 32, no. 1 (1932), p. 42–55.
This article is subtitled 'The adventures and accomplishments of the Joint Expedition
of the Natural History Society of Maryland and the American Museum that set sail in
the yawl *Basilisk* in November 1930 for scientific studies among the islands of the West
Indies'. Unfortunately, the yawl was wrecked on the northeast tip of Great Inagua
Island. Members of the expedition remained there for two weeks and made a thorough
herpetological study. The article provides a good description of the fauna of Inagua.

134 **A naturalist in the Bahamas: John I. Northrop, October 12, 1861–June
25, 1891; a memorial volume.**
Edited by Henry Fairfield Osborn. New York: Columbia University
Press, 1910. Reprinted by AMS Press, New York, 1967. 281p. 2 maps.
John Northrop was a zoologist who spent six months in the Bahamas in 1890. This
memorial volume contains all of his writings. Of the fourteen papers collected here,
ten pertain to the Bahamas and deal with such subjects as geology, birds, crustaceans,
shells, flora and sisal. There is a useful index to the Bahamian papers, which is unusual
in this kind of collection.

135 **The Bahama Islands.**
George Burbank Shattuck. New York; London: Macmillan, 1905.
630p. 13 maps.
Despite the publication date, this report of the Bahamas expedition sent out by the
Geographical Society of Baltimore in June 1903 is perhaps the best natural history of
the Bahamas. The object of the expedition, which included twenty scientists, was to
investigate the origin and natural history of the islands and to 'conduct studies along
lines intimately associated with the well-being of the inhabitants'. This document
contains a great deal of valuable information on geology, climate, soil and vegetation,
flora and fauna, health and history. The material, complete and authoritative, is highly
readable and contains excellent illustrations. The expedition visited Abaco, New
Providence, Andros, Green Cay, Eleuthera, Cat Island, Long Island, Rum Cay, and
Watlings Island.

136 **The natural history of Carolina, Florida, and the Bahama Islands:**
containing two hundred and twenty figures of birds, beasts, fishes,
serpents, insects, and plants . . . Volume one.
Mark Catesby, introduced by George Frick, notes by John Ewan.
Savannah, Georgia: Beehive, 1974. 107p. map.

Catesby's two volume work was first published in English in London in 1731–43 with
subsequent editions in 1754 and 1771. It was also published seven times in Germany
between 1749 and 1781. Both volumes offer descriptions and illustrations. Volume
one, covering birds, is considered to be the more important of the two volumes. The
second volume considers the remainder of the flora and fauna. This 1974 edition is a
reprint of volume one of the 1771 edition (London: B. White). It includes all of the
plates, reproduced in black-and-white. The introduction by Frick, coordinator of the
Winterthur Program at the University of Delaware, and notes by Ewan, Professor of
Biology at Tulane University, are valuable additions to this edition of Catesby's work,
making it a most useful volume for those who wish to consider only his period in the
Bahamas. Each copy of this edition includes reproductions of two colour plates.

137 **The natural history of Carolina, Florida and the Bahama Islands:**
containing the figures of birds, beasts, fishes, serpents, insects, and
plants: particularly, the forest-trees, shrubs, and other plants, not
hitherto described, or very incorrectly figured by the authors. Together
with their descriptions in English and French. To which are added
observations on the air, soil, and waters: with remarks upon agriculture,
grain, pulse, roots, etc. To the whole, is prefixed a new and correct map
of the countries treated of.
Mark Catesby. London: The Author, 1731–43. 2 vols.

Volume one contains the plates for the birds while volume two contains the plates for
sea life, reptiles, mammals, plants, and insects as well as the major text of the work
which is Catesby's account of Carolina and the Bahamas. The first volume of this
important work was reprinted in 1974 (q.v.) but the second volume is only available in
the original. Although this makes it difficult to obtain, it is necessary to consider the
second volume in order to appreciate the full extent of Catesby's work.

Vegetation

138 **Proceedings of the second symposium on the botany of the Bahamas.**
Edited by Robert R. Smith. Fort Lauderdale, Florida: College Center
of the Finger Lakes, Bahamian Field Station, 1987. 65p.

Included in this collection are papers on the genuses *Capiscum*, *Cocoloba* and *Anemia*,
as well as on Malpighiaceae, seagrasses, insect and plant relationships and the chemical
composition of various medicinal plants.

139 **Proceedings of the first symposium on the botany of the Bahamas.**
Edited by Robert R. Smith. Fort Lauderdale, Florida: College Center
of the Finger Lakes, Bahamian Field Station, 1986.
The papers in this collection cover the following topics: seagrasses, algae, *Scaevola*,
palms, plant communities, halophytes, ferns, bush medicine and *Canella alba*.

140 **Vegetation of North Point, San Salvador Island, Bahamas.**
Robert R. Smith, Kathleen Amatucci. Fort Lauderdale, Florida:
College Center of the Finger Lakes, Bahamian Field Station, 1986. 12p.
map. (Occasional Papers 1986, no. 6).
This booklet describes the various plants covering North Point, which extends out from
the northeast coast of San Salvador, and includes a detailed map showing the
distribution of the various plants and their relationships both to each other and to the
natural environment.

141 **Field guide to the vegetation of San Salvador Island, the Bahamas.**
Robert R. Smith. Fort Lauderdale, Florida: College Center of the
Finger Lakes, Bahamian Field Station, 1982. 135p.
This work offers a descriptive overview of the checklists of both vascular plants and
marine algae. It includes chapters, with illustrations, on economic plants, common
roadside plants and edible fruits.

142 **Flora of the Bahamian archipelago (including the Turks and Caicos
Islands).**
Donovan S. Correll, Helen B. Correll. Vaduz, Switzerland:
J. Cramer, 1982. 1692p. map. bibliog.
This work provides a means for the identification of the indigenous and naturalized
flowering plants and ferns in the Bahamian archipelago. The flora are divided into four
sections: ferns, flowering plants, grasses and palms, and trees. The families are
arranged phylogenetically while the genera and species are arranged alphabetically.
The entries are well written and very thorough. However, given its large size, this
guide cannot be used easily in the field. The work includes a glossary and 715
illustrations.

143 **Flowers of the Caribbean, the Bahamas, and Bermuda.**
G.W. Lennox, S.A. Seddon. London: Macmillan Caribbean, 1978.
72p.
This book is designed for individuals with little or no botanical training. The flora are
divided into three sections: herbs and shrubs, trees, and orchids. For each of the fifty
entries, the authors have provided a colour photograph, the common, local and
scientific names and a short description of each specimen. Although this handy guide
does not illustrate all species of flowering plants, it does discuss the more common
ones.

144 **Native trees of the Bahamas.**
Jack Patterson, George Stevenson.   Nassau: Jack Patterson, 1977.
128p. map.

The primary goal of this book is to stimulate interest in the native trees of the
Bahamas. For ease of use, the trees have been divided into sections on palms, pine
trees, simple alternative leaf trees, simple opposite leaf trees and compound leaf trees.
Each entry contains comments on the tree's trunk, crown, leafstem, leaves, flowers and
fruit. It is a thorough guide for the learned layperson.

145 **Flowers of the Bahamas.**
Hans W. Hannau, Jeanne Garrard.   Miami: Argos, 1972. 64p.

The text which accompanies this small book is short but informative. The main
purpose of the work is to highlight the thirty-four colour photographs which are
accompanied by useful, non-scientific descriptions.

146 **An introduction to some wild flowers of the Bahamas and the Caribbean.**
Margaret B. Rabley.   London: Collins, 1971. 64p.

Discusses the wild flowers under two main headings: 'Dicotyledons' (net veined leaves,
two seed leaves and flower parts generally in fives) and 'Monocotyledons' (parallel
veined leaves, one seed leaf and flower parts in threes or multiples of three). Each
entry gives the scientific and common names, a description and, in some cases, the
floral formula. This floral formula, which describes the flower section, is explained in
the book's introduction. Pen-and-ink drawings help to clarify each entry, though colour
illustrations would brighten up the book, which has been produced primarily as a
school text.

147 **Flowers of the West Indies: Caribbean and Bahamas.**
Hans W. Hannau, Jeanne Garrard.   Miami: Argos, 1970. 63p.

Combines an introductory text with thirty-four colour plates, each plate having its own
descriptive caption. These are good but do not appear immediately beside the
illustration. It is a picture book rather than a field guide or scientific treatise, and the
emphasis on high quality colour plates is typical of Hannau's books.

148 **Tropical blossoms.**
Dorothy Hargreaves, Bob Hargreaves.   Portland, Oregon: Hargreaves
Industrial, 1960. 62p.

This handbook includes entries for forty flowers and thirty-two trees from the
Bahamas, the Caribbean and tropical South America. A typical entry has a colour
photograph, both the common name and the botanical name, a description and an
indication of where the item might be found. This is not a scientific treatise but rather a
book for the traveller or resident.

149 **Vegetation of the Bimini Island group, Bahamas, British West Indies.**
Richard A. Howard.   *Ecological Monographs*, vol. 20, no. 4
(Oct. 1950), p. 317–49.

Howard discusses the general geographical features and history of Bimini as well as
individual areas in the group of islands. He also provides descriptions of individual
plant communities such as mangrove, coastal rock and tidal flat areas, and an extensive

check list of plants found on the islands. The article was published originally as a monograph by the Biological Laboratories of Harvard University, in 1948.

150 **Fifty tropical fruits of Nassau.**
Kendall Morton, Julie Morton.   Coral Gables, Florida: Text House, 1946. 118p.
This work is intended to acquaint the visitor with the types of fruits found in both Nassau and throughout the Bahamas. For each fruit, the authors provide a black-and-white photograph, the common and scientific names, a description and, in most cases, an indication of how the fruit should be eaten.

151 **The Bahama flora.**
Nathaniel Lord Britton, Charles Frederick Millspaugh.   New York: The Authors, 1920. Reprinted, New York: Hafner, 1962. 695p. bibliog.
This highly scientific ordering of Bahamian flora contains species that fall under the phylums of spermatophyta, pteridophyta, bryophyta and thallophyta as well as a list of explorations and collections of Bahamian flora from 1703 to 1911. There are no illustrations. It is a work for the scientist or well-informed layperson.

152 **Report on the continuation of the botanical exploration of the Bahama Islands.**
Nathaniel Lord Britton.   *Journal of the New York Botanical Garden*, vol. 8, no. 88 (April 1907), p. 71–81.
Presents an account of a collecting expedition in February and March 1907 to Eleuthera, Little San Salvador Island, Cat Island, Conception Island, Watling's Island and Long Island.

153 **Explorations in the Bahamas.**
Nathaniel Lord Britton.   *Journal of the New York Botanical Garden*, vol. 6 (1905), p. 78–85.
Offers a narrative of a collecting expedition from January to March 1905 on New Providence, Rose Island, the Berry Islands, Grand Bahama Island and the Exuma Cays. Britton found that Grand Bahama Island contained flora species not found in the southern Bahamas. The expedition brought back approximately 10,000 specimens, half of which were seaweed.

154 **Botanical exploration of the Inagua Islands, Bahamas.**
George V. Nash.   *Journal of the New York Botanical Garden*, vol. 6, no. 61 (Jan. 1905), p. 1–19.
An account of a collecting expedition to Great and-Little Inagua Islands in October and November 1904. Nash provides a detailed account of the expedition and good physical descriptions of the two islands. Over 1,000 specimens were brought back from the trip.

155 **Report on exploration of the Bahamas.**
Nathaniel Lord Britton. *Journal of the New York Botanical Garden*,
vol. 5, no. 59 (Nov. 1904), p. 201–09.
A botanical survey conducted in August and September 1904 on New Providence
Island is the subject of this article, which provides a good description of New
Providence and the flora of the seashore, the marsh lands, the pine barrens and the
coppice areas. The expedition returned with about 4,000 specimens.

156 **Flora of New Providence and Andros, with an enumeration of the plants
collected by John I. Northrop and Alice R. Northrop, in 1890.**
Alice Rich Northrop. New York: Torrey Botanical Club, 1902. 98p.
map. (Memoirs of the Torrey Botanical Club, vol. 12, no. 1).
This discussion of the botanical regions of New Providence and Andros provides
detailed descriptions of the 542 plant species collected by the Northrops.

157 **Provisional list of the plants of the Bahama Islands.**
John Gardiner, L.J.K. Brace, Charles S. Dolley. *Proceedings of the
Academy of Natural Sciences, Philadelphia*, vol. 41 (1889), p. 349–426.
This list of Bahamian plants includes 115 families, 410 genera and 621 species.

Marine life

158 **Sharks of the shallows.**
Samuel H. Gruber. *Natural History*, vol. 97, no. 3 (March 1988),
p. 50–59.
This investigation and description of lemon sharks off the Bimini Islands includes an
account and photographs of their birth.

159 **A field guide to coral reefs of the Caribbean and Florida: a guide to the
common invertebrates and fishes of Bermuda, the Bahamas, Southern
Florida, the West Indies, and the Caribbean coast of Central and South
America.**
Eugene Herbert Kaplan. Boston, Massachusetts: Houghton Mifflin,
1982. 289p. map. bibliog. (Peterson Field Guide Series, 27).
This book was sponsored by the National Audubon Society and the National Wildlife
Federation. Following a very good introductory chapter, Kaplan provides an overview
of coral reefs, their development and their ecology. The bulk of the work is devoted to
the animals of the lagoon and the reef. Technical terms are kept to a minimum as the
book is intended for laypeople, though a glossary is provided. Although Kaplan tries to
cover too much, and arguably should have dismissed invertebrates or fish, the book
does make interesting reading. The work is illustrated by thirty-seven coloured plates.
Stokes' *Handguide to the coral reef fishes* . . . (q.v.) may be more useful as a field guide
because the illustrations are accorded more attention than the text.

160 **Handguide to the coral reef fishes of the Caribbean and adjacent tropical waters including Florida, Bermuda and the Bahamas.**
F. Joseph Stokes. New York: Lippincott & Crowell, 1980. 160p.
The emphasis in this handguide is on the illustrations, which are paintings of colour photographs. The descriptions in the text are very short, often consisting of only one sentence or several short phrases. The fish described, 460 species, are the ones most likely to be seen by the snorkler and diver. This book, which includes a glossary, is useful for both professionals and amateurs.

161 **Fishes of the Caribbean reefs, the Bahamas and Bermuda.**
Ian F. Took. London: Macmillan, 1979. 92p. map.
Took's book is an introduction to some of the more common and spectacular fish to be found around the Caribbean and tropical west Atlantic reefs. For each of the eighty-five species covered, the author provides a description, including length, common and scientific names, a discussion of general habits and particular characteristics, and an indication of where the fish might be found. There are also sections on practical fish watching, underwater photography and conservation of the coral reef. The work is illustrated with seventy-two colour plates of fish and seven of coral.

162 **Caribbean reef invertebrates and plants: a field guide to the invertebrates and plants occurring on coral reefs of the Caribbean, the Bahamas and Florida.**
Patrick Lynn Colin. Hong Kong: T.F.H. Publications, 1978. 512p. map.
This book is designed to serve as an identification guide for the professional marine scientist and the amateur snorkler or scuba diver. It provides good introductory chapters on the natural history of Caribbean reefs and their organisms. The entries are arranged by phylum, with animals preceding plants. Within each phylum the individual species are considered by order and family. The descriptions given for each entry are very good, while the black-and-white and colour photographs are adequate. Sponges, sea fans and sea anemones, corals, marine worms, crustaceans, molluscs, starfish, sea urchins and sea cucumbers, and marine plants and algae are included.

163 **Shallow-water sponges of the western Bahamas.**
Felix Wiedenmayer. Basel, Switzerland: Birkhauser, 1977. 287p.
2 maps. bibliog. (Experientia Supplementum, 28).
A taxonomic study of the shallow-water sponges of the western Bahamas, particularly the Bimini area, supplemented with extensive ecological data. The sponges described are the most diverse of the known local West Indian fauna. There are eighty-two described species. This rather technical work includes a glossary and forty-three plates of black-and-white illustrations.

164 **Waterproof guide to corals and fishes of Florida, the Bahamas and the Caribbean.**
Idaz Greenberg, Jerry Greenberg. Miami, Florida: Seahawk, 1977. 64p.
This booklet provides coloured drawings and short descriptions for 206 fish and

amphibians, fifty-three corals and eleven dangerous corals and fish, such as jellyfish, stinging corals, sea urchins and electric rays.

165 **The many-splendored fishes of the Atlantic coast including the fishes of the Gulf of Mexico, Florida, Bermuda, the Bahamas and the Caribbean.**
Gar Goodson.   Palos Verdes Estates, California: Marquest Colorguide Books, 1976. 204p. 2 maps.

For each of the 408 entries, Goodson provides both the common name and the scientific name, a description, a distribution range and an indication as to whether it is edible. Though it is not as complete as Kaplan's *A field guide to coral reefs . . .* (q.v.) in terms of textual material, this volume is more useful than Stokes' *Handguide to the coral reef fishes . . .* (q.v.).

166 **Reef life in the Bahamas.**
Robert A. Martin.   *Oceans*, vol. 8, no. 6 (Nov. 1975), p. 44–53.

This description of the flora and fauna in the coral reefs of the Bahamas includes excellent colour photographs.

167 **Tropical marine fishes of southern Florida and the Bahama Islands.**
Warren Zeiller.   South Brunswick, New Jersey: A.S. Barnes, 1975. 125p. bibliog.

The author's objective is 'to present a series of photographs representative of the . . . fishes found from estuary to coral reef and to offer to interested persons identification references other than the usual taxonomic information' (Introduction). The bulk of the work consists of 289 colour plates; there are brief descriptions for each species. It is useful for the student of tropical fish as well as the tropical fish fancier. The information is accurate and accessible.

168 **In the coral reefs of the Caribbean, Bahamas, Florida, Bermuda.**
Hans W. Hannau.   Garden City, New York: Doubleday, 1974. 135p.

A general introduction to coral reefs which is accompanied by ninety-four coloured plates. Each chapter is by a different contributor which does lead to a patchy quality, and oversimplified material is combined with highly technical information. There are, however, useful chapters on corals, molluscs, fish and reef ecology. A picture-book for the 'armchair' explorer, it would be improved by maps and an index.

169 **Strange march of the spiny lobster.**
William F. Herrnkind.   *National Geographic Magazine*, vol. 147, no. 6 (June 1974), p. 818–31.

Presents an investigation of the unusual migrations of spiny lobsters on the sea bed of the Great Bahama Bank, off the shore of Bimini. The author speculates that the urge to migrate is an evolutionary anachronism, from glacial periods when warm water had to be found.

170 **Tropical marine invertebrates of southern Florida and the Bahama Islands.**
Warren Zeiller.   New York: Wiley, 1974. 132p. bibliog. (A Wiley-Interscience Publication).
Zeiller presents a series of colour photographs representative of the invertebrates found in coral reefs. Observations are confined to examples of six of the twenty-seven invertebrate phyla: Coelenterata (polyp animals), Platyhelminthes (flatworms), Mollusca (molluscs), Annelida (segmented worms), Arthropoda (arthropods) and Echinodermata (echinoderms). For each of the 183 examples, the author gives the phylum, class, order and family; the common and scientific names; the etymology of the scientific name; a short description; and a colour photograph. The work includes an appendix in which all the specimens are listed in phyletic sequence, from primitive to more specialized life forms. The book does not include plant life, microfauna or sponges.

171 **Beneath the seas of the West Indies: Caribbean, Bahamas, Florida, Bermuda.**
Hans W. Hannau, Bernd H. Mock.   New York: Hastings House, 1973. 104p.
Offers a discussion of reefs and reef ecology, marine archaeology in the West Indies and the International Oceanographic Foundation and Ocean Space Center in Florida. It includes fifty-four large colour plates and 120 small colour plates, as well as a picture portfolio for the identification of exotic, tropical fish which inhabit reef areas. This item is very similar to Hannau's *In the coral reefs* . . . (q.v.).

172 **The living reef: corals and fishes of Florida, the Bahamas, Bermuda and the Caribbean.**
Jerry Greenberg, Idaz Greenberg.   Miami, Florida: Seahawk, 1972. 110p.
This work consists chiefly of excellent colour photographs. However, there is nothing distinctively Bahamian about the book; the photographs could have been taken at another location.

173 **Bimini's concrete wreck.**
William M. Stephens.   *Oceans*, vol. 2, no. 1 (July 1969), p. 22–27.
The title of this article refers to the *Sapona*, one of seventeen cement-hulled vessels built during the First World War by Henry Ford. It was driven aground in 1926 and, during the period of American prohibition, it was used as a warehouse for illicit liquor. In the 1930s one entrepreneur conceived of turning it into a nightclub, but by the Second World War the ship was being used for target practice by the US Navy. Today, it is the basis for yet another coral reef in the Bahamas. Stephens provides a very good description of the reef in this article.

174 **Fishes of the Bahamas.**
James E. Bohlke, Charles C.G. Chaplin.   Wynnewood, Pennsylvania: Livingston, 1968. 771p. 2 maps. bibliog.
This excellent book lists approximately 700 species of fish found in the Bahamas. Each entry includes size, distinctions, colouring and distribution, and offers remarks. There

is also an introduction to the Bahamas which includes a history of the study of
Bahamian fish, a glossary and thirty-six colour plates. This work is very complete but,
because of its size, it cannot easily be used in the field.

175   **Shells at our feet: an introduction to shelling in the Bahamas.**
       Mary Baker Moulding.   Chicago: Sea Scapers, 1967. 102p. bibliog.
This informal, general introduction which is intended to answer the simple questions
that occur to most shellers also includes some scientific information to provide a good
foundation for shelling. Descriptions and definitions of various types of molluscs, and
of the techniques of shelling, a glossary of conchological terms and 130 colour plates
are among the contents.

176   **Descending the Andros reef.**
       C. Lavett Smith.   *Natural History*, vol. 75, no. 8 (Oct. 1966), p. 38–43.
Smith provides a vivid description of the Andros Barrier Reef which runs along the
eastern coast of the island on the edge of the Tongue of the Ocean.

177   **Stony corals from the vicinity of Bimini, Bahamas, British West Indies.**
       Donald F. Squires.   *Bulletin of the American Museum of Natural
       History*, vol. 115, no. 4 (1958), p. 217–62.
This article indicates the extent and variety of coral fauna and the factors involved in
its distribution. A discussion of the ecology and environment of corals and descriptions
of various species are included, as are forty-seven black-and-white photographs and a
good bibliography.

178   **Sponges of the western Bahamas.**
       M.W. de Laubenfels.   *American Museum Novitates*, no. 1,431
       (Nov. 3, 1949), p. 1–25.
In this very readable paper, Laubenfels discusses twenty-nine species.

179   **Coral castle builders of tropic seas.**
       Roy Waldo Miner.   *National Geographic Magazine*, vol. 65, no. 6
       (June 1934), p. 703–28.
Miner describes a barrier reef, one hundred miles long, bordering the eastern shore of
Andros Island and provides information on how reefs grow. The article includes eight
colour plates.

180   **Ecology of an oceanic fresh-water lake, Andros Island, Bahamas, with
       special reference to its fishes.**
       C.M. Breder.   *Zoologica*, vol. 18, no. 3 (Aug. 1934), p. 57–88.
An account of an expedition to Lake Forsyth on Andros Island describing habitat,
invertebrate fauna, reptiles, amphibians, fish and the lake's chemical nature. Lake
Forsyth supports twelve species of fish fauna, all of which are marine types which can
exist in the fresh-water environment because of the presence of calcium. At the same
time, the lake supports a relatively poor fauna of terrestrial vertebrates.

181 **The book about the sea gardens of Nassau, Bahamas.**
Stephen Haweis.   New York: Collier, 1917. 78p.
This early-twentieth century travel guide introduces the tourist to the Sea Gardens at
the east end of Hog (Paradise) Island between Hog Island and Athol Island, originally
the government quarantine station. There is good textual detail about the plants,
corals, sponges and fish that can be seen but the twenty pen-and-ink drawings are of
poor quality. The Sea Gardens still exist and can be viewed from glass bottom boats.

Birds

182 **The birds of Cat Island, Bahamas.**
Donald W. Buden.   *Wilson Bulletin*, vol. 99, no. 4 (Dec. 1987),
p. 579–600.
This study updates information on the distribution and status of the birds of Cat Island
and several offshore cays. It records ninety-seven species, forty-six for the first time.

183 **Underground parrots.**
Rosemarie Gnam.   *Animal Kingdom*, vol. 90, no. 5 (Sept./Oct. 1987),
p. 40–44.
The Bahama parrot once inhabited eight islands in the country but by the 1940s it was
only to be found on Great Abaco and Great Inagua, because of habitat destruction,
hunting, and capture for the pet trade. Gnam provides descriptions of nesting,
incubation, rearing of the young, habits and habitats. This is an informative article on
the subject, especially for the layperson.

184 **The birds of the southern Bahamas: an annotated check-list.**
Donald W. Buden.   London: British Ornithologists' Union, 1987.
119p. 3 maps. bibliog. (British Ornithologists' Union. Series of Checklists, no. 8).
Based largely on the author's 1979 PhD dissertation from Louisiana State University,
this work covers the major islands of the south: Crooked Island, Acklins Island,
Mayaguana, Little Inagua and Great Inagua as well as the numerous smaller islands
and cays in the region. An introductory chapter on the southern Bahamas provides
information on geography and geology, palaeontology, climate, vegetation and
previous ornithological explorations. The bulk of the book consists of a systematic list
of 183 species giving information on location of the species and breeding habits and
offering individual descriptions and other observations. This is a book for the specialist
rather than the weekend bird-watcher. There are no illustrations.

185 **The birds of Eleuthera Island, Bahamas.**
Harold A. Connor, Robert W. Loftin.   *Florida Field Naturalist*,
vol. 14, no. 4 (Nov. 1985), p. 77–93.
Observations on the 205 species listed were made over a five-year period. The authors

provide short, concise accounts for each species, and list seventeen species previously reported but not observed prior to this study.

186   **Catesby's birds of colonial America.**
Edited by Alan Feduccia.   Chapel Hill, North Carolina: University of North Carolina Press, 1985. 176p. map. bibliog. (The Fred W. Morrison Series in Southern Studies).

This work includes all of Catesby's 113 bird illustrations (thirteen of which are in colour) from his *Natural history* . . . (q.v.). For each, Feduccia has provided Catesby's full description, lightly edited and set in modern type. Each entry is followed by an editor's note commenting on the bird's habits and offering anecdotes and quotes from other early naturalists, especially John Lawson. Following the illustrations is the complete text of Catesby's work edited to be more easily read. Feduccia has produced a comprehensive volume of much historical interest. It is a good substitute for the original Catesby, considering that it is difficult to examine and the reprint is rather expensive.

187   **Birds of the West Indies.**
James Bond.   London: Collins, 1983. 5th ed. 256p.

This is a guide to the birds that inhabit the Greater and Lesser Antilles and the Bahama Islands. It is very complete and detailed in its coverage. Each species is presented by order, family and genus. There are two indexes, one of common names and one of local names, both of which are very useful. However, a geographical approach would have been appropriate as would the inclusion of maps.

188   **De fillymingo mon!**
Frank Graham, Jr.   *Audubon*, vol. 85, no. 1 (Jan. 1983), p. 50–65.

Graham describes the work of the National Audubon Society and the Bahamas National Trust in protecting over 30,000 flamingos on Great Inagua Island. The 'fillymingo mon' (or 'flamingo man') of the title is Alexander 'Sandy' Sprunt IV, National Audubon Society research director, who has worked with flamingos for over twenty years. There are excellent colour photographs.

189   **Biology and conservation of the Bahama parrot.**
Noel F.R. Snyder, Warren B. King, Cameron B. Kepler.   *Living Bird*, vol. 19, no. 1980/81 (1982), p. 91–114.

The authors explain that for the conservation of the species, future efforts will be required to: monitor the size of both the Abaco and Great Inagua populations; establish reserves for the species on Abaco; study the impacts of burning and lumbering on Abaco; and re-establish the species in parts of its former range elsewhere in the Bahamas. The article includes information on population estimates, feeding habits and reproduction.

190   **Notes on birds of San Salvador Island (Watlings), the Bahamas.**
J. Robert Miller.   *Auk*, vol. 95, no. 2 (April 1978), p. 281–87.

Breeding information is given for some resident species and some new records of non-resident species are noted. The total number of species known to be on the island is 132.

191   **Land bird communities of Grand Bahama Island: the structure and dynamics of an avifauna.**
John T. Emlen.   American Ornithologists' Union, 1977. 129p. 2 maps. bibliog. (Ornithological Monographs, no. 24).

Emlen analyses the population structure and dynamics of the Grand Bahama Island avifauna, focusing on the densities and ecological distributions of species through the habitats and foraging substrates of the vegetation. He also evaluates and interprets some of the factors underlying community structure and regulation. The dominant and most complex of the habitat types is the Bahamian pine forest, and this receives the most discussion in this very technical work.

192   **The birds of New Providence and the Bahama Islands.**
P.G.C. Brudenell-Bruce.   London: Collins, 1975. 142p. map.

This book is based on the author's four and a half years of residence on New Providence. There are entries and illustrations for nearly one hundred species. Each entry lists the common and scientific names and provides a description of the bird and a discussion of habits. The author also indicates the status of each bird by stating where it is found, whether or not it is a resident bird or a summer/winter visitor and, if a visitor, when it arrives and when it departs. For some species, he also comments on songs and nests. This work illustrates those species which are not found in Roger Tory Peterson's *A field guide to the birds* . . . (Boston, Massachusetts: Houghton Mifflin, 1980) and is therefore complementary. This book was also published under the title, *The birds of the Bahamas: New Providence and the Bahama Islands* (New York: Taplinger, 1975).

193   **Birds of the Bahamas.**
Andrew Paterson.   Brattleboro, Vermont: Durell, 1972. 180p. map.

Paterson lists only the more common species and all technicalities are kept to a minimum. Each entry gives the common name, the scientific name and, where appropriate, the Bahamian name. Good physical descriptions are given, as well as an indication of where each species can be found. Every entry is accompanied by a pen-and-ink drawing, though colour illustrations would have been more useful. The book includes a checklist of species which have been seen in the Bahamas. All of the species listed here are also present in Brudenell-Bruce's *The birds of New Providence and the Bahama Islands* (q.v.).

194   **New records of birds from the Bahama Islands.**
Dennis R. Paulson.   *Notulae Naturae of the Academy of Natural Sciences of Philadelphia*, no. 394 (Oct. 20, 1966), p. 1–15.

Paulson describes fifty-eight species and discusses in detail those found on Bimini, Cat Island and San Salvador Island.

195   **Pleistocene birds from New Providence Island, Bahamas.**
Pierce Brodkorb.   *Bulletin of the Florida State Museum*, vol. 4, no. 11 (June 1959), p. 349–71.

By examining bird fossils which he assigns to the pre-Pamlico portion of the Wisconsin glacial stage, Brodkorb finds that only four of fifteen species from the Pleistocene era still exist on the Island of New Providence and that the remaining eleven species are either extinct or occur farther south in the Bahamas and the Greater Antilles. He describes the fifteen species examined, and concludes that Bahamian avifauna have strong ties with the Greater Antilles and especially Cuba.

196 **Ballerinas in pink.**
Carleton Mitchell. *National Geographic Magazine*, vol. 112, no. 4 (Oct. 1957), p. 553–71.

Gives some background information on the flamingos in the Bahamas but primarily describes the 'marching' flamingos of Ardastra Gardens in Nassau. As a tourist attraction, this flock has been drilled to 'march' in circles, straight lines and figure formation.

197 **Observations and new records of birds from the Biminis, northwestern Bahamas.**
Charles Vaurie. *Auk*, vol. 70, no. 1 (Jan. 1953), p. 38–48.

Vaurie presents observations on the distribution and density of bird populations and an investigation of two tern colonies. There are also discussions of ecology and behaviour patterns and a list of seventy-nine of the species found on the Bimini islands.

198 **Flamingo hunt.**
Paul Arthur Zahl. Indianapolis, Indiana: Bobbs-Merrill, 1952. 270p.

Zahl was research associate of the conservation department of the Museum of Natural History in New York when this book was written. It is an account of his search for the breeding ground of the flamingo in the Bahama Islands. The book includes some description of the habits of the birds as well as of the local Bahamian social life during the late 1940s. It is recommended for the general reader and the nature lover.

199 **The flamingos of Inagua.**
Robert P. Allen. *Audubon Magazine*, vol. 53, no. 4 (July/Aug. 1951), p. 210–17, 264–65.

Allen describes the flamingo colonies of Inagua and calls for their preservation.

200 **Flamingos' last stand on Andros Island.**
Paul A[rthur] Zahl. *National Geographic Magazine*, vol. 99, no. 5 (May 1951), p. 635–52.

In this update to his 1947 article, 'The flamingos of Andros' (q.v.), Zahl describes the flamingo flocks on Andros Island and how they were forced to flee to Great Inagua Island. He provides information on their nesting and feeding habits.

201 **The flamingos of Andros.**
Paul A[rthur] Zahl. *Scientific Monthly*, vol. 64, no. 4 (April 1947), p. 277–88.

Zahl describes the flamingo colonies on Andros Island and provides information on their habits and habitat. He calls upon the reader to preserve the flamingo from man and technology.

202 **Bird remains from cave deposits on Great Exuma Island in the Bahamas.**
Alexander Wetmore. *Bulletin of the Museum of Comparative Zoology*, vol. 80, no. 12 (1937), p. 427–41.

Wetmore has examined a collection of bones from Great Exuma Island and found that the remains contain three extinct specimens (two hawks and a giant owl) and a crow and flicker which are both similar to species presently found in Cuba. Wetmore reaches the same conclusion as Brodkorb in his 1959 article (q.v.), that the Bahamian bird life of the past contained far more species than have survived into the twentieth century. The article contains detailed descriptions of the three extinct species found.

203 **Camps and cruises of an ornithologist.**
Frank Michler Chapman. New York: D. Appleton, 1908. 432p. map.

This work is divided into eight sections, each corresponding to a particular geographic area frequented by the author. Section four pertains to the Bahamas. Chapman provides a great deal of information on flamingos, egg birds, the booby and the man-o-war. There is also a very informative introduction to this section. The work is popular in style, though not lacking in seriousness and is one of the earliest studies of the Bahamian flamingo.

204 **Summer birds in the Bahamas.**
Glover Morril Allen. *Auk*, vol. 22, no. 2 (April 1905), p. 113–33.

Allen describes sixty-four of the species which only visit the Bahamas in the summer months.

205 **A flamingo city.**
Frank M[ichler] Chapman. *Century Illustrated Monthly Magazine*, vol. 69, no. 2 (Dec. 1904), p. 163–80.

Presents the account of an expedition to a flamingo rookery on an unnamed Bahamian island. Chapman provides vivid descriptions of the flamingos' habits including nesting, feeding and the birth and development of the young.

206 **On a collection of birds from the northern islands of the Bahama group.**
John Lewis James Bonhote. *Ibis*, series 8, vol. 3, no. 11 (July 1903), p. 273–315.

Bonhote lists and describes 104 species collected on Andros and Little Abaco Islands. He provides detailed descriptions for only some of the species listed, for others there being little or none.

207 **The origin of the avifauna of the Bahamas.**
Frank M[ichler] Chapman. *American Naturalist*, vol. 25, no. 294 (June 1891), p. 528–39.

Chapman discusses the 156 species and subspecies of birds recorded, up to the time of writing, in the Bahamas. He deals in more detail with the twenty-four native species, and offers a number of theories to explain their existence.

208 **The birds of the Bahama Islands, containing many birds new to the Islands, and a number of undescribed winter plumages of North American birds.**
Charles Barney Cory.   Boston, Massachusetts: Estes & Lauriat, 1890. rev. ed. 250p.

The author provides a personal rather than a scientific description of the birds. He discusses thirty-seven families and gives a distribution list showing where the birds are to be found. An appendix lists thirty-six birds which are not recorded by the author but which might occasionally occur in the Bahamas.

Insects

209 **Sandflies and tourism in Florida and the Bahamas and Caribbean area.**
John R. Linley, John B. Davies.   *Journal of Economic Entomology*, vol. 64, no. 1 (Feb. 1971), p. 264–78.

The authors present a comprehensive discussion of the relationship between sandflies and tourism; three species are considered in detail, being those most likely to be of economic significance. They deal with the biology of the three species, the realities of the sandfly problem as it affects tourism and the best-known control methods. The primary purpose of the article is to help those concerned with tourism to realize that sandflies present a serious threat, for which there is rarely any easy, cheap or totally effective remedy. The authors suggest that developers should fully investigate the sandfly situation before commencing a project.

210 **The butterflies of the Bahama Islands, British West Indies (Lepidoptera).**
Fredeick H. Rindge.   *American Museum Novitates*, no. 1563 (May 12, 1952), p. 1–18.

Describes fifty-four species and subspecies. Each includes a distribution range in the Bahamas.

Mammals

211 **Biology of the Bahaman hutia: geocapromys ingrahami.**
Garrett C. Clough.   *Journal of Mammalogy*, vol. 53, no. 4 (Nov. 1972), p. 807–23.

The hutia, an endangered rodent, which was thought until 1966 to be extinct, is found on East Plana Cay near the southeast end of the Bahamas. Clough provides information on population density and composition, feeding habits, reproduction and behaviour.

212   **The Bahaman hutia: a rodent refound.**
      Garret C. Clough.   *Oryx*, vol. 10, no. 2 (Sept. 1969), p. 106–08.
Clough describes the habits and behaviour of the hutia, found on East Plana Cay. This
is a preliminary article to Clough's 'Biology of the Bahaman hutia . . .' (q.v.).

213   **Notes on mammals of the Bahamas with special reference to the bats.**
      Karl F. Koopman, Max K. Hecht, Emanuel Ledecky-Janecek.
      Journal of Mammalogy, vol. 38, no.2 (May 1957), p. 164–74.
Brief mention is made of the Bahamian raccoon and the hutia. Of the eleven species of
bats described in detail, five are species originally from Cuba and another three are
from the Island of Hispaniola.

Molluscs

214   **Land and freshwater mollusks of Eleuthera Island, Bahama Islands.**
      William J. Clench.   *Revista de la Sociedad Malacológica*, vol. 8, no. 3
      (April 25, 1952), p. 97–116.
This is a list of forty-four species of molluscs found on Eleuthera, in which very little
description is given.

215   **Annulariidae of the Bahama archipelago.**
      Paul Bartsch.   In: *The operculate land molluscs of the family
      Annulariidae of the Island of Hispaniola and the Bahama archipelago.*
      Washington, DC: Smithsonian Institution, 1946, p. 182–252. (United
      States National Museum. Bulletin 192).
Offers descriptions of Bahamian land molluscs .Bartsch gives details of land molluscs
from three subfamilies, four genus and eight subgenus. This work is aimed at the
specialist.

216   **Land shells of the Bimini Islands, Bahama Islands.**
      William J. Clench.   *Proceedings of the New England Zoological Club*,
      vol. 19 (April 1942), p. 53–67.
Presents a list of twenty-three species, including locations and some short descriptions.

217   **Land and freshwater molluscs of Long Island, Bahama Islands.**
      William J. Clench.   *Memorias de la Sociedad Cubana de Historia
      Natural*, vol. 14, no. 1 (March 1940), p. 3–17.
Clench provides an account of the expedition to collect these specimens. He lists thirty-
four species, including eight only known to Long Island. Entries comprise details of
locations and, occasionally, short descriptions.

218 **Land and freshwater molluscs of Grand Bahama and the Abaco Islands, Bahama Islands.**
William J. Clench. *Memorias de la Sociedad Cubana de Historia Natural*, vol. 12, no. 4 (Sept. 1938), p. 303–33.
This article provides a history of explorations and collecting trips from the 1860s to the 1930s. It lists fifty-five species and subspecies, giving locations and, in some cases, a description.

219 **Origin of the land and freshwater mollusk fauna of the Bahamas, with a list of species occurring on Cat and Little San Salvador Islands.**
William J. Clench. *Bulletin of the Museum of Comparative Zoology*, vol. 80, no. 14 (1938), p. 481–541.
By basing his investigations on his study of land shells, Clench concludes that the fauna of the Bahamas possibly dates only from the Pleistocene era. He gives descriptions of the ecological areas (i.e., salt marsh ponds, blue holes, freshwater ponds) of Cat and Little San Salvador Islands and provides notes on the geology of the area. The article includes descriptions of thirty-nine species and lists the echinoderms, reptiles and amphibians collected by Clench.

220 **Shells of Mariguana Island with a review of the Bahama Helicinidae and descriptions of new Bahama species.**
William J. Clench. *Proceedings of the New England Zoological Club*, vol. 16 (July 31, 1937), p. 57–79.
Clench describes twenty-seven specimens of land species and includes a list of thirty-three marine species, all from Mariguana (Mayaguana) Island.

Reptiles

221 **Reptiles and birds of the Cay Sal Bank, Bahama Islands.**
Donald W. Buden, Albert Schwartz. *Quarterly Journal of the Florida Academy of Sciences*, vol. 31, no. 4 (Dec. 1968), p. 290–320.
The Cay Sal Bank is located 180 kilometres west of Andros Island and eighty-five kilometres north of Cuba. The authors have described in great detail five species of reptiles from Cay Sal Bank and have provided brief descriptions of seventy-four species of birds. There are no illustrations.

222 **The Anolis lizards of Bimini: resource partitioning in a complex fauna.**
Thomas W. Schoener. *Ecology*, vol. 49, no. 4 (early summer 1968), p. 704–26.
The object of this study is to describe and document those characteristics of four species of lizard which allow them to coexist on Bimini. Schoener discusses habitat, food, specialization, sexual dimorphism and the construction of an arboreal lizard fauna.

223 **Concerning some Bahaman reptiles, with notes on the fauna.**
Thomas Barbour, Benjamin Shreve. *Proceedings of the Boston Society of Natural History*, vol. 40, no. 5 (1935), p. 347–65.

In the first half of this article, the authors provide very detailed entries for fourteen Bahamian reptiles. In the second half, they discuss the origins and distribution of Bahamian fauna and conclude that they are varied and interesting but are only a remnant of the animal population which once existed in the area.

Prehistory and Archaeology

The Lucayans

224 **The ecology of Lucayan fishing practices.**
William F. Keegan. *American Antiquity*, vol. 51, no. 4 (Oct. 1986),
p. 816–25.
This analysis of prehistoric fishing practices in the Bahama archipelago brings together
ecological evidence, fishbone analysis, ethnohistoric reports for the prehistoric
Caribbean, experimental fishtrap samples and ethnographic reports of fishing in other
coral waters.

225 **Lucayan fishing practices: an experimental approach.**
William F. Keegan. *Florida Anthropologist*, vol. 35, no. 4
(Dec. 1982), p. 146–61.
Keegan discusses Lucayan subsistence living and fishing practices. He duplicated these
fishing practices by using Haitian-style basketry fish traps. The article includes lists of
fish species captured in the tidal flat environment and those caught in the reef
environment.

226 **Lucayan cave burials from the Bahamas.**
William F. Keegan. *Journal of New World Archaeology*, vol. 5, no. 2
(April 1982), p. 57–65.
In this article, Keegan presents information on skeletal collections from Freeport and
six other islands in the Bahamas and attempts to reconstruct Lucayan mortuary
practices from the available information. He gives an island-by-island summary of
twenty-two skeletal remains which are now housed in the Yale Peabody Museum.
Keegan's results show that no young children were represented, that the female
skeletons were all from the primary child-bearing years and that all the males
represented were adults. From the evidence examined, Keegan was not able to define
any rules for burial as practised by the Lucayans.

227 **Columbus's Arawaks: the sea and the virtuous savage.**
Vesta Rea-Salisbury. *Sea Frontiers*, vol. 26, no. 5 (Sept./Oct. 1980),
p. 279–86.
The author discusses Lucayans on San Salvador and includes a few pictures of artifacts.

228 **Spanish slave trade in the Bahamas, 1509–1530: an aspect of the
Caribbean pearl industry.**
Julian Granberry. *Journal of the Bahamas Historical Society*,
vol. 1 (Oct. 1979), p. 14–15; vol. 2 (Oct. 1980), p. 15–17; vol. 3 (Oct.
1981), p. 17–19.
Granberry examines the role played by the Lucayan Indians in the pearl industry which
was centred on the island of Cubagua, off the northeast coast of Venezuela. Spanish
slave raids to the Bahamas began around 1500 and between 1520 and 1530 the islands
had been completely depleted of all inhabitants. This piece, although it focuses on a
period later than the prehistorical, provides much useful information for the student of
Lucayan history and prehistory.

229 **Bahamas prehistory.**
William H. Sears, Shaun O. Sullivan. *American Antiquity*, vol. 43,
no. 1 (Jan. 1978), p. 3–25.
The authors' investigations of prehistoric excavations in the Bahamas reveal that
Antillean Lucayans migrated to the central Bahamas between AD 800 and 1000. They
conclude that the Lucayans originally visited the area in search of concentrations of
crystalline salt and shellfish and eventually established agricultural sites. Sears and
Sullivan also reason that cultural expansion throughout the Bahamas was primarily
limited by temperature and the rainfall requirements of manioc agriculture.

230 **On the trail of the Arawaks.**
Fred Olsen. Norman, Oklahoma: University of Oklahoma Press,
1974. 408p. 16 maps. bibliog. (The Civilization of the American Indian
Series, vol. 129).
This quite readable book is a personal account of the author's efforts to trace the origin
of the people who inhabited the Antilles at the time of the first European contact.
Although there is no specific mention of the Bahamas or the Lucayans, Olsen's book is
still useful as background information on the peoples of the Caribbean region.

231 **An anthropological reconnaissance of Bimini, Bahamas.**
Julian Granberry. *American Antiquity*, vol. 22, no. 4 (April 1957),
p. 378–81.
In order to solve the problem of the unknown origin of the pre-ceramic, pre-Arawak
people, Granberry surveyed the island of Bimini in 1955 in search of archaeological
sites. No sites were found and Granberry calls for further surveys on other islands. The
article provides a discussion of previous studies of this nature in the Caribbean.

232   **An anthropological reconnaissance of Andros Island, Bahamas.**
John M. Goggin.   *American Antiquity*, vol. 5 (1939/40), p. 21–26.
This is Goggin's report on archaeological and ethnological work done on Andros Island. No Lucayan habitation sites were found and it was determined that the island was sparsely populated in prehistoric times. Goggin deems this investigation to have been unsuccessful.

233   **Lucayan artifacts from the Bahamas.**
Theodoor Hendrik Nikolaas de Booy.   Lancaster, Pennsylvania: New Era Printing, 1913. 7p. (Contributions from the Heye Museum; vol. 1, no. 1).
This item has been reprinted from the *American Anthropologist*, vol. 15, no. 1, (Jan./March 1913). The author describes: a wooden paddle from Mores Island, one of the cays on the Little Bahama Bank; petroglyphs found in a cave on Rum Cay; a wooden stool (duho) from a cave at Spring Point on Acklins Island; and a ceremonial celt (a carved stone figure) from Mariguana (Mayaguana) Island. Descriptions of each of the four artifacts are accompanied by drawings. Unfortunately, de Booy gives little information about the Lucayans and does not provide a bibliography.

234   **Lucayan remains on the Caicos Islands.**
Theodoor Hendrik Nikolaas de Booy.   *American Anthropologist*, vol. 14, no. 1 (Jan./March, 1912), p. 81–105.
In this rather general discussion of the Lucayans, de Booy pays particular attention to excavations and finds on the Island of Providenciales, the Ambergris Cays, North Caicos Island and Grand Caicos Island. He gives much information that is of use to the study of Bahamian Lucayan prehistory.

235   **Traces of the Lucayan Indians in the Bahamas.**
Charles Johnson Maynard.   *Contributions to Science*, vol. 2 (1893), p. 23–34.
Maynard discusses both water wells and the hand axes used by Lucayans to remove conch meat from its shell. This is not a particularly substantial article but it does touch on one aspect of Lucayan studies.

236   **On the Lucayan Indians.**
William Keith Brooks.   Washington, DC: National Academy of Sciences, 1889. 9p. (Memoirs, vol. 4 (10th memoir), part 2).
Brooks offers a short introduction to the Lucayan Indians and provides a detailed examination of three Lucayan skulls, which are illustrated by twelve colour plates.

Archaeology

237   **New directions in Bahamian archaeology.**
William F. Keegan.   *Journal of the Bahamas Historical Society*, vol. 10 (Oct. 1988), p. 3–8.
Keegan examines the three types of archaeological study that he considers to be

needed in the Bahamas. These are studies in colonization, ceramics and subsistence living. The article has very good end-notes listing those studies already carried out on the archaeology of the Bahamas.

238 **The Long Bay site, San Salvador.**
Charles A. Hoffman. *American Archaeology*, vol. 6, no. 2 (1987),
p. 97–101.

Long Bay, on the west coast of San Salvador Island, is the site where Columbus first set foot in the New World, according to Samuel Eliot Morison in *Journals and other documents on the life and voyages of Christopher Columbus* (New York: Heritage, 1963. 417p.). Hoffman set out to find proof of Columbus' landfall by searching for traces of the items Morison listed as having been given by Columbus to the natives he met. He found at least forty-nine artifacts, including a Spanish dinaro (sic) from the reign of Henry IV, King of Castile, 1454–74. Hoffman concludes that until the appearance of evidence to the contrary, he believes the site is very close to the exact place on which Columbus first set foot in the New World.

239 **The Pigeon Creek Site, San Salvador, Bahamas.**
Richard Rose. *Florida Anthropologist*, vol. 35, no. 4 (Dec. 1982),
p. 129–45.

Rose presents archaeological findings from the Pigeon Creek Site on San Salvador and offers conclusions on chronology, ceramics, settlement and subsistence. He also investigates limestone, coral and shell tools, and the crushed shell used for pottery, and examines evidence of trade with other Caribbean regions.

240 **Bahamas archaeology project, reports and papers.**
Edited by Donald T. Gerace. Fort Lauderdale, Florida: College
Center of the Finger Lakes, Bahamian Field Station, 1980– . annual.

Presents annually a collection of papers and reports on site surveys and excavations throughout the Bahamas.

241 **A brief history of Bahamian archaeology.**
Julian Granberry. *Florida Anthropologist*, vol. 33, no. 3 (Sept. 1980),
p. 83–93.

Describes and discusses both archaeological investigations of the Bahamas and the collections of artifacts gathered since the late 1880s.

242 **The Gordon Hill Site, Crooked Island, Bahamas.**
Julian Granberry. *Journal of the Virgin Islands Archaeological
Society*, vol. 6 (1978), p. 32–44.

Granberry reports on Froelich G. Rainey's 1934 excavation on the island and discusses the artifacts (bones, shellware and ceramics) found in two burial sites, judged to be from the mid-thirteenth century. He indicates that Rainey's findings provide the basis for a reconstruction of Bahamian cultural history.

243 **Archeological investigations on Cat Island, Bahamas.**
James C. Maclaury.   Gainesville, Florida: University of Florida, 1970.
p. 27–50. map. (Contributions of the Florida State Museum. Social
Sciences, no. 16).

Cat Island was first inhabited between AD 1000 and 1500. The shell, stone and pottery artifacts discussed in this monograph were excavated from eighteen different sites and come from this time period. This item forms the second part of a volume containing Hoffman's *The Palmetto Grove site . . .* (q.v.).

244 **The Palmetto Grove site on San Salvador, Bahamas.**
Charles A. Hoffman.   Gainesville, Florida: University of Florida,
1970. p. 1–26. 2 maps. (Contributions of the Florida State Museum:
Social Sciences, no. 16).

These archaeological investigations on San Salvador Island was conducted to study the relationships between prehistoric cultures and their environments in general, and to add to the knowledge of the cultural prehistory of the Caribbean area. There is a discussion and description of stone, coral, bone, shell and pottery artifacts all dating from between AD 750 and 1200. This item was here bound with James C. MacLaury's *Archeological investigations on Cat Island, Bahamas* (q.v.).

245 **The cultural position of the Bahamas in Caribbean archaeology.**
Julian Granberry.   *American Antiquity*, vol. 22, no. 2 (Oct. 1956),
p. 128–34.

Granberry provides a short discussion of archaeological surveys carried out in the Bahamas between 1887 and 1955 and shows the close prehistory relationship with Haiti which is most evident in the southern Bahamas. He also points out that there appear to be no prehistoric cultural similarities between the Bahamas and the southeastern United States as has sometimes been thought.

246 **Origins of Tainan culture, West Indies.**
Sven Loven.   New York: AMS, 1979. 696p. map.

This volume was originally published in 1924 under the title, *Uber die wurzelm der tainischen kultur*. This is a reprint of the 1935 English edition published in Goteborg, Sweden. It is organized by topics, such as stone artifacts, ceramics, towns and houses, agriculture, social conditions and burial customs. There is some Bahamian information but like Joyce's *Central American and West Indian archaeology . . .* (q.v.), the work is more generally useful for background information. There is no index.

247 **Central American and West Indian archaeology; being an introduction
to the archaeology of the states of Nicaragua, Costa Rica, Panama and
the West Indies.**
Thomas Athol Joyce.   Freeport, New York: Books for Libraries Press,
1971. 270p. 2 maps. bibliog.

This book, a reprint of the 1916 edition (London: P.L. Warner; New York: G.P. Putnam's Sons), is divided into two sections: southern Central America and the West Indies. There is some information on the Bahamas and the Lucayans. Generally, the book is useful for background information and as an introduction to and summary of excavations and discoveries prior to 1916.

History

History of the Caribbean/West Indies

248 **A short history of the West Indies.**
John Horace Parry, Philip Manderson Sherlock.   London: Macmillan,
1971. 3rd ed. 337p. bibliog.
First published in 1956, this work is a valuable introduction to West Indian history. It
begins with the arrival of Columbus and traces West Indian history through to
independence in most of the British Caribbean. It also deals with the consolidation of
the Cuban revolution, the rise of the pro-statehood party in Puerto Rico, the
emergence of Black Power groups and efforts at regional cooperation. In their
introduction, Parry and Sherlock state that the 'history is worth studying for its own
sake and not merely as an appendix to the history of . . . European, African or Asian
homelands, or of the United States. Such a study, of the history of the West Indies in
its own right, is the object of this book'. This objective has been admirably achieved.

249 **From Columbus to Castro: the history of the Caribbean, 1492–1966.**
Eric Williams.   New York: Harper & Row, 1970. 576p. 3 maps.
bibliog.
Williams, Prime Minister of Trinidad and Tobago from 1956 to 1981, has written the
first complete history of the Caribbean as a whole. His purpose was to collate all
existing knowledge of the area in relation to the rest of the world and to provide,
through a greater awareness of its heritage, a foundation for the economic integration
of the region.

250 **The growth of the modern West Indies.**
Gordon K. Lewis.   New York: Monthly Review, 1968. 506p. map.
bibliog.
Lewis provides a decsriptive and interpretive analysis of the growth of the English-
speaking Caribbean from 1918 to 1966. This work, organized along territorial and

55

thematic lines, analyses in detail the various elements that have gone to make up the whole of West Indian society. There is a great deal of information about the Bahamas included.

251 **West Indies.**
Philip Manderson Sherlock. London: Thames & Hudson; New York: Walker, 1966. 215p. 3 maps. bibliog.
This is a well-written, informative and perceptive history of the British West Indies. The first half of the book gives a history of the region while the second half is a survey of social institutions such as the economy, the family, the Church, education, ways of life, folklore and the arts. Sherlock emphasizes three decisive dates: 1650, when the production of sugar started to dominate Barbados; 1834, when slave emancipation was enforced throughout the West Indies; and the period 1938 to 1944, which led to home rule, federation and subsequently independence for most West Indian nations in the latter half of the twentieth century.

252 **History of the British West Indies.**
Alan Cuthbert Burns. London: Allen & Unwin; New York: Barnes & Noble, 1954. 821p. 30 maps. bibliog.
Burns' book is designed to give the general reader an outline of the history of the West Indies, from discovery to 1952, with particular emphasis on the British West Indies. The work is based on source material and is well documented. References to the Bahamas, more than in most general history books, are numerous. This was the first book to treat the Caribbean as a unit.

253 **The history, civil and commercial, of the British West Indies. With a continuation to the present time.**
Bryan Edwards. New York: AMS, 1966. 5th ed. 5 vols.
This reprint of the 1819 London edition printed by T. Miller for G. and W.B. Whittaker is fascinating. A general description of the Bahama Islands by Daniel McKinnon appears in volume four. In it he provides information on early history, the Loyalists, geology, crops and government.

General history of the Bahamas

254 **The new Bahamian history: Africa's image revisited.**
Peter T. Dalleo. Decatur, Illinois: White Sound, 1988. 16p. (The Bahamas Research Institute. Occasional Papers Series, no. 2).
Dalleo highlights areas of historical distortion and the biased image of the Bahamian people as found in both modern and historical documents. He points the way to a new image for the country and gives examples of the reinterpretation of Bahamian history by members of three institutions: the College of the Bahamas, the Archives and the Historical Society. This new school of thought, which is gaining support, does not deny Bahamian participation in such nefarious affairs as piracy and smuggling, but rather

balances the previous misleading stereotypes by investigating other ignored aspects of the Bahamian past.

255   **A history of the Bahamas.**
Michael Craton.   Waterloo, Ontario: San Salvador Press, 1986.
3rd ed. 332p. 9 maps. bibliog.
First published in 1962, Craton's book is the most authoritative general political history of the Bahamas. The second edition, published in 1968, ends with the General Election of 1967 when a black political party first came to power under Lynden Oscar Pindling and formed a government which has been in power ever since. The third edition includes a new chapter dealing with events from 1967 to 1985. Craton provides excellent detail and a very useful bibliography. This work is an essential item for any Bahamian collection, large or small.

256   **Highlights in Bahamian history.**
Bahamas. Department of Archives.   Nassau: Department of Archives, 1985. 2 maps. [54p.].
This booklet, produced to accompany the exhibition held in the lobby of the Cable Beach Hotel, 16–22 October 1985, contains black-and-white photographs of all of the exhibits with captions for each. The exhibition, mounted in honour of the 1985 Commonwealth Heads of Government Conference, traces the highlights of Bahamian history from the landing of Columbus in 1492 to the present day.

257   **Homeward bound: a history of the Bahamas to 1850, with a definitive study of Abaco in the American Loyalist plantation period.**
Sandra Riley.   Miami: Island Research, 1983. 308p. 11 maps. bibliog.
This is a highly readable and very well-researched history of the Bahamas up to 1850, twelve years after the emancipation of slaves. The history of Abaco is skilfully intertwined with that of the rest of the country. Riley has included six appendices which are genealogical in nature. They are: surnames appearing on a list of baptisms and marriages, 1721–26; surnames from the 1731 and 1740 censuses; the Curry family genealogy, a typical Loyalist family; 'Book of Negroes', 1783, listing slaves sailing from New York and bound for Abaco between 31 July and 30 November 1783; a list of Loyalists emigrating to Abaco between 1783 and 1821; and the Bahamas slave register for 1834. The year of publication, 1983, also marks the bicentennial of the arrival of American Loyalists in the Bahamas.

258   **Pirates and plunderers: rethinking Bahamian history.**
Peter T. Dalleo.   *Africana Journal*, vol. 12, no. 4 (1981), p. 293–320.
The author reviews and augments historical literature on the Bahamas during the nineteenth century, focusing on regional, social and economic factors and African influences. He also re-examines the common interpretation of nineteenth century Bahamian development as predominantly a history of 'pirates and plunderers'.

259   **Nassau's historic buildings.**
C. Seighbert Russell.   Nassau: Bahamas National Trust, 1980. 110p. map. bibliog.
Russell describes seventy-seven public buildings, forts, hotels, churches, houses and

businesses, and provides a great deal of historical information about the structures and the people who built and owned them; the work is a very good social history of Nassau. Unfortunately, there is only one map, which does not show locations, and the eighty-one black-and-white photographs do not always do justice to some of the wonderful examples of architecture being presented. Some colour photographs would have been more than welcome. There is no table of contents, index or listing of buildings and sources for the photographs and prints are lacking. Despite these drawbacks, Russell's book is interesting and useful.

260 **Christ Church Cathedral tombstone and memorial plaque inscriptions.**
Jolton L. Johnson, Ruth M.L. Bowe.   Nassau: Public Records Office,
Archives Section, 1977. 17p.

The foundation stone for Christ Church Cathedral in Nassau was laid in 1837. The Cathedral, consecrated in 1845 and enlarged between 1864 and 1865, is the fifth church to occupy this site since the first was erected in 1670. This booklet transcribes the inscriptions from the forty-two tombstones and plaques on the interior walls, the twelve on the floor and furniture and the eighteen tombstones in the Cathedral's garden. The authors have included a plan of the Cathedral and its garden, a chronological index by death date and an alphabetical name index. This is a useful reference for genealogists.

261 **The Bahamian American connection.**
Bahamas. Public Records Office.   Nassau: Public Records Office,
1976. 51p.

This booklet of the Archives Exhibition held at the Art Gallery, Jumbey Village, 16 February–4 March 1976 contains black-and-white photographs of all of the pieces, with captions for each. The exhibition traced the connections between the Bahamas and the United States of America, from the arrival of Christopher Columbus in 1492 to Bahamian independence in 1973. It was mounted in honour of the US bicentennial.

262 **Bahamian symbols: the first five centuries.**
Whitney Smith.   Winchester, Massachusetts: Flag Research Center,
1976. 109p. (The Flag Bulletin, vol. 15, no. 2–3).

Written by the Executive Director of the Flag Research Center in Winchester, Massachusetts, this work outlines the symbols (flags, seals and coats of arms) that have been associated with the Bahamas from Columbus' discovery of the New World in 1492 to Bahamian independence in 1973. The work is profusely illustrated with colour and black-and-white photographs and illustrations.

263 **St. Matthew's Cemetery and the Eastern Burial Ground.**
Bahamas. Public Records Office.   Nassau: Public Records Office,
1976. 53p.

The St. Matthew's (Anglican) Cemetery was first consecrated in May 1826. It is composed of three burial grounds: the Churchyard and the Centre Burial Ground, which were both used for whites, and the North Burial Grounds used for blacks and 'persons of colour'. There are no tombstones visible in the latter. This booklet contains the visible transcriptions found on 329 plaques and tombstones in the Churchyard and the Centre Burial Ground. There are an additional 282 tombstones which have no inscriptions. Eight plans of the various sections of the cemetery and burial grounds are included. This item is useful for genealogists, though there are no indexes either chronological by death date or alphabetical by name.

264   **A selection of historic buildings of the Bahamas.**
Bahamas. Public Records Office.   Nassau: Public Records Office, 1975. 44p.

This booklet of the exhibition held at the Public Records Office, 17–25 February 1975 contains black-and-white photographs, with captions, of all the documents on show. There are photographs of thirty-two public buildings and private residences as well as of documents and architectural plans.

265   **The story of the Bahamas.**
Paul Albury.   London: Macmillan Caribbean; New York: St. Martin's, 1975. 294p. 6 maps. bibliog.

Albury, a Bahamian dentist and local historian, has written an overview of Bahamian history from Columbus to independence. He writes with enthusiasm and diligence and, if one disregards the rhapsodical prose, this non-scholarly work is enjoyable and easy to read. It augments Craton's *A history of the Bahamas* (q.v.) and treats tourism, nationalism and life in the Family Islands more fully.

266   **Discovery of a nation: an illustrated history of the Bahamas.**
Michael A. Symonette.   Nassau: Management Communication Services, 1973. 39p. map. bibliog.

This short, well-illustrated history of the Bahamas highlights ten major eras in Bahamian history including the arrival of Columbus (1492), the first European settlement (1648), emancipation (1838) and independence (1973). The work is aimed primarily at school children.

267   **By sail and wind: the story of the Bahamas.**
Jean Bothwell.   London; New York; Toronto: Abelard-Schuman, 1964. 152p. 2 maps. bibliog.

This very readable history of the Bahamas, written primarily for children in the age bracket of eight to ten years, not only covers the history from 1492 to 1964 but also provides chapters on geography and natural history, the people, the economy and industry and government. Although the bulk of this book is now out of date, the first six chapters which deal with history are still useful. Written for children, the bibliography nonetheless lists 'adult' books rather than insubstantial picture books. The photographs are flat and unimaginative.

268   **A short history of the Bahamas.**
A. Deans Peggs.   Nassau: Deans Peggs Research Fund, 1959. 3rd ed. 45p. map. bibliog.

Peggs, one-time Headmaster of the Government High School, has based his history on his original teaching notes. He provides short chapters on the highlights of Bahamian history: discovery, early English settlers, proprietors and pirates, Woodes Rogers, the Loyalists, emancipation, the American Civil War, the poverty of 1865–1918, prohibition, tourists and the Second World War. The first edition was published in

1951, followed by a second edition in 1955. Although now dated, this book is still used by students and researchers. In some respects, it was the first history of the Bahamas.

269 **Silent sentinels.**
Ronald Langton-Jones. London: F. Muller, 1944. 232p. map.
The bulk of this history of lighthouses is given over to a discussion of Bahamian lighthouses and the nation's Imperial Lighthouse Service. The author combines technical knowledge with stories and anecdotes.

270 **Bahamas; isles of June.**
Hugh MacLachlan Bell, foreword by Sir Bede Clifford. London: Williams & Norgate; New York: McBride, 1934. 226p. map.
Bell's work presents a romantic view of Bahamian history, wherein he focuses on the privateering role the Bahamas played in the American Revolution, the American Civil War, and the bootlegging and rum-running period of the 1920s. Clifford, the Governor of the Bahamas at the time of writing, states that, 'Major Bell has endeavored in his admirable book to restore to the privateers the distinction which they enjoyed among their contemporaries and to persuade law-abiding readers that although we may not be able to condone the privateers' morals, we have every reason to admire their courage and be proud of their achievements. These men represent the virility of our race'. This is an unusual look at Bahamian history.

271 **The early settlers of the Bahama Islands, with a brief account of the American Revolution.**
Arnold Talbot Bethell. Holt, England: Printed by Rounce & Wortley, 1930. 2nd ed. 166p.
Bethell provides a history of the Bahamas from the mid-seventeenth century to the early-twentieth century. A great deal of the book concentrates on and presents documents related to Bahamian history. Many of these, and other sections of the book, list the names of the early settlers, making Bethell's work an excellent resource for genealogists. Lists of Loyalists, of the inhabitants of New Providence (1671) and Eleuthera (ca. 1720) and of wills are included. There is no index. The title page of the volume advises that 'Most of the historical facts contained in this book are taken from the Archives of the Colony'.

272 **A history of the Bahamas House of Assembly.**
Harcourt Gladstone Malcolm. Nassau: The Nassau Guardian, 1921. 83p.
A history of the constitution, government and procedures of the House of Assembly written by the man who was then Speaker of the House. There are additional chapters on the mace, the speakers, the library, old government documents, royal portraits and governors' perquisites. A list of speakers of the House of Assembly up to 1921 is appended.

273 **Historical documents relating to the Bahama Islands.**
Harcourt Gladstone Malcolm. Nassau: The Nassau Guardian, 1910. 170p.
Malcolm's collection provides the full text of twenty-three documents (1647-1909)

from the Archives of the Colonial Office, the Records Office and the British Museum, London and the Governor's Office and the Records Office, Nassau. The book includes such documents as the Articles and Orders 'öf the Company of Eleutherian Adventurers (1647), the royal grant of the islands to the Lords Proprietors (1670) and the proclamation summoning the General Assembly (1729).

274 **List of documents relating to the Bahama Islands in the British Museum and Record Office, London.**
Harcourt Gladstone Malcolm. Nassau: The Nassau Guardian, 1910. 50p.
This work is divided into two sections. The first lists the documents housed in the British Museum. They consist of twenty-four manuscripts (1635–1824), ten printed books (1647–1720), thirteen acts of the Privy Council (1680–1720) and the official seal of George III to the Bahamas. The second lists the 212 Calendars of State Papers (1629-1700) in the Record Office. Malcolm's list is useful in accessing sources for the study of early Bahamian history.

275 **The Bahama Islands: notes on an early attempt at colonization.**
John T. Hassam. Cambridge, Massachusetts: J. Wilson & Son, 1899. 59p. map.
This is taken from the *Proceedings of the Massachusetts Historical Society* for March 1899. Hassam provides biographical sketches and traces the ancestry of all twenty-six Lords Proprietors of Carolina, an area which included the Bahamas. He also comments on the colonization of the Bahamas in the seventeenth century. The work is well documented and has excellent footnotes.

276 **The Bahamas; a sketch.**
John Thomas Watson Bacot. London: Longmans, Green, Reader, Dyer, 1869. 112p. bibliog.
According to the preface, Bacot wrote this book in order to set down a popular account of the Bahama Islands. In this, one of the earliest histories of the country, the author provides historical information concerning the Lucayans, the colonists and the pirates, comments on geography and geology, flora and fauna and climate, and includes a chapter which gives information and statistics on exports and imports, wrecking, education and government. Bacot limits his remarks to New Providence because he believes, erroneously, that 'The story of New Providence is the story of the whole group. There is no particular history attached to any other island of the Bahamas'.

Columbus' first landfall in the New World

277 Columbus and his world: proceedings of the first San Salvador Conference.
Compiled by Donald T. Gerace. Fort Lauderdale, Florida: College Center of the Finger Lakes, Bahamian Field Station, 1987. 359p. 18 maps.

These proceedings consist of twenty papers covering all aspects of Christopher Columbus: the man, the navigator, the ships he sailed and the lands and peoples he described. Of the fifteen articles included, there are five dealing with Columbus' first landfall in the New World. They are 'Egg Island is the landfall of Columbus: a literal interpretation of his Journal', by Arne B. Molander; 'The Turks and Caicos Islands as possible landfall sites for Columbus', by Robert H. Fuson; 'Columbus' first landfall: San Salvador', by Mauricio Obregon; 'Why we are favorable for the Watling-San Salvador landfall', by Paolo Emilio Taviani; and 'Additional comments relating Watlings Island to Columbus' San Salvador', by Donald T. Gerace.

278 The Columbus landfall in America and the hidden clues in his Journal.
Alejandro Raymundo Perez. Washington, DC: ABBE Publishers Association of Washington, DC, 1987. 113p. 4 maps. bibliog.

Perez's purpose was to seek a logical interpretation for some of the little-known passages in Columbus' *Journal* and to shed some light on the remaining obscure points regarding the first landfall. His findings reinforce the theory that Columbus first landed on Samana Cay. Perez's work was prompted by Joseph Judge's article in the November 1986 issue of *National Geographic Magazine* (q.v.).

279 The log of Christopher Columbus.
Christopher Columbus, translated by Robert Henderson Fuson. Camden, Maine: International Marine, 1987. 252p. 34 maps. bibliog.

Fuson has produced a modernized and more readable version of Columbus' log of his first journey to the New World from 3 August 1492–15 March 1493. Fuson accepts Samana Cay as Columbus' landfall in the New World and deals with the various landfall theories in an appendix. The work is well researched and provides excellent supporting chapters on Columbus himself, on the history of the log and on the technology of travel in Columbus' day. Columbus' journal has been published in English translation seven times; the first edition, in 1827, was entitled *Personal narration of the first voyage of Columbus* and was translated by Samuel Kettell (Boston, Massachusetts: T.B. Wait); the others appeared in 1893, 1903, 1960, 1963, 1987. Fuson's is the most recent version.

280 San Salvador: the forgotten island.
Pedro Grau Triana. Madrid: Ediciones Beramar, S.A., 1987. 71p., 79p. 18 maps. bibliog.

Grau Triana, a medical doctor, legislator, inventor and businessman, originally wrote this book in 1976. By examining Columbus' *Journal*, he concludes, quite categorically, that Watling Island was Columbus' first landfall in the New World. An interesting feature of the volume is a chart entitled, 'Features of Guanahani as described by Columbus', which lists twelve features of the landfall that Columbus noted in his *Journal*. Grau Triana compares six islands (Watling Island, Cat Island, Samana Cay, Mayaguana, Caicos Island and Grand Turk Island) for which the landfall has been claimed against these twelve features. He shows that Watling Island is the only one that encompasses all twelve. The book is written in English (71p.), but includes a Spanish version (79p.).

281 **Columbus and the New World.**
Edited by Wilbur E. Garrett (et al.). *National Geographic Magazine*, vol. 170, no. 5 (Nov. 1986), p. 562–605.

The editors of *National Geographic Magazine*, headed by Garrett, have gathered together articles by Joseph Judge, Luis Marden and Eugene Lyons which discuss Columbus' first landfall in the New World, the route he navigated and the structure of his ship, the *Nina*. They present a well-reasoned investigation, using both computers and centuries-old documents to conclude that Samana Cay, not the island of San Salvador, was Columbus' first landing site. A discussion of the nine landfalls suggested by various authors over the years is included.

282 **In the wake of Columbus: islands and controversy.**
Edited by Louis De Vorsey, Jr., John Parker. Detroit, Michigan: Wayne State University Press, 1985. 231p. 24 maps.

This collection of eight papers was originally published as volume fifteen of *Terrae Incognitae* (1983), the official publication of the Society for the History of Discoveries. All of the papers deal with the problem of the location of Columbus' first landfall. Pieter Verhoog argues for Caicos Island, while Oliver Dunn and James E. Kelley maintain that the government sanctioned official landing, Watlings Island, is correct. Arne B. Molander proposes Egg Island, off the coast of Eleuthera, and Robert H. Power identifies Grand Turk. The first paper, 'The Columbus landfall problem: a historical perspective' by John Parker, is one of the most interesting. He examines in detail all of the major theories from 1731 to 1981. There are also two papers concerned with the transcription and translation of Columbus' *Journal* on which most of the theories are based.

283 **Columbus' landfall and the Indian settlements of San Salvador.**
Ruth G. Durlacher-Wolper. *Florida Anthropologist*, vol. 35, no. 4 (Dec. 1982), p. 203–07.

The author uses Columbus' *Journal* to reconstruct his landfall and the days spent on and around San Salvador. She also provides descriptions of artifacts found at Pigeon Creek.

284 **The search for San Salvador.**
Arne B. Molander. *Journal of the Bahamas Historical Society*, vol. 4 (Oct. 1982), p. 3–8.

Using sixty-six clues from Columbus' *Journal*, Molander plots a new course for Columbus, to and through the Bahamas, in order to find the island Columbus named San Salvador. He identifies Royal Island/Egg Island, northeast of New Providence, as Columbus' first landfall.

285 **Columbus landed here – or did he?**
Arne B. Molander.   *Americas*, vol. 33, no. 10 (Oct. 1981), p. 3–7.
By studying topography, tidal currents, anchorages, flora and fauna and rainfall in comparison with extracts of Columbus's *Journal*, Molander concludes that Columbus first landed at Royal Island/Egg Island.

286 **Columbus's first landfall.**
L. Anthony Leicester.   *Sea Frontiers*, vol. 26, no. 5 (Sept./Oct. 1980), p. 271–78.
Leicester examines the five different San Salvador sites proposed by various authors since the nineteenth century. He also describes the three monuments which have been erected on San Salvador Island and the underwater one off the west coast of the same island.

287 **Christopher Columbus and the New World he found.**
John Scofield.   *National Geographic Magazine*, vol. 148, no. 5 (Nov. 1975), p. 584–625.
This is a collection of four short articles, each one dealing with one of the four voyages Columbus made to the New World between 1492 and 1504. Scofield states that on his first voyage, Columbus made his first landing on San Salvador Island.

288 **A new theory identifying the locale of Columbus's light, landfall and landing.**
Ruth G. Durlacher-Wolper.   Washington, DC: Smithsonian Institution, 1964. 41p. 3 maps. bibliog. (Smithsonian Miscellaneous Collections, vol. 148, no. 1, publication 4534).
On 21 October 1959, Wolper recreated Columbus's approach to the New World in order to determine where Columbus actually landed. Her tests centred around the light which was supposed to have been seen from the *Santa Maria* at about ten o'clock the night before Columbus's landing. This paper gives an account of her tests, which she believes prove that Watlings Island in the Bahamas is the San Salvador on which Columbus landed.

289 **Columbus never came.**
Kjeld Helweg-Larsen.   London: Jarrolds, 1963. 240p. 2 maps.
In this combination of history, description and travel guide, Helweg-Larsen contends that Columbus did not first land in the Bahamas but rather on one of the Caicos Islands, south of the Bahamas. The book also has general chapters on several of the major inhabited islands.

290 **Columbus landed on Watlings Island.**
Edzar Roukema.   *American Neptune*, vol. 19 (April 1959), p. 79–113.
Roukema's objective is to prove that Samuel Eliot Morison was correct in stating that Watlings Island was Columbus' first landfall in the New World, in his volume *Admiral of the ocean sea . . .* (q.v.). First of all, in order to plot Columbus' course, he discusses the *legua*, the measure of distance used. Secondly, he compares the descriptions of the landfall, as given by Columbus, to descriptions of the islands proposed as the place by

various authors. Thirdly, he describes the islands visited by Columbus after the initial landfall and shows their relationship to Watlings Island. Roukema is very confident and in particular criticizes the ideas of Edwin Link and Marion Link in *A new theory on Columbus's voyage through the Bahamas* (q.v.) and Pieter Verhoog in *Columbus landed on Caicos* (q.v.) and *Guanahani again* . . . (q.v.).

291   **A new theory on Columbus's voyage through the Bahamas.**
Edwin Albert Link, Marion C. Link.   Washington, DC: Smithsonian Institution, 1958. 45p. map. bibliog. (Smithsonian Institution. Smithsonian Miscellaneous Collections, vol. 135, no. 4).

Following up on the work of Verhoog in *Columbus landed on Caicos* (q.v.) and *Guanahani again*. . . (q.v.), the authors searched past and present charts, studied original source material, reflected on the studies and opinions of other historians and made a personal reconnaissance by air and by sea. In the light of their research, they mapped a new course for Columbus through the Bahamas and concluded that he landed on one of the Caicos Islands rather than on Watlings Island. On their expedition, the Links paid less attention to distances than to the elapse of sailing time according to the *Journal*.

292   **Columbus landed on Caicos.**
Pieter H.G. Verhoog.   *Proceedings of the United States Naval Institute*, vol. 80, no. 10 (1954), p. 1101–11.

Using what he considers to be the sailing directions found in Columbus' *Journal*, Verhoog concludes that South Caicos Island was Columbus' first landfall in the New World. His original book, *Guanahani again: the landfall of Columbus in 1492* (q.v.), and this more widely distributed article revived interest in the landfall problem and convinced many people that he was correct.

293   **Guanahani again: the landfall of Columbus in 1492.**
Pieter H.G. Verhoog.   Amsterdam: C. De Boer, 1947. 66p. 2 maps.

Verhoog rejected the use of old maps and notations in trying to determine Columbus' landfall and relied only on sailing directions, which he then plotted on a map in order to trace Columbus' voyage. Using this plotting chart, an entirely new methodology, he concluded that South Caicos Island was the first landfall. His book includes extensive notes but no bibliography.

294   **Admiral of the ocean sea: a life of Christopher Columbus.**
Samuel Eliot Morison.   Boston, Massachusetts: Little, Brown, 1942. 2 vols. 35 maps. bibliog.

Morison's admirable biography of Christopher Columbus received the Pulitzer Prize for biography in 1943. He has been criticized for being too uncritical of the explorer and some historians feel that the biography contains a number of controversial arguments, which Morison dealt with in one of two ways, either presenting both sides in order to let the reader choose, or, more characteristically, dismissing all possible answers but one. For example, he states, '. . . there is no longer any doubt that the island [on which Columbus made his first landfall] called Guanahani. . .was the present San Salvador or Watlings'. Despite the criticism, this book does remain a prime source of information on Christopher Columbus and his voyages to the New World. The two-volume work was also issued as a one-volume condensation, of the same title, in 1942

(Little, Brown. 680p.) and as an abridged volume, *Christopher Columbus, mariner* (Atlantic/Little, Brown, 1955. 224p.).

295 **The landfall of Columbus, an old problem restated.**
R.T. Gould. *Geographical Journal*, vol. 69, no. 5 (May 1927),
p. 403–29.
Gould discusses various landfall claims proposed over the years, from Catesby in 1731 in the first volume of his *Natural history* . . . (q.v.) to Murdock's *The cruise of Columbus* . . . (q.v.) in 1884. He concludes that Watlings Island was the site of the first landfall and praises Murdock for his work. He uses courses and distances sailed, evidence from various contemporary charts, Columbus' descriptions of the islands and sailing data in Columbus' *Journal* to reach this conclusion.

296 **The discovery of America and the landfall of Columbus.**
Rudolf Cronau. New York: The Author, 1921. 89p. 14 maps.
Cronau's investigations are based on Columbus' *Journal*. He concludes, most definitely, that Watling's Island is the landfall of Columbus. This monograph is bound together with *The last resting place of Columbus*, later published separately (New York: The Author, 1928. 32p.), in which Cronau tries to solve the mystery surrounding Columbus' burial place.

297 **The first landfall of Columbus.**
Jacques W. Redway. *National Geographic Magazine*,
vol. 6 (Dec. 29, 1894), p. 179–92.
Redway comments, at times quite critically, on the research of various nineteenth-century writers who have tried to establish Columbus' first landfall in the New World. He chooses Samana Island (or Cay) as the first landfall, basing his decision on a study of maps produced between 1500 and the mid 1700s.

298 **The cruise of Columbus in the Bahamas, 1492.**
J.B. Murdock. *Proceedings of the U.S. Naval Institute*, vol. 10,
(April 1884), p. 449–86.
Although he praises Fox's work in *An attempt to solve the problem of the first landing place of Columbus in the New World* (q.v.), Murdock disagrees with his choice of landfall. Using Columbus' *Journal* and modern rather than early charts, he concludes that Watlings Island is the correct site.

299 **An attempt to solve the problem of the first landing place of Columbus in the New World.**
Gustavus Vasa Fox. Washington, DC: Government Printing Office,
1882. 68p. map. (United States. Coast and Geodetic Survey. Methods and Results).
Using Columbus' *Journal* entries from 10 October 1492 to 28 October 1492 and an abridgement of his log book, Fox offers a careful analysis of the voyage and determines that Samana or Atwood Cay in the Bahamas was the place where Columbus first landed in the New World. Appendices include commentaries on the definitions and comparisons of miles and leagues as used by Columbus and variations of the compass in 1492.

300 **The landfall of Columbus.**
Richard Henry Major. *Journal of the Royal Geographical Society*,
vol. 41 (1871), p. 193–210.

In 1847, as editor of the *Select letters of Christopher Columbus* . . . (q.v.) for the
Hakluyt Society, Major concluded that Grand Turk Island was Columbus' first landfall
in the New World. However, in this paper, read to the Royal Geographical Society on
8 May 1871, he agrees with Becher's conclusions in *The landfall of Columbus on his
first voyage to America* (q.v.), in citing Watlings Island as the first landfall. He bases
his conclusions primarily on Columbus' *Journal* from which he quotes extensively.

301 **The landfall of Columbus on his first voyage to America.**
Alexander Bridport Becher. London: J.D. Potter, 1856. 376p. map.
bibliog.

This book includes accounts of Columbus' life before his first voyage, the journey and
landfall and the return voyage, along with excerpts from Columbus' *Journal*. Becher
concludes that Watlings Island was Columbus' first landfall in the New World.
However, he used the *Journal* when it suited him and ignored it when it did not. A
piece by Becher also appeared in the *Journal of the Royal Geographical Society*, vol. 26
(1856) p. 189–203, under the same title.

302 **Select letters of Christopher Columbus, with other original documents,
relating to his first four voyages to the New World.**
Christopher Columbus, translated and edited by Richard Henry
Major. London: Hakluyt Society, 1847. 240p.

In this first edition of *Select letters* . . . Major suggests that Columbus made his first
landfall on Grand Turk Island. He was heavily influenced by Gibbs' *Observations* . . .
(q.v.) and it was not until the publication of Becher's 1856 work, *The Landfall of
Columbus on his first voyage to America* (q.v.) that Major rethought his position and
concluded that Columbus first landed on Watlings Island. The second edition of *Select
letters* . . . (London: Hakluyt Society) was published in 1870; in it, Major announced
his change of opinion. Although both editions are important contributions to
Columbus scholarship, Major is not always viewed as an authoritative critical student
of the landfall issue because of this change.

303 **Observations tending to show that Grand Turk Island, and not San
Salvador, was the first spot Columbus landed in the New World.**
George Gibbs. *Proceedings of the New York Historical Society*,
(1846), p. 137–48.

In order to come to the conclusion of the title, Gibbs used Columbus' *Journal* and
visited various of the Bahamian and Turks and Caicos Islands. The San Salvador in the
title refers to Cat Island. He also discusses other claims for the first landfall throughout
his article. Gibbs was a resident of the Turks Islands which may have had some bearing
on his insistence that it was the landfall.

The first settlers, 1629–84

304 **The colonization of the Bahamas, 1647–1670.**
W. Hubert Miller. *William and Mary Quarterly*, vol. 2, no. 1
(Jan. 1945), p. 33–46.
Discusses Captain William Sayle (d. 1671), who promoted the first permanent
settlement of the Bahamas by leading the Eleutherian Adventurers from Bermuda to
Eleuthera. The author also considers the Bermudians who were the first settlers to
arrive on the Island of New Providence.

Buccaneers, 1684–1717

305 **Woodes Rogers: privateer and pirate hunter.**
M. Foster Farley. *History Today*, vol. 29 (Aug. 1979), p. 522–31.
This profile of Woodes Rogers (ca. 1679–1732) concentrates on his years as a privateer
but quite adequately outlines his career as Governor of the Bahamas.

306 **The funnel of gold.**
Mendel Peterson. Boston, Massachusetts: Little, Brown, 1975. 481p.
4 maps. bibliog.
This is a general history of pirates and privateers in the Caribbean. The Bahamas
section (p. 387–413) includes an account of Woodes Rogers' efforts to rid the Bahamas
of pirates. Other references to Bahamian islands, cities and waters are scattered
throughout the volume.

307 **Crusoe's captain: being the life of Woodes Rogers, seaman, trader,
colonial governor.**
Bryan D.G. Little. London: Odhams, 1960. 240p. 4 maps. bibliog.
Represents a biography of Woodes Rogers, one-time Governor of the Bahamas.
Following his circumnavigation of the world (1708–11), Rogers was appointed
Governor of the Bahamas in 1717. He was relieved of his duties in 1721 but was
reappointed Governor in 1728. He is best known in the Bahamas for ridding the
country of pirates and for giving the Bahamas its national motto, 'Expulsis Piratis,
Restituta Commercia', which may be translated as 'With the Expulsion of the Pirates,
Trade has been Revived'.

308 **The great days of piracy in the West Indies.**
George Woodbury. New York: Norton, 1951. 232p. bibliog.
Woodbury traces the beginnings of piracy in the Mediterranean and then describes the
events which led to its heyday in the Caribbean in the early eighteenth century. He
provides general information on buccaneers and pirates of the West Indies and specific
information on those of New Providence. Also, Woodes Rogers' efforts as Governor

to rid the Bahamas of these pirates are examined in this lively and not unsympathetic presentation of the 'great days'.

309   **Pirates and buccaneers of the Atlantic coast.**
Edward Rowe Snow.   Boston, Massachusetts: Yankee, 1944. 350p.
map. bibliog.
This book is useful for its information on Edward Teach, 'Blackbeard' (d. 1718), and on Mary Read (d. 1720) and Anne Bonney (1700–20), the 'lady pirates'.

310   **Mary Read: the pirate wench.**
Frank Shay.   London: Hurst & Blackett, 1934. 286p.
A fictional account of the female pirate, Mary Read, in which mention is also made of Anne Bonney, Edward Teach and Governor Woodes Rogers. This is an excellent narrative, historically accurate and straightforward.

311   **Under the black flag.**
Don Carlos Seitz.   Ann Arbor, Michigan: Gryphon Books, 1971.
341p. (The Rogue's Library).
Approximately one-fifth of this book deals with pirates and piracy in the Bahamas. The author gives a history of piracy in the Bahamas from 1670 to 1720 and an account of Governor Woodes Rogers' attempts to expel pirates from the islands. There are also separate chapters for the Bahamian pirates Edward Teach, John Martel, Edward England, Howell Davis, Charles Vane, Captain Condent and Thomas Anstis, though no mention is made of Mary Read and Anne Bonney. This vivid and authoritative work captivates the imagination and, in some respects, is superior to many novels which deal with the same subject. This is a reprint of the 1925 Dial Press edition.

312   **Woodes Rogers, privateer and governor.**
George Ernest Manwaring, edited by A. Deans Peggs.   Nassau: Deans
Peggs Research Fund, 1957. 48p. map.
This item was first published as an introduction to the 1928 Cassell reprint of Rogers' *A cruising voyage around the world* (1712). This booklet is a biography of Woodes Rogers, who was originally a British privateer preying on the Spanish. It was published on the 225th anniversary of Rogers' death.

The eighteenth century, 1717–1815

The American Revolution

313   **And take what we pleased.**
Charles R. Smith.   *By Valor and Arms*, vol. 3, no.1 (1977), p. 6–13.
Presents an account of the American raid on Nassau in 1778 by the *Providence* under Captain John Peck Rathbun and a contingent of Marines under Captain John Trevett. Rathbun managed to capture three ships in the raid while the Marines seized two forts.

However, the expedition was unsuccessful financially as there were few prize dollars given to the raiders.

314 **Ashore at New Providence.**
Jerry Keenan. *By Valor and Arms*, vol. 2, no. 3 (1976), p. 22–29.
Keenan discusses American Captain Samuel ·Nicholas (ca. 1744–90) and the Continental Marines' ambitious operations in taking Fort Nassau on New Providence Island during the American Revolution in 1776.

315 **The day the U.S. captured Nassau.**
Etienne Dupuch, Jr. *Mankind*, vol. 3, no. 6 (1972), p. 58–60.
Written in a conversational style, Dupuch's article describes the 1776 capture of Fort Montagu, which occurred without the firing of a shot.

316 **Rathbun's raid on Nassau.**
Frank H. Rathbun. *United States. Naval Institute Proceedings*, vol. 96, no. 11 (Nov. 1970), p. 40–47.
An account, written by one of his descendants, of Captain John Peck Rathbun's raid on Nassau in January 1778.

The Loyalists

317 **The Loyalist bi-centennial.**
Bahamas. Department of Archives. Nassau: Department of Archives, 1983. 80p.
This booklet of the exhibition of historical documents held in the foyer of the Post Office Building, 7–26 February 1983 contains black-and-white photographs of all of the exhibits with captions for each. The exhibition and this booklet trace the arrival of the Loyalists and their influences throughout the Bahamas.

318 **The Loyalists – general influences.**
D. Gail Saunders. *Journal of the Bahamas Historical Society*, vol. 5 (Oct. 1983), p. 3–10.
Saunders provides a description of the Bahamas prior to the arrival of the Loyalists, and information on several prominent Loyalists and their families. She also examines the Loyalist influences on the economy, society, culture and politics, and the impact of their slaves, a topic not often dealt with.

319 **Three Loyalist plantations on San Salvador Island, Bahamas.**
Kathy Gerace. *Florida Anthropologist*, vol. 35, no. 4 (Dec. 1982), p. 216–22.
Gerace investigates the plantations of Sandy Point, Farquharson's and Fortune Hill. She provides descriptions of general settlement patterns and the way of life in the late eighteenth and early nineteenth centuries.

320 **The first Loyalist settlements in Abaco, Carleton and Marsh's Harbour.**
Steve Dodge. Hope Town, Bahamas: Wyannie Malone Historical
Museum, 1979. 10p. 4 maps.
This is a revised version of an address given by the author in Hope Town, Abaco on 10
July 1979. It describes the founding of Carleton and Marsh's Harbour, both on Abaco
Island, by the Loyalists in the 1780s.

321 **The Loyalists of the American Revolution in the Bahamas and the
British West Indies.**
Wallace Brown. *Revista/Review Interamericana*, vol. 5, no. 4
(winter 1975/76), p. 638–47.
A small number of Southern Loyalists fled the United States after the American
Revolution to Dominica, Jamaica and the Bahamas. Although these refugees played a
role in the history of both Jamaica and Dominica, it was in the Bahamas that they left
their most permanent influence. Brown discusses where they settled and their impact
on their new homes.

322 **The American Loyalists in the Bahama Islands: who they were.**
Thelma Peters. *Florida Historical Quarterly*, vol. 40, no. 3 (1962),
p. 226–40.
Offers a study of individual families who fled to the Bahamas following the American
Revolution.

323 **The Loyalist migration from East Florida to the Bahama Islands.**
Thelma Peters. *Florida Historical Quarterly*, vol. 40, no. 2 (1961),
p. 123–41.
Peters outlines the circumstances which led Loyalists to migrate to the Bahamas and
the conditions under which they did so. She also provides a description of Nassau at
the time and a short discussion of crops and industries. The article points out that
although the Loyalists outnumbered the established inhabitants by almost two to one,
they soon adapted, and accepted the inhabitants' casual attitude toward agriculture and
a close dependence on the sea.

324 **The public life of George Chalmers.**
Grace Amelia Cockcroft. New York: Columbia University Press,
1939. 233p. bibliog. (Studies in History, Economics and Public Law,
no. 454).
George Chalmers (1742–1825) was a British civil servant, antiquarian and historian. He
was Colonial Agent for the Bahamas from 1792 until his death. A part of this
biography (p. 124–76) deals with trade and politics in the Bahamas during his tenure,
which coincided with the main Loyalist thrust.

325 **Loyalists in East Florida, 1774 to 1785: the most important documents
pertaining thereto.**
Wilbur Henry Siebert. Boston, Massachusetts: Gregg, 1972. 2 vols.
(The American Revolutionary Series. The Loyalist Library).
This is a reprint of the 1929 edition (De Land, Florida: Florida State Historical Society

(Society's *Publications*, no. 9, vols. 1–2)). In volume one, Siebert discusses the Loyalists in East Florida from March 1774 to December 1782 and their subsequent evacuation between February 1783 and November 1785. Included in this narrative is a section on those Loyalists who fled to the Bahamas. Volume two contains records and documents pertaining to Loyalists' claims for losses of property in Florida. This is a fascinating work, of particular interest to genealogists.

326 **The legacy of the American Revolution to the British West Indies and Bahamas: a chapter out of the history of the American Loyalists.**
Wilbur Henry Siebert. Boston, Massachusetts: Gregg, 1972. 50p.
(The American Revolutionary Series. The Loyalist Library).
Loyalists and their slaves from Florida and New York arrived in the Bahamas between 1783 and 1785. This is a discussion of their effects on population growth, agriculture, commerce, social conditions and slavery in the Bahamas. The author includes an account of Colonel David Fanning from Charleston to illustrate the plight of the Loyalists. This work was first published in 1913 by Ohio State University as vol. 17, no. 27 of the *Ohio State University Bulletin*.

The Seminole Negroes

327 **The Seminole Negroes of Andros Island, Bahamas.**
John M. Goggin. *Florida Historical Quarterly*, vol. 24, no. 3 (1946), p. 201–06.
Many runaway slaves from Georgia and South Carolina sought refuge among the Seminole Indians in Florida. At various times between 1812 and 1818 these runaways scattered, to avoid white slavers. Goggin attempts to trace the movements of Seminole Indians from Florida to Andros Island; although it is true that they did move to Andros, there is no functioning Indian culture to be found on the island.

328 **Notes on Seminole Negroes in the Bahamas.**
Kenneth W. Porter. *Florida Historical Quarterly*, vol. 24, no. 1 (1945), p. 56–60.
A number of Seminole Negroes fled to Andros and Bimini in the 1820s, with further groups arriving during and after the Seminole War in 1835. Porter explains how they may have arrived in the Bahamas but offers little evidence of their actually being there, beyond the existence of the family name of Bowlegs which is common to Seminole tribes in Florida and Blacks in Andros.

The nineteenth century, 1815–1914

329 The Bahamas in the mid-nineteenth century, 1850–1869.
Bahamas. Department of Archives. Nassau: Department of Archives,
1988. 43p.
An exhibition of historical documents was held in the foyer of the Post Office Building,
1–27 February 1988; this booklet contains black-and-white photographs of all of the
exhibits and captions for each. During this time period, various industries, such as the
pineapple, salt and wrecking industries, began to flourish in the Bahamas. Tourism
also established itself as a promising addition to the economy. The exhibition also
examines some of the problems which occurred at this time: a major cholera epidemic
swept the country in 1852, a devastating hurricane touched down in 1866 and the
bitterly debated Disestablishment Bill of 1869 ended government subsidies to the
Anglican and Presbyterian Churches.

**330 The ascendancy of Charles Rogers Nesbitt, politician, civil servant,
administrator.**
John M. Trainor. *Journal of the Bahamas Historical Society*, vol. 3
(Oct. 1981), p. 3–12.
Charles Rogers Nesbitt (1799–1876) was one of the most influential government
officials in the Colony of the Bahamas. He was both Deputy Colonial Secretary
(1818–38) and Colonial Secretary (1838–67). During his period of office the Bahamas
saw the end of slavery, the establishment of an educational system and the impact of
the blockade-running era. This biographical article provides a great deal of information
about the Bahamas of the nineteenth century.

331 The blockade running era in the Bahamas: blessing or curse?
D. Gail Saunders. *Journal of the Bahamas Historical Society*, vol. 10
(Oct. 1988), p. 14–18.
Examines blockade-running and its effects on Bahamian society. Saunders shows that
although imports and exports increased dramatically during the years of the American
Civil War, most of the benefits accrued to the residents of Nassau, many of whom were
not even Bahamian. The white merchant class benefited the most and eventually
consolidated their economic power by being elected to the House of Assembly, or
appointed to the Legislative Council or Executive Council.

332 "Cotton, cotton, everywhere!": running the blockade through Nassau.
John Pelzer, Linda Pelzer. *Civil War Times Illustrated*, vol. 19, no. 9
(Jan. 1981), p. 10–17.
The authors describe the transformation of the port of Nassau from a quiet village to a
great trading centre when, during the American Civil War, it became a haven for
blockade-runners. The article also contains descriptions of the type of steamers used to
run the blockades.

333 Blockade-running from Nassau.
Richard Drysdale. *History Today*, vol. 27 (May 1977), p. 332–37.
Drysdale discusses trade from the port of Nassau during the American Civil War,

1861–65. Although trade and the economy flourished during this period, the country quickly sank into obscurity following the end of the war.

334 **Blockade runners of the Confederacy.**
Hamilton Cochran.   Westport, Connecticut: Greenwood, 1973. 350p. bibliog.
This general history of blockade-running during the American Civil War contains numerous references to Nassau. It is a reprint of the 1958 Bobbs-Merrill edition.

335 **Blockade-running in the Bahamas during the Civil War.**
Thelma Peters.   *Tequesta*, vol. 5 (1945), p. 16–29.
Peters examines the historical ties between the Bahamas and the United States and the origins of blockade-running in the light of these ties. She provides descriptions of a number of the better-known blockade ships and investigates the economics of blockade-running. There are also descriptions of the social life in Nassau during this period.

336 **Running the blockade: a personal narrative of adventures, risks and escapes during the American Civil War.**
Thomas E. Taylor.   Freeport, New York: Books for Libraries Press, 1971. 180p. 2 maps.
Taylor was an assistant to a firm of Liverpool merchants trading chiefly with India and the United States. During the American Civil War, Taylor elected to take part in running commercial blockades established by the Northern forces. This is his account of shipping goods to Bermuda, Havana and the Bahamas and then running them into blockaded ports in the southern United States. It was first published in London by John Murray in 1896.

337 **The Bahamas in the late nineteenth century, 1870–1899.**
Bahamas. Department of Archives.   Nassau: Department of Archives, 1987. 47p.
An exhibition of historical documents was held in the Post Office Building, 2–28 February 1987. This booklet was produced to accompany it, and contains black-and-white photographs of all of the exhibits, with captions. Prior to 1870, in the years 1861–65 the Bahamas had experienced an economic boom, as a result of the American Civil War; between 1865 and 1870, however, the economy lagged seriously. The colony entered a kind of reconstruction phase from 1870, which saw increased growth in the pineapple industry and the rise of the sponging and sisal industries. The emphases in this booklet are on the growth of industry; communications (such as the 1892 telegraphic cable linking New Providence to the United States); education (compulsory education was introduced for children aged six to twelve, in 1878); emigration and immigration; and social development and reform (for example, in 1882 Nassau gained city status, and the Post Office Savings Bank and the Bank of Nassau were formed, in 1885 and 1888 respectively).

338 **Social control and the colonial state: the reorganisation of the police force in the Bahamas, 1888–1893.**
Howard Johnson. *Slavery and Abolition*, vol. 7, no. 1 (1986), p. 46–58.
Johnson describes the introduction of Barbadian constables to police the Bahamas. Members of the Bahamian white ruling class took this step to protect themselves and their property from the black population. Prior to this, the West Indian Regiment had provided police protection.

339 **The Bahamas during the early twentieth century, 1900–1914.**
Bahamas. Department of Archives. Nassau: Department of Archives, 1986. 46p.
Many new technologies were introduced into the Bahamas during this time period and an exhibition was held in 1986 to highlight several of them. In this booklet containing captioned black-and-white photographs of all the exhibits, topics covered include communication (1913 saw the opening of the first wireless-telegraphy station); education; industry (in 1905 the Bahamas Timber Company was formed); technology (in 1906 the first telephone system was established); and the treatment of blacks (the 1907 Truck Systems Act guaranteed monetary payments for workers).

The twentieth century to independence, 1914–73

340 **The Bahamas during the Great War.**
Frank Holmes. Nassau: The Tribune, 1924. 180p.
This chronicle of events in the Bahamas between August 1914 and July 1919 was written in 1920 at the request of Sir William Allardyce, Governor of the Bahamas (1914–20). A short digest of it is included in *The Empire at war*, edited by Sir Charles Prestwood Lucas (London: Oxford University Press, 1921–26, section X, part III, volume II). Holmes outlines the activities of the Bahamas War Relief Committee which gathered money, clothing and fruit to be sent to England during the war. The Bahamas also sent three contingents and five units of fighting men to serve with other forces from the Empire. The names of those who served and those who died are listed.

341 **The Bahamas during the World Wars, 1914–1918 and 1939–1945.**
Bahamas. Department of Archives. Nassau: Department of Archives, 1985. 55p.
Historical documents from the war years were exhibited in the foyer of the Post Office Building 4–23 February 1985. Black-and-white photographs of all of the exhibits are contained in this booklet, with captions for each. The Bahamas' war efforts during both of the World Wars are outlined.

342 **The real McCoy.**
Frederic Franklyn Van de Water.   Garden City, New York:
Doubleday, Doran, 1931. 305p.
Bill McCoy was a daring and successful rum-runner from 1920 to 1925. Dubbed 'King of Rum Row', he was the inventor of many of the rum-running techniques employed during the days of prohibition in the United States. Van de Water has written this interesting account of McCoy's escapades in the form of an autobiography. The phrase, 'the real McCoy', meaning all that is best and genuine, was inspired by Bill McCoy.

343 **Colonial civil servant.**
Alan Cuthbert Burns.   London: Allen & Unwin, 1949. 339p. 5 maps.
Burns was Colonial Secretary to the Bahamas (1924–28) just prior to Sir Charles Dundas. In this book, he comments at length on the Colonial Office in the Bahamas and the difficulty of being an 'imported' civil servant. He also discusses agriculture and industry. Burns was never very happy in the Bahamas and this is clear in his comments on the Bahamian natives themselves and on the role of the legislature and government in the islands.

344 **Proconsul: being incidents in the life and career of the Honourable Sir Bede Clifford.**
Bede Edmund Hugh Clifford.   London: Evans Brothers, 1964. 327p. 2 maps.
Sir Bede Clifford (1890–1969), a New Zealander, was Governor of the Bahamas from 1932 to 1937. He was subsequently Governor of Mauritius, and then of Trinidad. This autobiography includes information about the Bahamas during the Depression and the pre-Second World War years.

345 **African crossroads.**
Sir Charles Cecil Farquharson Dundas.   Westport, Connecticut: Greenwood, 1976. 242p.
This is an honest and modest book, reminiscent of the old colonial service. Sir Charles Dundas was both Colonial Secretary (1928–34) and Governor (1937–40) of the Bahamas. This autobiography includes diplomatic accounts of both of these stays in the islands. Among other things, he comments on the form and style of government in the Colony, agriculture, tourism, prohibition, and the death of the sponging industry. Dundas' term as Governor was cut short by two years to allow the Duke of Windsor to take over the governorship in 1940. This is a reprint of the 1955 edition published in London by Macmillan.

346 **The Duke of Windsor's war: from Europe to the Bahamas, 1939–1945.**
Michael Bloch.   London: Weidenfeld & Nicolson; New York: Coward-McCann, 1982. 397p. 2 maps. bibliog.
From 1940 to 1945, the Duke of Windsor (formerly King Edward VIII of Great Britain) was Governor of the Bahamas. In contrast to many other accounts of this period, Bloch's presents a very sympathetic picture of the Duke and Duchess. As assistant to the Duchess' lawyer, Maitre Suzanne Blum, Bloch had access to a great many private papers and pieces of correspondence on which he bases this work. Blum

requested that this book be written and the reader should realize that she selected which documents Bloch should use. The Duke of Windsor emerges as very naïve – socially, politically and personally. This work should be contrasted with Michael Pye's *The King over the water* (q.v.) which Bloch calls 'a venomous volume' guilty of 'grotesque distortions'.

347 **The king over the water.**
Michael Pye.   London: Hutchinson, 1981. 279p. map. bibliog.

Pye's account of the sojourn of the Duke and Duchess of Windsor in the Bahamas between 1940 and 1945 is much harsher than Michael Bloch's *The Duke of Windsor's war* (q.v.). While Bloch gives an overall view of the Duke's tenure as Governor, Pye concentrates on the three major problems faced by the Duke – political scandal, the 1942 riot, and the sensational murder of Sir Harry Oakes. Pye's book is a good study of the Windsors in the Bahamas, the politics of the colony and the influence of the white ruling merchant class. Meticulously researched, the book draws a chilling picture of a colony where repressive white supremacy was an accepted fact.

348 **The 1942 riot in Nassau: a demand for change?**
D. Gail Saunders.   *Journal of Caribbean History*, vol. 20, no. 2 (1985/86), p. 117–46.

Saunders describes the workers' riot in Nassau of 31 May and 1 June 1942 and indicates that the riot was a spontaneous outburst by a group of disgruntled labourers. She notes that socio-economic change was slow to come to the Bahamas, partly because of the lack of black leadership and partly because economic conditions were generally better than elsewhere in the Caribbean.

349 **King's X: common law and the death of Sir Harry Oakes.**
Marshal Houts.   New York: Morrow, 1972. 334p.

This book concerns the murder of Sir Harry Oakes (1874–1943) in the Bahamas and the subsequent trial of his son-in-law, Alfred de Marigny. Houts' thesis is that there existed a deliberate conspiracy to convict an innocent man and that there was also a plan of non-involvement on the part of many others who wanted to see the case closed as expeditiously as possible. Houts' account of the trial concentrates on the forensic evidence. Bocca's *The life and death of Sir Harry Oakes* (q.v.) is more interesting and provides more information about Oakes. A bibliography and notes would have proved useful in Houts' volume.

350 **The life and death of Sir Harry Oakes.**
Geoffrey Bocca.   Garden City, New York: Doubleday; London: Weidenfeld & Nicolson, 1959. 238p.

Ostensibly a biography of Sir Harry Oakes, nearly half the book is given over to his murder in 1943, the trial of his son-in-law and the aftermath of the trial. Bocca insists that an impartial inquiry should be established to reinvestigate the murder (this was never done) and suggests that Sir Harry was murdered by a syndicate of financial adventurers involved in an intricate plot to get their hands on Oakes' fortune. Unfortunately, Bocca presents very little evidence to support his claim.

351 The murder of Sir Harry Oakes, Bt.
Eugene A.P. Dupuch.   Nassau: Nassau Daily Tribune, 1959. 481p.

This account of the murder of Sir Harry Oakes and the subsequent trial of the accused, Alfred de Marigny, comes from the files of the *Nassau Daily Tribune* (q.v.). At that time, Eugene Dupuch was Assistant Editor and provided most of the coverage of this event for the news media. This book consists of extracts from the *Tribune* between July 8, 1943, the day on which Sir Harry's body was found, and November 11, 1943, the day on which de Marigny was found not guilty of murder. The book includes some accounts from the *Miami Herald* and a few items which do not come from the court proceedings but are related to the case. This is perhaps the most accurate account of de Marigny's trial next to the court transcripts themselves. The work is fascinating reading and provides an immediacy not found in other accounts which have often been written years after the fact by persons not present at the time.

352 More devil than saint.
Marie Alfred Fouquereaux de Marigny.   New York: B. Ackerman, 1946. 256p.

Marigny, a mid-century dandy, examines his life from his youth in Mauritius up to the day of his acquittal from the charge of the murder of his father-in-law, Sir Harry Oakes. Marigny's book demonstrates that he was naïve and had little awareness of those he met and the world around him. The autobiography was also published in French under the title, *Ai-je tué? Le monde est ma prison: autobiographie* (Montreal: S. Brousseau, 1946. 437p.).

353 Who killed Sir Harry Oakes?
James Leasor.   Boston, Massachusetts: Houghton Mifflin; London: Heinemann 1983. 248p. bibliog.

Leasor presents the murder of Sir Harry Oakes and the trial of the Count de Marigny in a novelistic style. He theorizes that Oakes was killed while spurning a Mafia attempt to launch a casino in Nassau. This is not a traditional crime analysis nor does it solve the Oakes mystery, but it does provide for interesting speculation.

The twentieth century after independence, 1973– .

354 Bahamas in international politics.
Vaughan A. Lewis.   *Journal of Interamerican Studies and World Affairs*, vol. 16 (May 1974), p. 131–52.

The Bahamas became independent from Great Britain in 1973 but remains economically dependent on the United States as a result of its tourism and banking industries. Lewis presents four issues to be faced by the new nation: economic dependency, territorial jurisdiction, immigration, and human and non-human resources.

355 **Amazing new-country caper.**
A. St. George. *Esquire*, vol. 83, no. 2 (Feb. 1975), p. 60–64, 151–54.
Outlines the plan, which was never carried out, for Abaco to secede from the Bahamas following independence. The article also profiles the personalities behind this plan.

356 **The Bahamas ten years after independence, 1973–1983.**
Bahamas. Department of Archives. Nassau: Department of Archives, 1983. 80p.
This booklet covers the first decade of nationhood and is filled with self-congratulatory praise. It was produced to accompany the exhibition of historical documents held at the Senate Building, 27 June–16 July 1983, and contains black-and-white photographs of all of the exhibits, with captions for each.

Individual islands

Abaco

357 **Wilson City and the coming of the twentieth century in Abaco.**
Steve Dodge. *Journal of the Bahamas Historical Society*, vol. 8 (Oct. 1986), p. 3–7.
Dodge outlines the role of Wilson City in the history of Abaco and the Bahamas. In 1906, construction was begun on this settlement, named after Governor William Grey Wilson, although Governor Sir Gilbert Thomas Carter had made the original agreement in 1900. It was built, ten miles south of Marsh Harbour, by the Bahamas Timber Company, a consortium of lumber merchants from the United States, and was visualized as a utopian socialist community. In 1916 the company closed down operations because of machinery deterioration, rising costs and declining production. The equipment that remained was broken up and sold for scrap while the houses and other buildings were dismantled and moved to Nassau.

358 **A guide and history of Hope Town.**
Steve Dodge, Vernon Malone. Decatur, Illinois: White Sound, 1985. 48p. 2 maps.
This booklet includes a walking tour and a history of Hope Town, Abaco. The first settlers were Loyalists, who arrived around 1785. At various times throughout history the inhabitants of this settlement have engaged in wrecking, pineapple and sisal growing and, most successfully, sponging. This booklet, which also includes the Hope Town classified directory, is definitely for the visitor, but is particularly useful for the history provided.

359 **Abaco: the history of an out island and its cays.**
Steve Dodge. North Miami, Florida: Tropic Isle Publications, 1983. 172p. 12 maps. bibliog.
The history of Abaco is unique in that its insular nature forced the inhabitants to

develop their own distinctive society. This is the first general comprehensive history of Abaco. Although the emphasis is on the post-Loyalist period, there are two chapters on pre-Columbian and early-British culture and geography. Dodge explores two themes: the extreme isolation of Abaco during the nineteenth and early-twentieth centuries and the fact that modernization has been delayed in Abaco (the first automobile did not appear on the island until the 1950s). This book is well researched, with good footnotes and illustrations. There is a very good article on boat-building and the chapter on the Abaconian independence movement of 1973 is an enlightening addition to other accounts of Bahamian independence.

360   **From sand banks to Treasure Cay.**
Marjorie W. Brown in collaboration with Elsie Porter.   [n.p.]: The Author, 1977. 109p. 1982. rev. ed. 127p. map.
This book is particularly useful for the sections on the history of the area and on the Owens-Illinois Company of Toledo, Ohio which came to Abaco in 1959 to conduct timbering operations. The work provides a very good outline of the growth of a Bahamian resort, but a map of Treasure Cay itself would have been useful.

361   **Man-O-War, my island home: a history of an outer Abaco island.**
Haziel L. Albury.   Hockessin, Delaware: Holly Press, 1977. 167p. map.
This is the first comprehensive description and history of Man-O-War Cay, Abaco. It is a personal memoir that tells the stories of the people who have contributed to the wealth and progress of the settlement. Albury describes in detail old habits, customs, and occupations, especially boat-building which is the main livelihood. Albury's source for all his material is oral history. He includes a genealogy of the Albury family (the majority of the inhabitants), a glossary and ten Abaconian recipes.

362   **The innocent island: Abaco in the Bahamas.**
Zoe Durrell.   Kennebunkport, Maine: Durrell Publications, 1972. 157p. 2 maps. bibliog.
Durrell presents the history of the Bahamas as it has affected Abaco and discusses the development of Abaco from 1960 to 1972. There are also descriptions of the birds, plants and shells found on and around the island.

Eleuthera

363   **Arawaks and astronauts: twenty years on Eleuthera.**
Kjeld Helweg-Larsen.   London: Jarrolds, 1970. 192p. 2 maps.
This is an account of the author's twenty years on the island of Eleuthera. He provides amusing anecdotes and shrewd observations of the social and political evolution of the Bahamas. As a history and description of Eleuthera, the book throws light on the ways of life, as well as manners and customs of the past.

364   **Eleuthera: the island called "Freedom".**
Everild Young.   London: Regency, 1966. 181p. 3 maps.
Presents a geography and romanticized history of the island of Eleuthera from the mid-

seventeenth century to the 1960s. Young includes a discussion of industry and development on the island and a look at some of the island's personalities. There is no index or bibliography.

Exuma

365   **Exuma, historical/pictorial guide.**
Jeffery Kevin Thompson.   Nassau: The Author, 1983. 138p. 7 maps.
This is a good reference guide to Exuma, comprising 365 islands and cays, which begin thirty miles southeast of Nassau and stretch in that direction for 130 miles. Seventeen of the islands are inhabited. Thompson provides sections on geography, history (the Exumas were first settled by Loyalists in 1783), government, agriculture, transportation and communication, business and statistics. There are also descriptions of nineteen of the settlements found in the Exumas.

Grand Bahama

366   **Freeport, Bahamas: a dream come true.**
Jolene Prewit-Parker.   Moore Haven, Florida: Rainbow, 1983. 112p. map. bibliog.
Prewit-Parker has written an uncritical history of Freeport and of the role played by Wallace Groves who began the planning and development of Freeport as a modern city.

367   **Grand Bahama.**
Peter J.H. Barratt.   Newton Abbot, England: David & Charles; Harrisburg, Pennsylvania: Stackpole, 1972. 206p. 3 maps. bibliog. (The Island Series).
This is a general discussion of the history and development of the island of Grand Bahama. Early native history is well covered and there is particular emphasis on the phenomenal development in the 1960s. A section on treasure and its recovery is very interesting. An appendix contains a useful ten-page list of settlements on Grand Bahama. Barratt was a one-time planner in the development of Freeport.

368   **The truth about Freeport/Lucaya.**
Needham Christopher Hines.   Miami, Florida: Florida Research Press, 1964. 77p. map. bibliog.
This history and guidebook to Freeport/Lucaya was written for the businessperson or prospective resident rather than the tourist.

New Providence

369 **Settlements in New Providence.**
Bahamas. Department of Archives. Nassau: Department of Archives, 1982. 67p.

This booklet contains black-and-white photographs of all of the historical documents which were exhibited in the Post Office Building's foyer, 8–27 February 1982, and offers captions for each. It outlines the development of Nassau and other settlements on the Island of New Providence, and contains twelve plans of Nassau and the other settlements.

370 **A guide to African villages in New Providence.**
Patrice M. Williams. Nassau: Public Records Office, 1979. 13p.

The African villages of New Providence were settled by blacks from slave ships captured by the Royal Navy after the abolition of the slave trade. The slaves were brought to the Bahamas and declared free. Williams discusses the three major villages: Adelaide, Carmichael and Gambier, as well as six minor ones: Grant's Town, Bain Town, Fox Hill, Sandiland's Village, Headquarters and Delancey Town. This short, well-referenced document contains useful information on a little-researched topic.

371 **Historic Nassau.**
D. Gail Saunders, Donald Cartwright. London: Macmillan Caribbean, 1979. 54p. 4 maps. bibliog.

This work by the archivist of the Bahamas (Saunders) and a local architect (Cartwright) traces the city's beginnings and discusses the major influences which have contributed to Nassau's growth and present-day appearance. In particular, the authors consider the effects of the American Loyalists and developments in the nineteenth century. The authors' intention is to give the reader a quick look at Nassau's main historic buildings. Their text and numerous black-and-white photographs and illustrations more than accomplish this.

372 **Bain Town.**
Cleveland Wilmore Eneas. Nassau: Timpaul, 1976. 52p.

A social history and nostalgic look at the section of Nassau where the author was born and raised. Bain Town was originally settled by members of the Yoruba tribe of Nigeria. Eneas is a good story-teller and provides a book that is not only very useful and interesting to Bahamians but also to non-Bahamians who want to know something of the social history of the islands. A map of the area would have been a useful addition.

373 **Historic forts of Nassau in the Bahamas.**
Bahamas. Development Board. Nassau: Commonwealth of the Bahamas, 1952. 2nd ed. 31p.

This is a well-illustrated book about the early English-built forts (there were none built by the Spanish) in Nassau and elsewhere on New Providence Island. Particular note is made of Fort Nassau, built in 1697 and demolished in 1837, and the three forts still standing, Fort Charlotte (1789), Fort Montagu (1741) and Fort Fincastle (1789). Also mentioned are four smaller fortifications no longer standing: Fort Winton, Potter's Cay

Battery, Hog Island Battery and Old Fort. Plans of Fort Charlotte and Fort Nassau are
included.

374   The history of the Isle of Providence.
John Oldmixon.   London: J. Culmer, 1949. 30p.
This reprint of a chapter from Oldmixon's 1741 edition of *The British Empire in
America* is a history of the Bahamas from 1667, when the islands were granted to the
Lords Proprietors of Carolina, to 1736. The author obtained a great deal of his
information from Governors Nicholas Trott and Woodes Rogers and provides a picture
of life in the Bahamas during the time of the pirates. Oldmixon (1673–1742) was a
writer of poems, plays, books, pamphlets and memoirs.

Paradise Island

375   Paradise Island story.
Paul Albury.   London: Macmillan Caribbean, 1984. 121p. 7 maps.
From the seventeenth century up to 1962, Paradise Island, off the northeast shore of
the Island of New Providence, was known as Hog Island. Albury discusses the history
of Hog/Paradise Island from its initial use as a means of defence (barracks were built
and guns erected, in the 1790s, but no shots were fired and they had been deserted by
1834). He considers its later uses, as a site for shipyards, dockyards and agriculture,
through to its present function as a mecca for tourists. Though a notes section is
included, a bibliography and index would make this easily-read book more useful.

San Salvador

376   The outermost island: an oral history of San Salvador, the Bahamas.
Virginia White.   Fort Lauderdale, Florida: College Center of the
Finger Lakes, Bahamian Field Station, 1985. 70p. map.
This book describes San Salvador's subsistence life style based on agriculture and
fishing, and how it was affected by the installation of two United States military bases
during the 1950s and the establishment of self-government for the Bahamas in 1973
after 325 years of British rule. White has based her work on the recorded recollections
of natives of San Salvador, and has included a short history of the Catholic Church on
San Salvador as well as several bush medicine remedies.

Slavery

377 A modified form of slavery: the credit and truck systems in the Bahamas in the nineteenth and early twentieth centuries.
Howard Johnson. *Comparative Studies in Society and History*, vol. 28 (Oct. 1986), p. 729–53.
Examines the control mechanisms which enabled the white minority to consolidate its position as a ruling élite in the post-emancipation period. The elements contributing to this élite's economic and social control were a monopoly on the credit available to the majority of the population and the operation of a system of payment in truck, in goods rather than in money. This is a well-researched paper and although there is no bibliography, there are excellent notes.

378 Slavery in the Bahamas, 1648–1838.
D. Gail Saunders. Nassau: The Author, 1985. 249p. map. bibliog.
This is a well-documented and detailed picture of slavery in the Bahamas. The author examines the demographic structure of the Bahamian slave population from 1648 to emancipation and analyses the growth and decline of slavery, patterns of mortality and fertility, family structure, occupational distribution and health patterns of the slave population. There are also brief descriptions of life on a plantation, slave resistance, liberated African settlements on New Providence and the apprenticeship system which followed emancipation. This work, the author's 1978 MPhil thesis rewritten, was published to commemorate the 150th anniversary of the abolition of slavery in the British Empire.

379 Africans in the Caribbean: a preliminary assessment of recaptives in the Bahamas, 1811–1860.
Peter T. Dalleo. *Journal of the Bahamas Historical Society*, vol. 6 (Oct. 1984), p. 15–24.
Recaptives were Africans taken from their homeland by slavers and either captured by the British anti-slavery naval squadron or wrecked and subsequently freed in the

Bahamas. Dalleo offers suggestions as to their origins and how many came to the Bahamas. He also seeks to better understand their contributions to the building of Bahamian society in the first half of the nineteenth century. The article investigates immigration, resistance and African retentions from a Bahamian perspective.

380 Aspects of slavery, part II.
Bahamas. Department of Archives.   Nassau: Department of Archives, 1984. 52p.

An exhibition of historical documents was held in the Post Office Building, 6–25 1984, to commemorate the 150th anniversary of the abolition of slavery. This booklet is a very good introduction to the history of Bahamian slavery but, unfortunately, the captioned black-and-white reproductions which are given for each of the exhibits are not very good. Six of the exhibits are duplicates from *Aspects of slavery* (q.v.).

381 From punishment to cruelty: treatment of slaves in the Bahamas, 1723–1832.
Patrice M. Williams.   *Journal of the Bahamas Historical Society*, vol. 6 (Oct. 1984), p. 30–33.

Williams examines the laws pertaining to slavery prior to 1784 and finds that these laws, which reflect the fears felt by whites, protected the interests of the whites and are marked by brutality and repression. She then compares these early laws with those passed in the late-eighteenth century and early-nineteenth century and finds that the later laws set out to protect the slaves from cruelty though they were still harsh in their outlook.

382 The share system in the Bahamas in the nineteenth and early twentieth centuries.
Howard Johnson.   *Slavery and Abolition*, vol. 5, no. 2 (1984), p. 141–53.

Johnson examines the operations of the sharecropping system in the Bahamas from its origins after the abolition of slavery up to the early years of the twentieth century. He notes that the system improved neither the social status nor economic conditions of ex-slaves. The sharecropping system became an effective mechanism by which landowners retained a reliable and dependent labour force. He also provides a description of the economic structure of the colony in the years before the abolition of slavery.

383 Slave resistance in the Bahamas.
D. Gail Saunders.   *Journal of the Bahamas Historical Society*, vol. 6 (Oct. 1984), p. 25–29.

Slave resistance in the Bahamas took many forms including refusal to work, general inefficiency, deliberate laziness, running away and suicide. Saunders describes four of the slave revolts which took place between 1829 and 1833. She also provides a brief discussion and description of slave society.

Slavery

384 **Trades and occupations of runaway slaves in the Bahamas, 1784–1834.**
Roderick J. MacIntosh. *Journal of the Bahamas Historical Society*,
vol. 6 (Oct. 1984), p. 7–14.
MacIntosh has made a study of 412 runaway slave announcements that appeared in
Bahamian newspapers between 1784 and 1834. Of this total number, ninety-eight
indicate the occupation of the runaway. Slaves who possessed a particular skill were
valuable because they could be hired out and thus provide their owners with a source
of income. The author has reproduced twenty-nine runaway notices in this fascinating
article.

385 **Bahamian Loyalists and their slaves.**
D. Gail Saunders.   London: Macmillan Caribbean, 1983. 81p. 5 maps.
bibliog.
The Bahamian National Archivist has written this book, based on research for her
MPhil thesis, to commemorate the 200th anniversary of the coming of the Loyalists
and their slaves to the Bahamas between 1783 and 1800. The work traces their
settlements and considers the influence that both the Loyalists and their slaves had on
the Bahamas' development. Those influences were economic (cotton and salt
production and stock-raising); social (architecture, bush medicine, Junkanoo, story-
telling, and obeah); and political. In particular, Saunders details the racial barriers
raised by the Loyalists which were to affect Bahamian society for over 150 years. A
useful glossary is also included.

386 **Health of Bahamian slaves in 1834.**
D. Gail Saunders.   *Journal of the Bahamas Historical Society*, vol. 2
(Oct. 1980), p. 11–14.
For the most part, Bahamian slaves enjoyed good physical health. Saunders attributes
this to a reasonable diet, a temperate climate and favourable working and living
conditions. In examining the Registration of Slaves for 1834, she found that only 1.2
per cent of the slave population suffered from disease and that the female population
was healthier than the male. The most common diseases and ailments suffered by the
slaves were blindness, lameness, hernias, mental illness, ulcerated legs and tuberculosis.
The article also provides some information about medicine and physicians in the early-
nineteenth century.

387 **Hobbesian or Panglossian?: the two extremes of slave conditions in the
British Caribbean, 1783 to 1834.**
Michael Craton.   *William and Mary Quarterly*, vol. 35, no. 2 (1978),
p. 324–56.
Craton examines slave conditions at Great Exuma, particularly at the plantation of
Denys Rolle and that of his son, John, and contrasts this with the Worthy Park
plantation in Jamaica. There is a discussion of sex ratios, fertility of women, family
groupings and miscegenation. The Rolle slaves were found to be more fertile, and this
is attributed to stable families, an absence of miscegenation, spacing between births
and an early peak of fertility. They were also better fed and experienced less cruelty.

388 **Aspects of slavery.**
Bahamas. Public Records Office.   Nassau: Public Records Office,
1974. 28p.
This booklet, which covers the exhibition of historical documents held at the Bahamas
Public Records Office, 12–16 February 1974, contains black-and-white photographs of
all of the exhibits; each is given a caption. Slaves were used on plantations throughout
the Bahamas until the Emancipation Act of 1834, which provided for a compulsory
apprenticeship, or transmission period, between slavery and full freedom. The
Emancipation Act of 1838 abolished the apprenticeship period and gave all ex-slaves
complete freedom. Emancipation Day, the first Monday in August, is still celebrated
throughout the Bahamas.

389 **A relic of slavery: Farquharson's journal for 1831–32.**
Charles Farquharson, introduced by A. Deans Peggs.
Nassau: Deans Peggs Research Fund, 1957. 84p. 2 maps.
Farquharson owned a 2,000 acre estate on Watlings Island; the chief crop was sorghum
and cattle were also raised. This is a working, not a romantic, diary; its short, pertinent
entries describe the running of a self-sufficient estate in the Bahamas. It includes useful
descriptions of land preparation, harvesting, home building and repairs and road
mending. The introduction is very good.

Population

General

390 **Population projections for the Bahamas until 2015.**
Bahamas. Department of Statistics. Nassau: Department of Statistics,
1987. 64p.
Population projections are calculated through the use of fifty-four tables, eight age-sex
pyramids and two graphs.

391 **Report of the 1980 census of population.**
Bahamas. Nassau: Ministry of Finance, 1986– .
The 1980 census was the sixteenth decennial census to be conducted in the Bahamas.
Of the five volumes published to date volume one, *Demographic and social
characteristics*, provides 204 tables, seventeen for the Bahamas as a whole and eleven
tables each for the seventeen inhabited islands or island groups; volume two covers
Economic activity and income; volume three, *Migration*; volume four, *Education*; and
volume five, *Union status and fertility*.

392 **Some aspects of fertility in New Providence.**
Azella Major. Nassau: Department of Statistics, 1981. 38p. bibliog.
This is the first ever study of fertility in the Bahamas. The objectives of the survey,
which was conducted between September 1978 and September 1979, were fourfold, to
provide: information on fertility levels and patterns and the factors affecting fertility; a
framework for the study of fertility and other economic and social factors affecting the
community; information for government and social planners; and a basis for a national
fertility survey. The study includes eighteen tables which compare fertility levels with
marital status, age of entry into sexual unions, use or non-use of contraception, levels
of education, occupation, employment status, religion and cultural factors. Although
the study does not provide a fertility level for the Bahamas, a fertility rate of 97.4 per
thousand women (based on 1980 data, the most recent available) is given in the United

Nations *Demographic yearbook* (New York: UN, Department of International Economic and Social Affairs, Statistical Office, 1988. 1233p.).

393 **Census of population and housing, 1980: preliminary review.**
Bahamas. Department of Statistics. Nassau: Commonwealth of the Bahamas, 1980. 17p.
This booklet provides preliminary results of the 1980 census and, in particular, comments on the definite shift of population to New Providence and Freeport. It also gives six tables, a description of the census divisions and comparisons with the 1970 figures.

394 **The 1980 census of population and housing: an overview.**
J. Egbert Tertullien. Nassau: Department of Statistics, 1979. 11p. (Census Bulletin, no. 1/79).
Written prior to the 1980 census, this item describes how the census will be conducted, for what purposes census data are used and the problems of census taking. Tertullien also provides some commentary on the questions to be asked.

395 **Demographic aspects of the Bahamian population, 1901–1974.**
Azella Major. Nassau: Department of Statistics, 1976. 53p. (Census Monograph, no. 2).
This monograph provides much more text than is usual in a Department of Statistics publication. There are sections on general population growth, sex and age distribution and fertility, mortality and migration. The report found that: population increased three-fold between 1901 and 1974; the Bahamian population is a youthful one with 43.6 per cent under fifteen years of age; there is a predominance of males at birth but females live longer; there is a low crude death rate; migration plays a more significant role in population growth than any other demographic component; one quarter of the work force is non-Bahamian; and inter-island migration is mainly to Freeport and Nassau.

396 **Report of the 1970 census of population.**
Bahamas. Nassau: Commonwealth of the Bahamas, 1972. 481p. 17 maps.
Contains general statistics and statistics for labour, education, migration and income. There are 754 tables of data.

Internal migration

397 **The characteristics of internal migration to and from New Providence Island (Greater Nassau), Bahamas, 1960–1970.**
Thomas D. Boswell. *Social and Economic Studies*, vol. 35, no. 1 (March 1986), p. 111–50.
Boswell examines migration to and from New Providence Island during the 1960s, and

investigates the spatial patterns of in-migration to and out-migration from Greater Nassau, the selectivity characteristics of internal migrants and the impact of internal migration on the demographic composition of Nassau. Twelve data tables are provided.

398 **Internal migration in the Commonwealth of the Bahamas, 1960–1970.**
Thomas D. Boswell, Anderson K. Chibwa. Nassau: Clyde-Berren Associates, 1981. 205p. 7 maps. bibliog.
This book is designed to investigate the characteristics of internal migration in the Bahamas in the 1960s. Census data from 1963 and 1970 show that ten of the seventeen most inhabited islands decreased in population while Grand Bahama and the Berry Islands increased by 214 per cent and sixty-seven per cent respectively. Nassau, the capital, experienced a small decrease, which is unusual in a developing country.

399 **A comparison of net migration patterns and their spatial correlates in Puerto Rico and the Bahamas during the 1960's.**
Thomas D. Boswell, Anderson K. Chibwa. *Geographical Survey*, vol. 8, no. 3 (July 1979), p. 16–29.
Discusses the factors influencing internal migration. This is the first migration study designed for comparative purposes dealing with two separate island entities in the Caribbean.

Minorities

400 **Safeguarding our traders: the beginnings of immigration restrictions in the Bahamas, 1925–33.**
Howard Johnson. *Immigrants and Minorities*, vol. 5, no. 1 (March 1986), p. 5–27.
An analysis of the reasons behind the demands for controls on immigration between 1925 and 1933. This restrictive legislation was designed mainly to limit economic competition from 'trading minorities' and, to a lesser extent, the immigration of skilled West Indian labourers. This article documents the involvement of these minorities in the economy of the islands, the reactions of 'native' Bahamians and the nature and language of their opposition to the incursions of the immigrants. The culmination of these tensions was the legislation which led to the reassertion of local control over the economy.

401 **Haitians in the Bahamas face a new wave of massive deportations.**
Max Dominique. *Migration Today*, vol. 13, no. 5 (1985), p. 30–32.
Haitian migration to the Bahamas began in the 1960s and was welcomed as a source of cheap labour. However, in the late 1970s and early 1980s it came to be seen as a social and economic problem. Dominique discusses roundups of illegal Haitian immigrants and pleads for understanding and compassionate treatment of them.

402   **The Haitian problem: illegal migration to the Bahamas.**
Dawn I. Marshall.   Mona, Kingston, Jamaica: Institute of Social and
Economic Research, University of the West Indies, 1979. 239p. 3 maps.
bibliog.

This study of the illegal entry of Haitians into the Bahamas focuses primarily on the
individual immigrant rather than on the problem in general because there was little
information available to Marshall on the volume, frequency, duration or routes of
migration. The study describes the environmental background of the Haitian migrant,
the problems he or she faces on reaching the Bahamas and Haitian migration over
time. The work concludes with a case study of Haitians living in Carmichael, a small
settlement on New Providence Island south of Nassau. As most figures used by
Marshall are pre-1970, this study is now only useful for background research.

Overseas population

403   **Black immigrants: Bahamians in early twentieth-century Miami.**
Raymond A. Mohl.   *Florida Historical Quarterly*, vol. 65, no. 3
(1987), p. 271–97.

Bahamians, attracted by job prospects and cash wages, were among the first
immigrants to Miami, especially after its incorporation in 1896. The Bahamians were
unused to the obsequious behaviour expected of Southern blacks; they consequently
roused the ire of the local whites who appealed to the Miami police and the British
Foreign Office to help stem racial problems. Despite these problems, the city of Miami
continued to attract Bahamians and their presence helped to swell the city's
population.

Folklore

404   **Old stories and riddles: Bahamiana culturama #1.**
Mizpah C. Tertullien.   Nassau: The Author, 1977. 52p.
A collection of six Bahamian folk stories and eighteen Bahamian riddles written
exclusively for elementary-age school children.

405   **Once was a time, a wery [sic] good time: an inquiry into the folklore of**
the Bahamas.
Basil C. Hedrick, Cezarija Abartis Letson.   Greeley, Colorado:
University of Northern Colorado, Museum of Anthropology, 1975.
48p. bibliog. (Museum of Anthropology. Miscellaneous Series, 38).
This examination of folklore is set in the context of the history and the geography of
the Bahamas. Hedrick and Letson outline the typical features of Bahamian folklore:
the opening and closing formulae; the personalities of the characters (both animal and
human); the joke structure of the plot; the most common motifs; and some of the most
graphic linguistic devices. They comment at length on oral performance, which is
ignored by Edwards in his *Bahama songs and stories . . .* (q.v.) and only occasionally
alluded to by Parsons in *Folk tales of Andros Island, Bahamas* (q.v.), the two early
major collections of Bahamian folklore.

406   **I could talk old-story good: creativity in Bahamian folklore.**
Daniel J. Crowley.   Berkeley, California: University of California
Press, 1966. 156p. map. bibliog. (University of California Publications.
Folklore Studies, 17).
Looks at Bahamian folktales and methodology and the oral tradition in the Bahamas.
Crowley corroborates Parson's view in *Folk tales of Andros Island, Bahamas* (q.v.)
that these tales were learned in Africa and not America. He discusses regional
variations from island to island, individual variation by the narrator and the folk tale as
theatre. He maintains that stories from Andros are the most numerous, the longest,
the most varied in motif structure and stylistic presentation, and are the richest in all

those attributes that Bahamians value highly in the folktale. The work includes sixty-three tales scattered throughout the book, accessible through a separate index. There is also an index of types and motifs but no general index for the book itself.

407   **Form and style in a Bahamian folktale.**
Daniel J. Crowley.   *Caribbean Quarterly*, vol. 3, no. 4 (Aug. 1954), p. 218–34.
Crowley analyses eleven major components of the Bahamian folktale by comparing two variants of the same folktale as told in the Bahamas of the 1950s.

408   **Bahamian proverbs.**
Basil Peek.   London: J. Culmer; Nassau: Providence Press, 1949. [n.p.].
This is a collection of twenty-three one-line Bahamian proverbs, each accompanied by a line drawing. Proverbs such as: 'E'ry day fishin' day but no e'ry day catch fish', 'When eye no see, mout' no talk' and 'Man can't whistle and smoke one time' exemplify the Bahamian proverb tradition.

409   **Bahamian lore.**
Robert Arthur Curry.   New York: Gordon, 1978. 125p. 4 maps. (Bahamas Series).
This is a reprint of the limited edition originally published privately (Paris: Lecram, 1928). Curry has penned an impressionistic word picture of the Bahamas recreating lore relating to Columbus, the Lucayan Indians, 'Blackbeard' (Edward Teach) and various aspects of island life. The work includes two native songs and two Bahamian folktales. It is fascinating in its own way though not very factual.

410   **Folklore from Eleuthera, Bahamas.**
H.H. Finlay.   *Journal of American Folk-Lore*, vol. 38, no. 148 (April/June 1925), p. 293–99.
This collection includes: two stories, 'Rabbit makes Bookie murder' and 'Fake message: take my place'; twenty-four proverbs; twelve riddles and puzzles; and twenty-four toasts. Finlay provides no commentary for these examples of Bahamian folklore.

411   **Riddles and proverbs from the Bahama Islands.**
Elsie Worthington Clews Parsons.   *Journal of American Folk-Lore*, vol. 32, no. 125 (July/Sept. 1919), p. 439–41.
Presents a collection of twenty-four riddles from Eleuthera and Watlings Island and twelve proverbs from Eleuthera.

412   **Folk tales of Andros Island, Bahamas.**
Elsie Worthington Clews Parsons.   Millwood, New York: Kraus Reprint, 1976. 170p. (American Folklore Society Memoirs Series).
This reprint of the 1918 American Folklore Society publication is the next major collection of Bahamian folktales after Edwards' *Bahama songs and stories . . .* (q.v.) published in 1895. Parsons finds that these Andros tales are of a distinctly Bahamian character rather than being merely local, that the characters in the tales are possessed

of fixed attributes and names and that Bahamian tales were learned in Africa not America. The book is well foot-noted and contains 115 Bahamian folktales.

413 Four folk-tales from Fortune Island, Bahamas.
W.T. Cleare. *Journal of American Folk-Lore*, vol. 30, no. 116 (April/June 1917), p. 228–29.
Cleare presents four tales: 'Bartering mothers', 'The buried tail', 'Dead or asleep' and 'Getting the other fellow to take your place'.

414 Proverbs from Abaco, Bahamas.
Hilda Armbrister. *Journal of American Folk-Lore*, vol. 30, no. 116 (April/June 1917), p. 274.
Presents a collection of fifteen proverbs from Abaco, such as 'Beeg eye choke puppy', meaning 'Don't bite off more than you can chew'. Critical analysis of the proverbs does not appear.

415 Riddles from Andros Island, Bahamas.
Elsie Worthington Clews Parsons. *Journal of American Folk-Lore*, vol. 30, no. 116 (April/June 1917), p. 275–77.
Presents a collection of twenty-one riddles from Andros Island. One example is 'De black man settin' on de red man head', the answer being a pot sitting on fire.

416 Bahamian folk lore.
James Fitz-James. Montreal: The Author, 1906. 64p.
Contains six Bahamian folktales written in dialect: 'The race between Brother Horse and Brother Conch'; 'The courting of Brother Rabbit and Brother Bookie'; 'Brother Elephant and Brother Paroquet'; 'Brother Devil and Brother Lobster'; 'Cadoel'; and 'Brother Cat and Brother Dog'.

417 Items of folk-lore from Bahama Negroes.
M. Clavel. *Journal of American Folk-Lore*, vol. 17, no. 64 (Jan./March 1904), p. 36–38.
Clavel discusses folklore and the miscellaneous superstitions surrounding Bahamian 'hags', that is, old Congo women of between eighty and one hundred years old.

418 Bahama songs and stories: a contribution to folklore.
Charles Lincoln Edwards. Millwood, New York: Kraus Reprint, 1976. (American Folklore Society Memoirs Series).
This is a reprint of the 1895 New York edition. Edwards divides Bahamian folktales into two classes, the old stories which are part of Negro folklore and the fairy stories which are Bahamian stories that use the same sources as English fairy tales. The thirty-eight stories are presented in dialect as are the forty songs. The stories use animal characters imported from Africa and America and deal mostly with animal themes while the songs are mostly spirituals. In an appendix, Edwards discusses Negro music in general. This collection has very little commentary.

419　**Some tales from Bahaman folk-lore.**
Charles Lincoln Edwards.　*Journal of American Folk-Lore*, vol. 4,
no. 12 (Jan./March 1891), p. 47–54; vol. 4, no. 14 (July/Sept. 1891),
p. 247–52.

These two collections with the same title follow up an earlier article, 'Folk-lore of the
Bahama Negroes' (q.v.) in the *American Journal of Psychology*. The January/March
instalment contains seven old stories and the July/September segment contains five
fairy stories.

420　**Folk-lore of the Bahama Negroes.**
Charles Lincoln Edwards.　*American Journal of Psychology*, vol. 2,
no. 4 (Aug. 1889), p. 519–42.

Offers a collection of twelve stories from Green Turtle Cay. There is also a description
of the Cay and the people who live there, but there is no real analysis of the stories.

Religion

421 **Early history of Baptists in the Bahamas.**
Antonina Canzoneri. *Journal of the Bahamas Historical Society*, vol. 4 (Oct. 1982), p. 9–16.
Canzoneri provides a history of the Bahamian Baptist Church from 1800 to the mid-twentieth century and examines, in particular, the early church buildings and the early preachers, including Brother Amos, Sambo Scrivens, Frank Spence and Prince Williams. She also offers some remarks on religious liberty in the Bahamas and points out that the Baptist Church was not recognized on official occasions until after the Progressive Liberal Party came to power in 1967.

422 **His light for an island nation: a missionary account of God's faithfulness to His Word in the Bahama Islands.**
Eleanor Ford.　Sayre, Pennsylvania: Bible Lighthouse Press, 1982. 318p. 10 maps.
This history of the Island Missionary Society (IMS), founded in 1941 by Paul Dean Ford (1893–1968), is Ford's personal, evangelical account of her missionary experience in the Bahamas. She provides a view of Bahamian religious life and social life.

423 **Baptists in the Bahamas: an historical review.**
Michael Carrington Symonette, Antonina Canzoneri.　El Paso, Texas: Baptist Spanish Publishing House, 1977. 79p. bibliog.
A brief but valuable introduction to the Baptist religion in the Bahamas. Symonette and Canzoneri investigate the areas of confrontation between the Baptists and the Anglicans and explain how the Anglican church, oriented toward the white population, retained social and political status in spite of the numerical advantage held by the Baptists.

424 Research on the history of Baptists in the Bahamas.
Antonina Canzoneri. *Caribbean Archives*, no. 5 (1976), p. 41–50.
This article is primarily a bibliography, listing materials from the Public Records Office
in Nassau, the Registrar General's Department (Bahamas) and the Bahamas Land
Grants Office which pertain to the history of the Baptists in the islands. The author
provides a useful guide for others researching this area and for those who wish to
investigate other denominations. There is also a short, two-page history of the Baptists
preceding the bibliography.

425 Let the church roll on: a collection of speeches and writings.
Cleveland Wilmore Eneas. Nassau: The Author, 1974. 114p.
A collection of speeches presented by Eneas on religion in the Bahamas, religious
philosophy, Bahamian politics, emancipation, education and the Kiwanis Club (an
international service club) in the Bahamas. There is also some biographical material
which not only provides information about Eneas but also about the Bahamas in the
first half of the twentieth century.

426 A new beginning.
Philip A. Rahming. Nassau: Family Island, 1973. 73p.
This is a collection of thirteen sermons and addresses delivered by the author in the
Bahamas and the United States, his intention being to encourage Christian behaviour
in society. The majority of the addresses were delivered in the Bahamas and offer a
glimpse of society and religion in the country.

427 Upon these rocks: Catholics in the Bahamas.
Colman James Barry. Collegeville, Minnesota: St. John's Abbey
Press, 1973. 582p. map.
Father Colman Barry, one-time president of St. John's University in Collegeville,
Minnesota, provides a detailed history of the Catholic Church in the Bahamas. Father
Chrysostom Schreiner was the first permanent Catholic missionary in the Bahamas,
arriving in Nassau in 1891. Prior to this the Bahamas was served by a stream of priests
from the United States. The first Bahamian to be ordained as a priest was Father Carl
Thomas Albury in the 1920s, while the first black priest in the Bahamas was the
American Father Prosper Meyer who arrived in 1948. Barry also seeks to analyse why
Catholic influence was minimal until 1858 when the Bahamas became part of the
Vicariate of South Carolina. This work is well researched and foot-noted but lacks a
bibliography.

428 The hermit of Cat Island: the life of Fra Jerome Hawes.
Peter Frederick Anson. New York: P.J. Kennedy; London: Burns &
Oates, 1957. 212p.
Born John Cyril Hawes, Fra Jerome (1876–1956) originally studied as an architect but
entered theological college in 1901. He was posted to the Bahamas as a minister of the
Church of England in 1908 and remained until 1911. In that same year he converted to
Roman Catholicism in the United States and subsequently went to Australia until 1939
when he returned to the Bahamas and settled on Cat Island; he remained there until
his death. Because of his architectural background Fra Jerome designed six secular
buildings, forty-one churches and fifteen religious structures other than churches.
Thirteen of these churches and St. Augustine's Monastery and College were built in

the Bahamas. Anson has written an interesting biography based on his own knowledge of him and on Fra Jerome's own papers and correspondence.

429 **Ups and downs in a West Indian diocese.**
Roscoe George Shedden.   London: A.R. Mowbray, 1927. 188p. map.
This is an interesting and detailed history of the Church of England in the Bahamas which was written at the request of the Nassau Council in England 'to stimulate interest in our Mission' (Preface).

430 **The Church in the West Indies.**
Alfred Caldecott.   London: Cass, 1970. 275p. map. bibliog. (Cass Library of West Indian Studies, no. 14).
A reprint of the 1898 edition published in London by the Society for Promoting Christian Knowledge as one of the series of Colonial Church Histories, and in New York by E. & J.B. Young. Caldecott outlines church history from 1605 to 1897 with emphasis on the nineteenth century and provides an objective commentary on the failure of the Church of England clergy in the West Indies to help the slaves. Although there is only slight mention of the Bahamas this work is good for an overall view of religion in the Caribbean.

431 **In sunny isles; chapters treating chiefly of the Bahama Islands and Cuba.**
George Lester.   London: Charles H. Kelly, 1897. 144p. bibliog.
Lester prepared this book in honour of the coming centenary of the commencement of the Wesleyan-Methodist mission in the Bahamas in 1800. He presents a very good look at the beginnings of organized, European and American religion in the country and, at the same time, makes comparisons with the introduction of Methodism into Cuba. There are fascinating illustrations and appendices, including a list of Wesleyan missionaries in the Bahamas from 1800 to 1897. Before the arrival of the missionaries, black Bahamians had followed obeah and remnants of African religions.

432 **Classified digest of the records of the Society for the Propagation of the Gospel in Foreign Parts, 1701–1892 (with much supplementary information).**
Compiled by Charles Frederick Pascoe.   London: Society for the Propagation of the Gospel in Foreign Parts, 1895. 5th ed.
Describes (p. 217–27) the work of the Society in the Bahamas from 1731 to 1892. This is a useful resource documenting ministers and missionaries in the Bahamas.

433 **Addington Venables, bishop of Nassau: a sketch of his life and labours for the church of God.**
William Francis Henry King.   London: W. Wells Gardner, 1878. 123p. map.
Addington Robert Peel Venables (1827–76) was born in England and educated at Eton, Exeter College, Oxford and the Theological College at Wells. At the age of thirty-six he was consecrated a bishop and arrived in Nassau the following year to become the second Church of England bishop of the See of Nassau. Venables

remained Bishop of Nassau until his death. He was a missionary bishop and spent a great deal of his time visiting the Out Islands and concerning himself with the welfare of the people. King has produced a book which gives some useful information concerning the Church of England in the Bahamas but primarily praises the life and work of Bishop Venables.

434 **A mission to the West India Islands: Dowson's journal for 1810–17.**
William Dowson, edited by A. Deans Peggs.   Nassau: Deans Peggs Research Fund, 1960. 118p.

Dowson's journal, which was begun on 20 April 1810 and ended on 29 April 1817, chronicles his trip to the Caribbean and his time spent in the Bahamas (1812–17). It is doubtful that the diary was written with publication in mind but it has been produced with care and attention to detail. Dowson provides, among other things, a history of early Bahamian Methodism.

Obeah

435 **It's a natural fact: obeah in the Bahamas.**
Basil C. Hedrick, Jeanette E. Stephens. Greeley, Colorado:
University of Northern Colorado, Museum of Anthropology, 1977.
38p. bibliog. (Museum of Anthropology. Miscellaneous Studies, 39).
Hedrick and Stephens provide a brief description and history of obeah followed by a
longer section on the practice of obeah. There is also reference to obeah's relation to
bush medicine.

436 **Ten, ten the Bible ten: obeah in the Bahamas.**
Timothy O. McCartney. Nassau: Timpaul, 1976. 192p. map. bibliog.
This discussion of obeah in the Bahamas considers its beliefs, practices, superstitions
and taboos. Following a brief introduction to the Bahamas, McCartney begins an in-
depth look at obeah. He explains the origins of obeah, what it is and how it is practised
in the Bahamas. He describes the rituals and provides a number of spells and case
histories. There are two chapters of particular interest. The first looks at the psycho-
social aspects of obeah, comparing it to religion, medicine and folklore in the
Bahamas. The second enumerates Bahamian beliefs and superstitions surrounding
dreams, birth and childhood and male-female relationships. The title refers to a
Bahamian chant used as protection against spirits. In the Bahamas, the number ten is
significant because it is forbidden to spirits and is considered a magic number for
success and protection. This is the most complete look at obeah available. It is written
by a Bahamian psychologist which gives it some added validity.

437 **Conflict and communication: the social matrix of obeah.**
Keith F. Otterbein. *Kansas Journal of Sociology*, vol. 1, no. 3
(summer 1965), p. 112–18.
An analysis of Bahamian field magic, or obeah, as it is practised on Andros Island,
where its function is to prevent the stealing of fruit and other crops.

438   **Witches and fishes.**
Henry Hesketh Joudou Bell.   London: Edward Arnold, 1948. 187p.

This is partly a travel book and partly a collection of sketches and reminiscences. Bell's *Obeah: witchcraft in the West Indies* (q.v.) is probably more useful, although this item should not be entirely overlooked as it contains fascinating stories which help to explain obeah and show how it is often used.

439   **Voodoos and obeahs: phases of West Indian witchcraft.**
Joseph John Williams.   New York: AMS, 1970. 257p. bibliog.

A reprint of the 1932 edition (New York: Dial Press), this work concentrates on the African origins of voodoo in Haiti and obeah in Jamaica. Although it does not focus on the Bahamas, it can be used as a good background source. It is a thorough, scholarly work with a useful bibliography.

440   **The man with the wart: an obeah story.**
Henry Christopher Christie.   London: Press Printers, 1928. 38p.

This is the story of Wilburn Wilshere who is plagued by an obeah-induced wart which appears in the middle of his forehead. Christie has filled his story with obeah lore but because it is written in dialect, it is difficult to read. This is probably the only lengthy Bahamian obeah story that is available.

441   **Obeah: witchcraft in the West Indies.**
Henry Hesketh Joudou Bell.   Westport, Connecticut: Negro
University Press, 1970. 200p.

This reprint of the 1889 edition (London: Sampson Low, Marston, Seale & Rivington) is a good introduction to obeah. Although it deals principally with Grenada, the information presented is fairly representative.

Social Conditions

442 **Social insurance: the experience of three countries in the English-speaking Caribbean.**
Carmelo Mesa-Lago. *International Labour Review*, vol. 127, no. 4 (1988), p. 479–96.
This article is based on a 1987 report prepared for the International Labour Organization. It deals with social insurance programmes in the Bahamas, Barbados and Jamaica, presents the historical evolution of social insurance in these three countries and deals with coverage and non-compliance, benefits, administrative issues and financing.

443 **Custom and conflict on a Bahamian Out-Island.**
Jerome Wendell Lurry-Wright. Lanham, Maryland: University Press of America, 1987. 188p. bibliog.
The author's investigations look at the kinds of disputes that occur between individuals on the island of Mayaguana. He examines how historic, ecological, economic and social factors might lead to the development of disputes and the settlement management of them. He also considers the roles played by political organizations, religion and folk beliefs, especially obeah. His research, based on observations of both formal and informal levels of legal systems in action, shows that the inhabitants of Mayaguana attempt to avoid the courts at all possible costs.

444 **Masters of Paradise Island: organized crime, neo-colonialism and the Bahamas.**
Alan A. Block, Patricia Klausner. *Dialectical Anthropology*, vol. 12, no. 1 (1987), p. 85–102.
The authors describe the recent growth of organized crime in the Bahamas and contend that it exercises neo-colonial power in the country by controlling tourism and casino gambling. They also point out that one cannot understand the range and dynamics of contemporary neo-colonialism, as well as the politics of the Caribbean in

general, without considering the power of organized crime. There are sections on the tourist industry, politics, the formation of Resorts International and the organized crime connection. The authors have also appended excellent end-notes.

445   **The role of the coloured middle class in Nassau, Bahamas, 1890–1942.**
D. Gail Saunders.   *Ethnic and Racial Studies*, vol. 10, no. 4
(Oct. 1987), p. 448–65.
Saunders attempts to define the role of the Bahamian coloured middle class during the late-nineteenth and early-twentieth centuries and to describe how this segment of society changed over a period of time. She points out that the coloured middle class despised manual labour and acted as a divisive element more apt to perpetuate than to eliminate colour prejudice. The article deals with business, politics and education as well as some of the personalities of the times. It is extensively researched and foot-noted.

446   **Writers, social scientists, and sexual norms in the Caribbean.**
Dean W. Collinwood.   *Tsuda Review*, no. 31 (Nov. 1986), p. 45–57.
An examination of sexuality and family life which is based on data drawn from the published and unpublished works of contemporary Bahamian poets, playwrights, novelists, lyricists and essayists. Collinwood investigates the Bahamian perception of the family structure and finds that Bahamian writers see their home lives as ugly and repressive. He also examines Bahamian sexual practices as seen by these authors, and concludes that the majority of the authors see contemporary sexual practices as wrong and morally sinful. At the time of writing two volumes by Collinwood, a comparative sociologist, were at press: *Modern Bahamian society*, edited with Steve Dodge (Parkersburg, Iowa: Caribbean Books, [1989]. 278 p.) and *The Bahamas between worlds* (Decatur, Illinois: White Sound, [1989]. 118 p.). Neither has been reviewed by the compiler, but both promise to be valuable.

447   **Green Turtle Cay: an island in the Bahamas.**
Alan G. LaFlamme.   Prospect Heights, Illinois: Waveland, 1985.
110p. 2 maps. bibliog.
After having spent seven months on Green Turtle Cay, the author produced a work which details race, class, economy, politics, social organization, religion and tourism in this community.

448   **Tryin' to make it: adapting to the Bahamas.**
John Bregenzer.   Lanham, Maryland: University Press of America,
1982. 88p. 5 maps. bibliog.
The author's objective is to explore and document the implications of an idea concerning the nature of human adaptation to a minor island in the Caribbean. The island under study is Eleuthera. Bregenzer's starting point is the myth that tropical islands are a sort of Eden. He shows that the ecology and environment of Eleuthera are far from idyllic and that the people are not noble savages. By looking at the history of Eleuthera, he shows that these Bahamians have had, and will continue to have, no control over the cycles of boom and bust that affect their lives. There are also detailed discussions of the present cultural system of Eleuthera. Throughout this work, the author shows how Bahamians have adapted to an island life.

Social Conditions

449 **The handbook on alcoholism in the Bahamas.**
Edited by Colin B. Archer. Nassau: Colmar Publications, for the
Bahamas Council on Alcoholism, 1981. 65p.
This book brings together a collection of articles and lectures dealing with alcoholism
and drinking patterns in a Bahamian context.

450 **Origin and persistence of an inner-city slum in Nassau.**
Michael F. Doran, Renee A. Landis. *Geographical Review*, vol. 70,
no. 2 (April 1980), p. 182–93.
Examines the development of the Over-the-Hill district of Nassau which the authors
term, at first, an inner-city slum. They conclude that Over-the-Hill may be so,
according to American-derived definitions, but that the area in no sense corresponds to
the clichés of inner-city slum formation taken for granted in many textbooks and in the
minds of many urban theorists. For the authors, 'Over-the-Hill is instead a testimony
to the power with which social controls maintain particular districts to the ends that
they were intended by the power elite' (Conclusion). This article also provides a
history of the growth of Nassau and the villages of Bain Town, Grants Town and
Delancey Town.

451 **Aspects of Bahamian culture.**
Anastasia Elaine Smith. New York: Vantage, 1978. 78p.
This work is based on the author's MA thesis from Fisk University in which she
discusses Bahamian culture and the influences bearing on it in colonial and post-
colonial times. These discussions are placed, in the main, in three contexts: Bahamian
government, politics and history; Bahamian Out Island societies; and particular aspects
of Bahamian culture. It provides a useful introduction to Junkanoo (the Bahamian
Boxing Day and New Year's Day festival with African origins), Bahamian bush
medicine, obeah (the voodoo-like occult practised throughout the West Indies) and
Bahamian folk songs and stories. Junkanoo and obeah are discussed in other sections
of this bibliography.

452 **The Church as an agent for dispute settlement: a Bahamian Out-Island
example.**
Jerome Wendell Wright. *Journal of Religious Thought*, vol. 53
(spring/summer 1978), p. 27–34.
Wright investigates the role of the Church as an informal agent in dispute settlement.
His research was carried out on the island of Mayaguana. The author has investigated
this more closely in his 1987 book *Custom and conflict on a Bahamian Out-Island*
(q.v.).

453 **Stranger's no more: anthropological studies of Cat Island, the Bahamas;
report of an ethnographic research project conducted in 1977.**
Edited and introduced by Joel S. Savishinsky. Ithaca, New York:
Department of Anthropology, Ithaca College, 1978. 349p. 6 maps.
A collection of twenty-six papers written by graduate students following research on
Cat Island in the east central Bahamas. Besides the introduction by Savishinsky and
nine personal essays by some of the students, detailing their experiences, there are also
eleven descriptive essays and five analytic studies, which make up the bulk of this

work. The descriptive essays deal with such topics as family life, farming, fishing, boat-building, straw plaiting (for baskets, purses and hats) and bush medicine. The analytic studies focus on dyadic relationships in the Bahamian family, childhood socialization, Bahamian women, kinship, society, poverty and alcohol consumption.

454 **Bahamian sexuality.**
Timothy O. McCartney.   Nassau: Timpaul, 1976. 101p.
Deals with normal and abnormal human sexuality in a coherent, readable, easy to understand manner. McCartney has written this study for parents, educators, physicians and teenagers and has placed his views in a Bahamian context, dealing with local and common situations. This book can be used, not so much as a study of sexuality, but rather as a useful source of information about Bahamian society and the Bahamian view of sexuality.

455 **Psychologically speaking: attitudes and cultural patterns in the Bahamas.**
Mizpah C. Tertullien.   Boynton Beach, Florida: Star Publishing, 1976. 244p. bibliog.
The essays which make up most of this book originated as a radio programme of the same name which was broadcast in the Bahamas between 1973 and 1975. Tertullien deals with personality, with special emphasis on the role parents and other adults have in shaping the personality of children; work; family life; anxiety; guilt; aggression; violence; and community development. In all instances, she discusses concepts in a Bahamian context, notably so in the sections on family life and community development. This is a useful item for understanding the Bahamian psyche.

456 **Black and white on Green Turtle Cay.**
Alan G. LaFlamme.   *Caribbean Review*, vol. 7, no. 1 (Jan./Feb./March 1975), p. 13–17.
Offers an analysis of changing race relations in one of the Bahamian Out Island communities. LaFlamme discusses such factors as economics, black consciousness, tourism and politics.

457 **Changing house types in Long Bay Cays: the evolution of folk housing in an Out Island Bahamian community.**
Keith F. Otterbein.   New Haven, Connecticut: Human Relations Area Files Press, 1975. 123p. map. bibliog. (HRAFlex Books, SW1-001. Ethnography Series).
Long Bay Cays in southern Andros was settled in the latter half of the nineteenth century by freed Negro slaves from other Bahamian islands. This study is devoted to a detailed description of the types of houses which were built in the community. Otterbein traces the evolution of the three stages of development: the nineteenth-century house, the Georgian house and the modern house. He also makes an effort to distinguish the factors and processes responsible for the change from one type of house to another.

458 **Believers and beaters: a case study of supernatural beliefs and child rearing in the Bahama Islands.**
Charlotte Swanson Otterbein, Keith F. Otterbein. *American Anthropologist*, vol. 75, no. 5 (Oct. 1973), p. 1670–81.
Twenty adults who care for children in Congo Town on Andros Island were interviewed about the training given to the forty-eight children and grandchildren in their charge, as well as about their beliefs in the supernatural. The authors conclude that adults who fear the supernatural will inflict more pain on the children in their charge than will those who do not.

459 **From Adam's rib to women's lib.**
Basil Cooper. Nassau: The Author, 1973. 204p.
A rambling, not very well-organized collection of thoughts, comments and interviews concerned with women's fight for equality. The author is especially concerned with the problems women have with the traditional concept of the female role. The text of this work is not particularly Bahamian in content but the views and unsubstantiated opinions are Bahamian. There is no index.

460 **Neuroses in the sun.**
Timothy O. McCartney. Nassau: Executive Printers, 1971. 166p. bibliog.
This comprehensive and sympathetic study of mental health in the Bahamas investigates the attitudes, mores and traditions of past and contemporary Bahamian life. The book deals with such concerns as the family, childhood and adolescence and the problems of the Bahamian adult. It also touches on drugs, alcoholism and marital difficulties. This readable text is not only for the interested Bahamian but also provides a discussion of Bahamian psychology for the interested foreigner.

461 **Cooper's Town, Bahamas: a statistical survey.**
Keith F. Otterbein. *Social and Economic Studies*, vol. 19, no. 2 (June 1970), p. 263–77.
Describes some of the social characteristics of Cooper's Town, Great Abaco Island, particularly patterns of courtship and marriage and household composition. Cooper's Town is atypical of Bahamian settlements in its low illegitimacy rate and the predominance of male-headed households. The differences appear to be due to missionary activity and earlier marriages have been influenced by a better economic situation.

462 **The development cycle of the Andros household: a diachronic analysis.**
Keith F. Otterbein. *American Anthropologist*, vol. 72, no. 6 (Dec. 1970), p. 1412–19.
Otterbein focuses on the changes in household composition that occurred between 1930 and 1970 in four villages located on southern Andros Island.

463 **Linked changes in values and behavior in the Out Island Bahamas.**
William B. Rodgers, Richard E. Gardner. *American Anthropologist*, vol. 71, no. 1 (Feb. 1969), p. 21–35.
Rodgers and Gardner examine the relationships between culture and behaviour in two communities on Great Abaco Island. They hypothesize that in a community exposed to economic development there would be concomitant value changes as opposed to a community which has been more isolated. Murphy Town is used as an example of the former, Crossing Rocks the latter.

464 **Household atomism and change in the Out Island Bahamas.**
William B. Rodgers. *South-Western Journal of Anthropology*, vol. 23, no. 3 (autumn 1967), p. 244–60.
By examining three communities on Great Abaco Island, Rodgers provides an in-society test of some hypotheses pertaining to household composition change and a case study of the effects of developmental change on household composition.

465 **The Andros Islanders: a study of the family organization in the Bahamas.**
Keith F. Otterbein. Lawrence, Kansas: University of Kansas Press, 1966. 152p. 6 maps. bibliog.
Otterbein undertook his research in 1959 and 1961. He describes the economic and demographic conditions, courtship and mating system, household composition and inter-personal relationships of the residents of Long Bay Cays, Andros. His research is based on the concept of New World Negro family organization and focuses on its three primary features: the close ties between mothers and their children; domestic units dominated by females; and the high frequency of female-headed households.

466 **Courtship and mating system of the Andros Islanders.**
Keith F. Otterbein. *Social and Economic Studies*, vol. 13, no. 2 (June 1964), p. 282–301.
A highly detailed account of the courtship and mating system at Long Bay Cays, Andros. Courtship information includes marriage preparations, mate selection and the engagement while the section on the mating system provides information on extra-residential mating, separation, outside (illegitimate) children, remarriage and consensual (unmarried) habitation.

467 **The household composition of the Andros Islanders.**
Keith F. Otterbein. *Social and Economic Studies*, vol. 12, no. 1 (1963), p. 78–83.
Otterbein analyses the various forms or phases of the southern Andros household during its life cycle and discusses the factors contributing to these changes. His article provides more information on methodology than actual findings.

468 **The study of a small and isolated community in the Bahama Islands.**
T. Wesley Mills. *American Naturalist*, vol. 21, no. 10 (Oct. 1887), p. 875–85.
An early sociological study of the Bahamas conducted on Green Turtle Key (or Cay) a

Social Conditions

settlement of, at that time, about 600 people with equal proportions of blacks and whites. Mills discusses agriculture and fishing, nutrition, housing and hygienic conditions. There is, however, a very patronizing view of humanity and a distinct bias in favour of the whites: 'The best part of the town and the more eligible dwellings are occupied by the Whites, it need hardly be said. . .' and '. . .the Blacks accepting an inferior *status* in society without a murmur'. The article does provide interesting descriptions of late-nineteenth century living conditions in the Bahamas.

Drug Trade

469   **Drug barons take over Bahamas island.**
Polly Whittell.   *Motor Boating and Sailing*, vol. 161 (May 1988),
p. 54–59, 108, 110, 112.

In 1978, Carlos Lehder arrived on Norman's Cay, a small (six miles long by two miles
wide) island thirty-five miles southeast of New Providence. He bought half the island,
including the 3,300 foot long airstrip, the good harbour and the yacht club. This article
outlines how Lehder, a cocaine dealer and one of the leaders of Colombia's Medellín
cartel, removed the island's residents, scared off visiting yachtspeople and established
an armed camp supervising the shipment of drugs into the United States. Lehder was
arrested in 1987 and in 1988 was sentenced to 135 years in prison, in addition to a life
sentence without parole. Whittell reports that Norman's Cay is beginning to return to
normal.

470   **How drugs turned the tide against Bahamas' banks.**
Pete Engardio, Gail DeGeorge.   *Business Week*, no. 3053
(May 23, 1988), p. 142.

The authors claim that the Bahamas has allowed itself to become a virtual free-zone
for drug smugglers, causing new banking business to bypass the country in search of
safer ground.

471   **Caught in a Bahamas drug war.**
Ralph Naranjo.   *Motor Boating and Sailing*, vol. 157, no. 6
(June 1986), p. 46–49, 122–24.

Describes one yachtsman's encounter with a drug drop that went awry off the Exuma
Islands. Naranjo also lists precautions for recreational boaters travelling throughout
the Bahamas.

472 **The cocaine crisis.**
Edited by David Franklyn Allen. New York; London: Plenum, 1987.
253p. bibliog. (International Cocaine Symposium. Bahamas. 1985).
These twenty-one papers are from the First International Cocaine Symposium held
November 21–22, 1985 in the Bahamas and sponsored by the American Embassy there
and the nation's Ministry of Health. The papers which deal in particular with the
Bahamas are: 'Public health approaches to the cocaine problem: lessons from the
Bahamas'; 'The Bahamas and drug abuse'; 'Epidemic freebase cocaine abuse: a case
study from the Bahamas'; 'Drug abuse 1975–1985: clinical perspectives of the
Bahamian experience of illegal substances'; 'Cocaine and the Bahamian woman:
treatment issues'; and 'Treatment approaches to cocaine abuse and dependency in the
Bahamas'.

473 **Paradise lost.**
Sunday Times Magazine, (29 Sept. 1985), p. 24–49.
This issue investigates allegations that the Prime Minister is a corrupt liar, who allowed
the Bahamas to become a drug traffickers haven. Contents include discussions of the
Prime Minister's life style, investigations of drug king-pin, Carlos Lehder, and
comments on those government officials who resigned or were dismissed following a
Commission investigation, published as *Report of the Commission . . .* (q.v.), into drug
trafficking in the Bahamas.

474 **Report from the Bahamas.**
Bonnie Waitzkin. *Motor Boating and Sailing*, vol. 153, no. 1
(Jan. 1984), p. 42–47, 158–59.
Waitzkin outlines the problems created by drug trafficking through the Bahamas from
South America to the United States. As she points out, the Royal Bahamas Defence
Force has been increased to deal with the situation and the Ministry of Tourism has
increased its budget to override the problems. Although she plays down reports of
piracy, Waitzkin does indicate what forms of precaution can and should be taken by
boaters in the area. Along with this article, Waitzkin has included a short piece
entitled, 'Misadventures on the Great Bahama Bank' which describes being caught in
the middle of an impending drug drop.

475 **Report of the commission of inquiry appointed to inquire into the illegal
use of the Bahamas for the transshipment of dangerous drugs for the
United States of America.**
Bahamas. The commission. Nassau: The commission, 1984.
2 vols. in 1.
In 1983, a commission was appointed to investigate the drug trade in and through the
Bahamas. The members of the commission were charged with four responsibilities: to
investigate the involvement of government officials or employees; to determine the
adequacy of existing law enforcement in the Bahamas; to investigate the activities of
law enforcement officials of the United States in the Bahamas; and to determine the
adequacy of existing Bahamian legislation in this area. The report outlines: the nature
and extent of drug smuggling in the Bahamas; corruption of the police, politicians and
the legal system; influence peddling; laundering of funds; the adequacy of law
enforcement; and Bahamian-United States relations. There were also investigations of
several highly-placed government officials. Among the officials investigated were the

Minister of Youth, Sports and Community Affairs and the Minister of Agriculture, Fisheries and Local Government who were among the four officials who resigned following the publication of the commission's report. This document also includes the minority report by one commission member who criticized the Prime Minister's handling and accounting of his own finances. The appendices include lists of witnesses and exhibits and statistics concerning drug seizures in the Bahamas between 1980 and 1984.

476 **U.S. narcotics interdiction programs in the Bahamas.**
United States. Congress. House of Representatives. Committee on Foreign Affairs. Washington, DC: US Government Printing Office, 1984. 211p.

This document provides verbatim reports of three meetings of the Task Force on International Narcotics Control held on September 28, October 19 and November 2, 1983. Over the course of these meetings, the Task Force reviewed the cooperation between US federal agencies and State and local agencies in interdicting narcotics in transit through the Bahamas. It also examined the effectiveness of the programmes and activities of the US Department of State, the US Drug Enforcement Administration and the South Florida Task Force in the quest to interdict this narcotics traffic. The cooperation among these agencies and with State and other local officials was also considered by the Task Force. The second meeting of the Task Force dealt in particular with drug trafficking through the Bahamas while the third meeting examined the role of the National Narcotics Border Interdiction System and the role of the US Coast Guard. This item includes the prepared statements of witnesses.

Health and Bush Medicine

Health

477 **Changing patterns of health and health care on a small Bahamian island.**
Robert A. Halberstein, John E. Davies. *Social Science and Medicine*, vol. 13B, no. 2 (April 1979), p. 153–67.

Examines the biocultural, demographic and ecological variables that have shaped the rapidly changing profile of health and disease on Bimini. The authors have outlined the three major health problems (hypertension, haemoglobinopathis and excessive infant mortality) which had been influenced, for the worse, by economics, mate selection, sanitation, dietary habits and the use of local medicinal plants. The article also shows that the improvement of the drinking water supplies, the increased use of contraceptives and the introduction of 'orthodox' medical care have had a positive impact on the health of the island. There is an extensive bibliography.

478 **Out-Island doctor.**
Evans W. Cottman. New York: Dutton, 1963. 248p. 3 maps.

Cottman, an American high school science teacher with a Master's degree in biochemistry and some knowledge of optometry, visited the Bahamas six times between 1939 and 1944. He moved to Crooked Island in 1945 and eventually received a licence as an Unqualified Medical Practioner. This is his account of practising medicine and living on an Out Island in the 1940s and 1950s.

479 **Memoir on the topography, weather, and diseases of the Bahama Islands.**
Peter S. Townsend. New York: J. Seymour, 1826. 80p.

Records Townsend's observations during a year's residence and medical practice in the Bahamas. The book was published to show a comparison between the diseases of the tropical and northern latitudes and to demonstrate the influence of climate on the human constitution. It is now useful because it provides a fascinating catalogue of diseases and cures of that time.

Bush medicine

480 **Herbal medicine and home remedies: a pot pourri in Bahamian culture.**
Portia Brown Jordan. Nassau: Nassau Guardian, 1986. 172p. bibliog.
This somewhat bizarre but fascinating collection of information includes a list of
ailments and bush medicine remedies, food and drink recipes, proverbs, games and
songs, a list of local herbs and their uses, and a list of fruit trees. Poetry by Jordan's
uncle, Raymond Waldin Brown, the author of *Bahamas in poetry* (q.v.) and *Bahamas
in poetry and poems of other lands* (q.v.) appears, as do a treatise on sexual and
asexual plant propagation by Karra Subba Reddy, an appendix of illustrations and a
glossary.

481 **Love potions of Andros Island, Bahamas.**
Susan A. McClure, W. Hardy Eshbaugh. *Journal of Ethnobiology*,
vol. 3, no. 2 (1983), p. 149–56.
The use of herbal love potions on Andros Island is examined, and the various species
and plant parts used. The methods of preparation and the social and medicinal
functions of the love potions are also reviewed. The information is based on interviews
with seven bush medicine practitioners.

482 **Traditional medical practices and medicinal plant usage in a Bahamian
island.**
Robert A. Halberstein, Ashley B. Saunders. *Culture, Medicine and
Psychiatry*, vol. 2, no. 2 (June 1978), p. 177–203.
The traditional medical system of Bimini is analysed on the basis of a survey of eighty-
three per cent of the residents of the island and of the activities and materials of the
two main native 'professionals' – a healing specialist and a herbalist. Islanders
demonstrate a resourceful utilization of indigenous medicinal plants, several of which
contain chemicals with genuinely curative effects. The article includes a list of twenty-
five medicinal plants commonly used on Bimini with information on physical
characteristics, medicinal uses and chemical components.

483 **Bush medicine in the Exumas and Long Island, Bahamas: a field study.**
Joan Eldridge. *Economic Botany*, vol. 29, no. 4 (Oct./Dec. 1975),
p. 307–32.
This is a study of the folk uses of native and introduced plants for medicinal purposes.
The report provides a description of pertinent background material and personal
observations made during the field work and presents data collected on those plants
that are used by native inhabitants. It includes a list of plants used for medicinal
purposes with information on how they are prepared and what they cure.

484 **Bush medicine in the Bahamas.**
Helen Burns Higgs. Nassau: Nassau Guardian, 1969. 20p.
This booklet discusses some of the major medicinal plants found in the Bahamas.
Higgs explains how they are used and the belief system that surrounds their use. Sixty
medicinal plants are shown in drawings.

485   **Medicinal uses of plants by native Inaguans.**
      William H. Sawyer.   *Scientific Monthly*, vol. 80, no. 6 (June 1955),
      p. 371–76.

Sawyer provides a table of information about thirty plants used by Inaguans for medicinal purposes. For each plant, he gives the common name, the Latin name, details of its preparation and the dosage required. The plants are listed under headings describing their use, such as: coughs and colds, fevers, toothaches, jaundice and rheumatism. There are twenty-one such headings. Sawyer also provides a brief description of Inagua in the text of the article.

Politics and Government

486 **Leadership in the Bahamas.**
Parliamentarian, vol. 68, no. 1 (Jan. 1987), p. 24–25.
Gives a short profile of the Prime Minister, Sir Lynden Oscar Pindling (1930– .) and examines some of the issues which faced him prior to the 1987 general election, which he won.

487 **My political memoirs: a political history of the Bahamas in the 20th century.**
Henry Milton Taylor. Nassau: The Author, 1987. 410p.
Taylor was first elected to the Legislature in 1949 and in 1953 was a co-founder of the Progressive Liberal Party (PLP). This well-written and interesting personal memoir details the whole of his political life and, in some respects, is a memoir of the political life of the Bahamas from the 1940s to the mid 1980s.

488 **Political leadership in the Bahamas: interviews with the Prime Minister of the Commonwealth of the Bahamas and Leader of the Opposition.**
Dean W. Collinwood, Steve Dodge. Decatur, Illinois: Bahamas Research Institute, 1987. 26p. (Occasional Papers Series, no. 1).
This monograph consists of two sections: 'The Bahamas for the short-term', an interview with the Prime Minister, Sir Lynden Pindling; and 'The Bahamian opposition and moral authority', an interview with Kendal Isaacs, the Leader of the Opposition, the Free National Movement (FNM). In these interviews, conducted in late-May 1985, the Prime Minister points out that unexpected turns of events preclude anything but short-term planning for the nation and his own political party, while Isaacs stresses the need for a nation to be governed by those who have not only the formal authority but also the moral authority to govern.

Politics and Government

489 **Declaration of commitment.**
Free National Movement. Nassau: Free National Movement, 1982.
34p.
This booklet outlines the 1982 platform of the Free National Movement and presents the political philosophy of the FNM concerning twenty-one different areas. The most important are economy, education, external affairs, finance, health, national insurance, tourism, works and utilities and youth.

490 **The new Bahamians.**
Michael A. Symonette. Nassau: Bahamas International, 1982. 136p.
Symonette's title refers to those Bahamians who have come of age since independence in 1973. This collection of thirty-two essays, originally written by Symonette between 1975 and 1982 speak to these 'new' Bahamians about their past and their future.

491 **Race and politics in the Bahamas.**
Colin A. Hughes. New York: St. Martin's; St. Lucia, Windward Islands: University of Queensland Press, 1981. 250p. 7 maps.
Hughes shows the transformation of the Bahamas from majority white rule to majority black rule. The focus is on change and the means by which it was brought about. Hughes discusses the rise of party politics (1953–57), white power (1963–66) and black power (1967–77). There is an appendix of the national election results for 1956, 1962, 1967, 1968, 1972 and 1977. Although there is no bibliography, this work is well footnoted.

492 **The struggle for freedom in the Bahamas.**
Vanguard Nationalist and Socialist Party of the Bahamas. Nassau: The Vanguard Party, 1980. 73p.
The Vanguard Party was formed in 1971 and has yet to play a significant role in Bahamian politics. This treatise is an analysis of the political and economic situation in the Bahamas and an attack against the ruling PLP as well as the Opposition, FNM. This work contains a great deal of rhetoric but is still one of the better presentations of the Vanguard Party's philosophy.

493 **The U.S.-Bahamian lobster dispute: international perspectives.**
Ken I. Boodhoo, Ivan C. Harnanan. *Caribbean Studies*, vol. 20, no. 1 (March 1980), p. 57–67.
Examines the significance of the lobster in the international law of the sea, and considers the basis of the claims made by the Bahamian government and claims by the Cuban-Americans, and the US constitutional rights of the latter. The authors provide information about this dispute from 1942 to 1978, when thirty-five US-based boats were intercepted, a fourteen year old Cuban-American was shot, twelve boats were confiscated and twenty-five Cuban-Americans were arrested. The study has some relevance to similar law of the sea problems elsewhere in the Caribbean.

494 **Imperialism and class struggle in the Bahamas.**
Kermit Scott. *Appeal to Reason*, vol. 5, no. 4 (winter 1979/80),
p. 3–17.

Scott argues that while Bahamians are building a stable community and culture with a strong sense of national identity, the country is being exploited by imperialists and outlaws. He calls upon socialists in the United States to lend support to a country whose hope of independence is being thwarted by the exploiters.

495 **Conflicts toward liberation.**
Gladys Manuel. Bridgetown, Barbados: Cedar, 1979. 34p.

Manuel provides a forceful and thought-provoking account of tensions within the PLP from 1953 to 1972 and an analysis of the Nationalist Movement during the same time period. The movement was propelled by the PLP who sought to wrest control from the white minority, although the Vanguard Party views the PLP as similar to the whites in outlook.

496 **The faith that moved the mountain.**
Sir Randol F. Fawkes. Nassau: The Author, 1979. 292p.

Part biography and part political history, this is a study of the transition from colonial dependence to internal self-government, 1930–67. Sir Randol, knighted in 1977, has always been active in politics and the labour movement. He was leader of the Labour Party and sided with the PLP after the 1967 general election, which saw the first black government come to power in the Bahamas.

497 **Who's who in the Bahamas government, 1953–1978.**
Progressive Liberal Party. Silver Jubilee Research Committee.
Nassau: PLP, 1978. 20p.

This booklet is primarily a biographical dictionary of all those politicians who served the Bahamas from 1953 to 1978. There are also lists of cabinet ministers, and a chronology and summary of political events.

498 **Progressivism and independence: a selection from the writings of L.O.**
Pindling, 1969–1978.
Lynden Oscar Pindling. Nassau: Progressive Liberal Party, 1978.
100p.

These are selections from the Prime Minister's speeches. Topics include the rise of the PLP, economic and educational development, international affairs, trade unions, Bahamianization (the training of Bahamians to assume jobs held by foreigners) and immigration.

499 **The Bahamas: a review of post-independence foreign relations.**
Ramesh F. Ramsaran. *Caribbean Yearbook of International*
Relations, (1976), p. 311–23.

Ramsaran discusses the rationale for independence in the Bahamas, the economy and its implications on foreign policy and relations with the United States and the Caribbean region. In order to persuade the country to embrace independence, the PLP equated it with enhanced development. Ramsaran points out that after independence in 1973, the PLP, having inherited a United Bahamian Party (UBP) development strategy and economy, pursued a foreign policy which permitted little scope for the promised development.

500 What is the relevance of Black Power to the Bahamas?
Timothy O. McCartney. In: *Is Massa day dead?: Black moods in the Caribbean*. Edited by Orde Coombs. Garden City, New York: Anchor/Doubleday, 1974, p. 165–86.

McCartney examines the influence of the Black Power movement in the US on the Bahamas. He initially provides a history of protest movements in the Bahamas, of which there were very few. The significant ones were the riot of 1942, which Saunders discusses in more detail in her article, 'The 1942 riot in Nassau: a demand for change?' (q.v.) and the 1958 general strike. McCartney also looks at the economic and social situation of the late 1960s and early 1970s and enumerates the various social and political groups which were formed. The article concludes with some personal views. He states that Bahamians must reject the racial nomenclature of the Black Power movement and emphasize unity in the Bahamas in which leaders must project a sense of pride and objectivity in being Bahamian rather than black Bahamian.

501 The best of Pot Luck.
Edward A. Minnis. Nassau: Nassau Guardian, 1972. 204p.

A collection of 205 editorial cartoons originally published in the *Nassau Guardian* between February 1970 and October 1972. The cartoons by Minnis, who is also a painter, song-writer and singer, reflect the social, political, educational and commercial life of the Bahamas. Although not all the cartoons may be readily understood, they will be of use to those well-versed in Bahamian politics of the early 1970s.

502 Civics for the Bahamas.
Vivian Carrington, Harcourt Turnquest. Port of Spain, Trinidad; Kingston, Jamaica: Longman Caribbean, 1972. 114p.

The authors discuss the rights and duties of citizens and government, and government in general, using the Bahamas to illustrate their points. The book is well illustrated with Bahamian subjects. Although published just before independence, it is not necessarily out of date or inaccurate. It was originally published for school children as an introduction to civics and government in anticipation of independence.

503 The quiet revolution in the Bahamas.
Doris Louise Sands Johnson. Nassau: Family Islands, 1972. 177p. map. bibliog.

The 'quiet revolution' of this important political history refers to the rise of a black Bahamian government and, in particular, the rise of the PLP. It is divided into two sections. The first provides historical background to politics in the Bahamas. It explores the effects of slavery and colonialism on the black population and their resulting exploitation and degradation by the white minority. Section two examines in detail the philosophy, goals and techniques of the PLP leadership. The work concludes by outlining problems faced by the Bahamas' first black government and the solutions proposed and those that were implemented. This book contains a wealth of information on attitudes, values and political manoeuvring and is especially useful for an understanding of the Nassauvian ambience during the late 1960s and early 1970s.

504 **Scandal in the Bahamas.**
Richard Oulahan, William Lambert. *Life*, vol. 62, no. 5 (Feb. 3, 1967), p. 58–74.
This article investigates corruption prior to and during the 1967 general election in the Bahamas. The corruption was said to include insurance fraud, secret bank accounts and laundered money, sales of worthless securities and gambling traps controlled by the Mafia. The authors examine alleged Mafia connections and the development of gambling in Nassau and Freeport. They also discuss in detail the Bay Street Boys and their involvement in this corruption.

505 **Plan for progress and prosperity.**
Progressive Liberal Party. Nassau: PLP, 1962. 24p.
This booklet presents the PLP's platform written nine years after the Party was formed. It was produced just prior to the 1962 general election.

506 **What the UBP has done for you.**
United Bahamian Party. Nassau: UBP, 1960. 31p.
This is a collection of editorials from the *Nassau Guardian* (q.v.) outlining what the UBP has done for the Bahamas in the past and what is planned for the future.

507 **Nassau's bustling Bay Street Boys.**
Spencer Klaw. *Fortune*, vol. 59, no. 1 (Jan. 1959), p. 92–96. 126, 130.
Describes the activities of various of the Bay Street Boys, including: tourism, which rose from 32,000 people per year in 1949 to 175,000 in 1958; real estate (a two-acre lot rose from $3,000 in 1934 to $100,000 in 1959); foreign investment; off-shore companies; and the relationship between the Bay Street Boys and the black community.

508 **Politics in Paradise.**
Alexander T. Jordan. *American Mercury*, vol. 77, no. 6 (Dec. 1953), p. 55–58.
Looks at corruption in the Bahamas in the early 1950s when the Colony was controlled by the Bay Street Boys.

509 **You should know your government.**
Randol F. Fawkes. Nassau: The Author, 1949. 50p. map.
This book was written for the young Bahamian man since Bahamian women did not receive the right to vote until 1962. The body of the work explains democracy and government, and outlines the constitution of the Bahamas and the role of the Governor, the House of Assembly and the judiciary. There are also chapters on administration and the civil service, taxation and citizens' rights, duties and responsibilities. The work is, of course, out-dated now but was very good in its time and is still a useful background book for those exploring politics and government in the Bahamas.

Constitution and Legal System

Constitution

510 **Constitutional development of the Bahamas.**
Bahamas. Public Records Office. Archives Section.   Nassau: Public
Records Office. Archives Section, 1979. 47p.

This booklet accompanied the exhibition of historical documents held at the Senate
Building, Parliament Square, 24 September–26 October 1979. It contains black-and-
white photographs, with captions, for all the exhibits. The exhibit was held to
commemorate the 250th anniversary of Parliament in the Bahamas; the first assembly
met on 29 September, 1729.

511 **The Bahamas independence order 1973.**
London: HMSO, 1973. 84p. (Great Britain. Statutory Instruments,
1973, no. 1080: Caribbean and North Atlantic Territories).

This is the constitution upon which the Bahamas became an independent nation on 10
July, 1973.

512 **Report of the Bahamas Independence Conference, 1972.**
London: HMSO, 1973. 18p. (Great Britain. Parliament. Papers by
Command, 5196).

A report on the conference which set out the constitution of the Bahamas and outlined
the date for independence. This report includes the constitution and speeches by the
Secretary of State for Foreign and Commonwealth Affairs, the Prime Minister of the
Bahamas and the Leader of the Opposition.

513 **Independence for the Commonwealth of the Bahamas.**
Nassau: Cabinet Office, 1972. 32p.

A White Paper on independence which sets out the principles to govern the natural and orderly development of a new country. This document outlines the constitutional and legal factors of independence, external relations and foreign policy and plans for social and economic development.

514 **The Bahamas and independence.**
Parliamentarian, vol. 53, no. 3 (July 1972), p. 209–13.
A summary of the Government's Green Paper on independence which was introduced into the House of Assembly on 8 March, 1972. This Green Paper was followed by the Government's final proposal on independence in the form of a White Paper entitled *Independence for the Commonwealth of the Bahamas* (q.v.).

515 **The Bahama Islands (Constitution) order 1969.**
London: HMSO, 1969. 81p. (Great Britain. Statutory Instruments, 1969, no. 590: Caribbean and North Atlantic Territories).
Known as the 'Fifth Constitution', this document, though substantially the same as that of 1964 (q.v.), not only provided for some minor changes but also gave the Bahamian government more responsibility for internal security and limited responsibility in external affairs. This document took the Bahamas as far as the British government would allow, short of complete independence.

516 **Report of the Bahamas Constitutional Conference, 1968.**
London: HMSO, 1968. 20p. (Great Britain. Parliament. Papers by Command, 3792).
This report on the proposals of the 'Fifth Constitution' of the Bahamas includes comments and remarks by the Secretary of State for Commonwealth Affairs, the Premier of the Bahamas, the Leader of the United Bahamian Party and the Leader of the Labour Party.

517 **The Bahama Islands (Constitution) order in Council, 1963.**
London: HMSO, 1964. 73p. (Great Britain. Statutory Instruments, 1963, no. 2084: Caribbean and North Atlantic Territories).
The 1963 Constitution came into effect on 7 January, 1964 and gave the Bahamas complete internal self-government. The proposals abolished the Executive Council and established a Senate. Ministerial government was introduced and power was vested in a Cabinet formed by the majority party of the House of Assembly. This is sometimes known as the 'Fourth Constitution'.

518 **Report of the Bahamas Constitutional Conference, 1963.**
London: HMSO, 1963. 12p. (Great Britain. Parliament. Papers by Command, 2048).
A report on the proposals of the 'Fourth Constitution' of the Bahamas.

Legal system

519 **The Bahamas consolidated index of statutes and subsidiary legislation to . . .**
Faculty of Law Library. University of the West Indies. Barbados.
Holmes Beach, Florida: Wm. W. Gaunt & Sons, 1985– . annual.
This is one of a series in the West Indian Legislation Indexing Project (WILIP) compiled in cooperation with the British Development Division. The index lists statutes in force since 1 April, 1965.

520 **Elements of Bahamian law.**
Leonard J. Knowles. Nassau: Business & Law Publishers (Bahamas), 1978. 133p.
Sir Leonard Knowles, Chief Justice of the Bahamas, 1973–78, explains Bahamian law by using examples from actual cases. He deals with the constitution, the judiciary, statute law and common law, contracts, torts, persons and property, finance, criminal law and procedures and the law of the sea. This book is a very useful introduction to the law but it is not always easy to read or understand and is best suited to the well-informed layperson. An introductory essay and index would have proved useful.

521 **The statute law of the Bahama Islands, 1799–1987; in force on the 30th June 1987.**
Edited by Sir Gordon Bryce. Exeter, England: A. Wheaton, 1988.
8th ed. 8 vols. supplement.
This edition consists of eight main volumes and a supplementary volume which together set out the statute laws of the Bahamas. Previous editions were published in 1846, 1855, 1868, 1877, 1901, 1929, 1957 and 1965.

522 **The subsidiary legislation of the Bahama Islands, 1799–1965; in force on the 1st August 1965.**
Edited by Sir Ralph Hone. Nassau: Government of the Colony of the Bahama Islands, 1965. rev. ed. 3 vols.
These volumes contain all the subsidiary legislation, Orders, Orders in Council, Regulations and Rules in force on 1 August, 1965. The material has been arranged according to the pattern adopted for the 1965 edition of *The statute law of the Bahama Islands, 1799–1965*.

Economy

523 Bahamas: looking to the future.
Norman Peagam. *Euromoney*, supplement (Dec. 1987), p. 1–29.
This supplement, sponsored by the Central Bank of the Bahamas, contains articles on economy, banking, foreign investment, tourism, industry, insurance, agriculture and fisheries. There are also interviews with the Prime Minister and the Governor of the Central Bank.

524 The Bahamas: economic report.
World Bank. Washington, DC: World Bank, 1986. 117p. map. (A World Bank Country Study).
This report is based on an International Bank for Reconstruction and Development economic mission to the Commonwealth of the Bahamas in May 1985. It reviews the performance of the Bahamian economy during the early 1980s and analyses the development issues and prospects facing the Bahamas at that time. The report predicts positive economic growth with no balance of payment problems. It includes thirty-seven tables of statistical data with information from the mid 1970s to the mid 1980s.

525 A general information guide on the economy of the Bahamas.
Central Bank of the Bahamas. Nassau: Central Bank of the Bahamas, 1986. 60p.
This booklet was originally produced in response to a request from Junior Achievement (Bahamas) to provide information on the economy for secondary school students and the general public. The guide contains seven sections, each pertaining to a different sector of the economy (tourism, banking and finance, manufacturing, agriculture and fisheries, the public sector, the external sector and general economic questions). In each section, the information has been presented in a series of questions and answers. This approach is effective and the information is easy to understand. Although the Central Bank has tried to keep the terminology non-technical, there is a glossary for the few technical terms which it was necessary to use.

526 **Caribbean economic handbook.**
Peter D. Fraser, Paul Hackett. London: Euromonitor Publications,
1985. 241p. 10 maps.
The section on the Bahamas (p. 37–47) offers discussions and data tables on the
economy, agriculture, industry, finance, tourism and trade. There are also data tables
comparing the Bahamas with the rest of the Caribbean and general chapters on the
Caribbean as seen in a world context, along with an overview and future outlook for
the region.

527 **Bahamas.**
Roger De Backer. *Courier: African-Caribbean-Pacific Community*,
no. 88 (Nov./Dec.1984), p. 23–36.
This is primarily an economic survey with discussions of business, industry and
banking. It includes an interview with the Prime Minister, Lynden Pindling, in which
he reviews the country's global economic outlook. The article points out that the
Bahamas has a reputation as a tourist spot, a tax haven and an offshore business
centre, all of which have overshadowed agriculture and fisheries, two industries with
good potential for growth.

528 **The Caribbean basin to the year 2000: demographic, economic, and
resource-use trends in seventeen countries.**
Norman A. Graham, Keith L. Edwards. Boulder, Colorado:
Westview, 1984. 166p. (A Westview Replica Edition).
A comparative analysis of projected long-term trends in seventeen Caribbean
countries, including the Bahamas. More than 100 clearly readable tables and figures
provide information on a wide range of topics, including fertility rates, income
distribution, energy consumption, arable land per capita, receipts from tourism,
foreign trade, oil and mineral resources and military assistance from the US. The
authors discuss the potentially destabilizing roles of rapid population growth, limited
natural resources, weak national economic performances and income disparities and
examine the impact of these factors for each country to the year 2000. The study is
written for an American audience and concludes with a discussion of the ways in which
the trends under discussion affect the policies of the US in the Caribbean.

529 **An economic history of the Bahamas.**
Anthony A. Thompson. Nassau: Commonwealth Publications, 1982.
292p. map. bibliog.
The purpose of this book is quite clearly stated in the preface, in which the author
writes that this work 'is merely a collection of facts concerning commercial and
industrial policies, activities, and developments arranged in a time sequence with
emphasis on the period beginning in the early 1950's. It is not intended to and does not
apply the principles of economics to the Bahamian economy. Nor does it attempt to
analyze the economy in terms of generally accepted economic blueprints for
developing countries'. One does wish for some analysis but the information on
Bahamian economics from 1492 to 1982 is useful. The book also lists Members of
Parliament, senior government officers and officials of government corporations and
government boards for 1982.

530 **The IDB in the Bahamas.**
Inter-American Development Bank. Washington, DC: IDB, 1980.
10p. map.
This report briefly outlines the Bahamas' contributions to the Inter-American Development Bank (IDB) and, in more detail, its activities in the Bahamas in the areas of agriculture, fisheries, tourism, transportation and industry.

531 **Economics applied to the Bahamas.**
H.M.H.A. Van Der Valk. Nassau: Central Bank of the Bahamas, 1979. 163p.
In this book, written primarily for students, Van Der Valk deals with the characteristics, development and problems of the Bahamas and stresses those parts of economics which are of importance to the country. Contents include the public and private sectors, savings and investment, natural resources, the service economy and tourism.

532 **External dependence and national development: a case study of the Bahamas.**
Ramesh F. Ramsaran. In: *Contemporary international relations of the Caribbean*. Edited by Basil A. Ince. St. Augustine,
Trinidad/Tobago: Institute of International Relations, University of the West Indies, 1979, p. 166–217. bibliog.
Ramsaran's purposes in this article are: to examine the nature of the development the Bahamas has achieved in the post-war period; to identify the main instigators of growth, the character of the policies that have been pursued and their general economic and social impact on the country; to draw attention to some of the major difficulties facing the development of the country; and to examine the economic policy of the Bahamas in relation to its external policy. In exploring these issues, he provides background material on the Bahamian economy and the government's approach to development; information on industry and agriculture; an outline of political developments since 1967; and an overview of the Bahamas' relations with other Caribbean countries. Ramsaran comes to three conclusions: more Bahamian involvement and less foreign ownership is needed in the tourist industry; the government must encourage a larger number of locally-owned, small-scale manufacturing enterprises; and the government must rethink its tax haven status.

533 **An expanding economy.**
J. Crocker. *West Indies Chronicle*, no. 1532 (1976), p. 20–23.
Crocker discusses the Bahamian government's encouragement of tourism, prompted by the desire to supplement earnings in the traditional sectors of the economy.

534 **Focus on the Bahamas.**
Compiled Alan Bowden. *New Commonwealth*, vol. 48, no. 2
(Feb. 1969), p. 5–12.
Presents a collection of four short articles: 'Keeping pace with this phenomenal tourist growth spiral' by Lynden Oscar Pindling, then Premier of the Bahamas; 'The diversity of Bahamas' industry' by Arthur D. Hanna, then Deputy Prime Minister; 'The rapid economic growth of the Bahamas' by Carlton E. Francis, then Minister of Finance; and

an unsigned article entitled 'The Bahamas Monetary Authority'. All of the articles deal with the economic progress of the Bahamas in the mid to late 1960s.

535 Review of Bahamian economic conditions and post-war problems.
John Henry Richardson.   Nassau: Nassau Guardian, 1944. 150p.

Directs attention to the main economic problems and emphasizes long-term developments. Richardson reviews population, imports and exports, employment, wages and the cost of living, banking and currency, public revenue and expenditure, occupations and industries, programmes for Out Island development, vocational training, social welfare and social security. He then makes recommendations for the post-Second World War Bahamas in the areas of tourism, agriculture, forestry, fishing and other industries. This is useful background information for late-twentieth century studies.

Finance and Banking

536 **Household income, 1986– .**
Bahamas. Department of Statistics. Nassau: Department of Statistics,
1987– . annual.
These are the results of the first survey undertaken by the Household Survey Section of
the Department of Statistics. The survey provides data on the composition and
characteristics of the labour force and comprehensive, reliable and regular statistics on
social, demographic and economic characteristics of households. The information has
been collected from households in New Providence, Grand Bahama, Abaco, Andros,
Eleuthera, Harbour Island, Spanish Wells and Exuma.

537 **Tax and investment profile: Bahamas.**
Touche Ross International. London: Touche Ross International,
1987. 17p.
This guide, written in general terms, was prepared by the staff of the Touche Ross
International firm in the Bahamas. It includes general information, a discussion of
investment factors and exchange controls, procedures for establishing a business in the
Bahamas and a review of taxation.

538 **Banking in the Bahamas.**
Peat, Marwick, Mitchell. Nassau: Peat, Marwick, Mitchell, 1986.
2nd ed. 91p.
This very thorough booklet is concerned primarily with wholesale (or offshore)
banking activities, though certain matters covered are equally applicable to commercial
banks serving the Bahamian public. It also deals with matters relating to trust company
operations in the Bahamas.

Finance and Banking

539 **The offshore banking sector in the Bahamas.**
Carlene Francis. *Social and Economic Studies*, vol. 34, no. 4 (1985), p. 91–110.
Examines the structure of the banking system and the factors, both external and internal, which accounted for the emergence and development of the Bahamas as a major offshore banking centre. Francis also discusses the role of the Central Bank *vis-à-vis* offshore and domestic banking operations and evaluates the gross economic benefits from offshore banking.

540 **The Bahamas: banking and beyond.**
Norman Peagam. *Euromoney*, supplement (Oct. 1984), p. 1–36.
This special supplement, sponsored by the Central Bank of the Bahamas contains information on: the growth of offshore banking, insurance, the shipping registry, tourism, agriculture and real estate. It also includes two interviews, one with the Prime Minister, Sir Lynden Pindling, and another with William Allen, the Governor of the Central Bank of the Bahamas.

541 **The monetary and financial system of the Bahamas: growth, structure and operation.**
Ramesh F. Ramsaran. Kingston, Jamaica: Institute of Social and Economic Research, University of the West Indies, 1984. 409p. bibliog.
Discusses all aspects of Bahamian financial life. The author provides information on Bahamian economy and society, the commercial banking system and finance companies. He examines government policies and strategies, analyses the insurance industry and reviews the factors which have contributed to the emergence of Nassau as a Euro-currency centre. The status of the Bahamas as a tax haven is also discussed.

542 **Doing business in the Bahamas.**
Price, Waterhouse. New York: Price, Waterhouse, 1981. 41p. (Information Guide).
Discusses the investment climate, exchange controls, banking and local finance, exporting and importing, labour relations and social security, accounting and taxation. The appendices list current import duties and immigration fees. This guide has been updated with a July 1988 supplement.

543 **Private sector investment in the development of the Bahamas: lessons learned from successful programme implementation.**
Weston H. Agor. *Public Administration and Development*, vol. 1, no. 1 (Jan./March 1981), p. 35–46.
Outlines the lessons learned from a successful government programme which encouraged foreign private sector investment in the country. The article outlines the plan, describes the basic approaches and techniques and shows the potential for other developing countries.

544 **The growing respectability of the Bahamas.**
Jenny Ireland. *Banker*, (Dec. 1979), p. 55–61.
Ireland examines the banking situation in the Bahamas in the late 1970s and outlines how the Bahamas has grown and will continue to grow in the banking field.

545 **Aspects of public finance in a tax haven: the case of the Bahamas.**
Ramesh F. Ramsaran. *Social and Economic Studies*, vol. 26, no. 4
(Dec. 1977), p. 514–30.
Ramsaran discusses the fiscal structure of the Bahamas and some of the financial
problems facing the country in the context of its tax haven policy.

546 **The Commonwealth of the Bahamas: profile of an offshore investment
centre.**
Central Bank of the Bahamas and the Banker Research Unit, edited
by Philip Thorn. London: Banker Research Unit, 1976. 134p. map.
This work examines, in detail, the Bahamas as an offshore centre, and covers the
relationship of the offshore financial community to the Euromarkets. Though now out
of date, this book is useful for background research. Much of the information is
updated in Francis' 'The offshore banking sector in the Bahamas' (q.v.).

547 **Household expenditure in the Bahamas, 1973.**
Bahamas. Department of Statistics. Nassau: Department of Statistics,
1975. 98p.
This is the second of a two-part document detailing the results of the first National
Household Sample Survey conducted by the Department of Statistics in late 1973. This
part of the report, which is made up chiefly of data tables, gives information on
household expenditure and savings. Part one of the report is entitled *Labour force and
income distribution, 1973* (q.v.).

548 **The Central Bank of the Bahamas: origin, functions, activities.**
Central Bank of the Bahamas. Nassau: Central Bank of the Bahamas,
1974. 42p.
This is a clear and simple guide to the Central Bank of the Bahamas and banking in the
country in general. Although this is not a current publication, it does provide useful
background material.

Industry, Trade and Labour

General

549 **Bahamian labor migration to Florida in the late nineteenth and early twentieth centuries.**
Howard Johnson. *International Migration Review*, vol. 22, no. 1 (spring 1988), p. 84–103.
In the period 1880–1920, a great many Bahamians migrated to Key West and Miami in order to find work. Johnson examines the economic structure of the Bahamas which, with the decline of major agricultural exports, prompted this outward migration. He discusses the implications for the Bahamas by looking at the effects of this labour migration on the family and Out Island agriculture. He also measures the impact of remittances from the workers abroad on economic development in the country.

550 **The Bahamas: when will the time come?**
McKinley Conway. *Site Selection Handbook*, vol. 31 (June 1986), p. 752–56.
Conway investigates why industries have not moved to the Bahamas, and sizeable investments have not been forthcoming. He concludes that industrial development can only progress if government corruption, especially in the area of drug trafficking, can be cleaned up and if the Bahamas can raise its profile with corporate facility planners in the United States and elsewhere. Conway also provides a brief discussion of the Bahamas Agricultural and Industrial Corporation which has been instituted to oversee economic development.

551 **Bahamian labor migration, 1901–1963.**
Klaus De Albuquerque, Jerome L. McElroy. *New West Indian Guide*, vol. 60, no. 3/4 (1986), p. 167–202.
From the turn of the twentieth century up to 1963, many Bahamians left the country for periods of nine months to two years to find employment elsewhere in the

Caribbean and in the United States. As well as working in Florida as farm labourers (1908–24 and 1943–66), Bahamians also migrated to Panama (1895–1908) to help build the canal; to Costa Rica, Honduras and Guatemala (1904–06) to work fruit plantations; to the Dominican Republic (1900–12) to cut cane; to Tampico, Mexico (1909–10) to work on the docks; and to Charleston, South Carolina (1918–19) to engage in construction work on naval installations. The authors examine this temporary and recurrent migration, and discuss the fragility of the Bahamian resource base, the circumstances under which labour migration took place and the influences of colonial policy and regional labour demand on this movement of Bahamians. In one of the first studies of this sort, they investigate the number of migrants and their reasons for leaving, their conditions of service and the impact of labour migration on the Bahamas. The article contains good notes and an extensive bibliography.

552 **Bahamas business guide: a guide to doing business in the Bahamas and the government's economic and financial policies.**
Nassau: Commonwealth Publications, 1980– . annual.
Provides general background data for local and foreign businesspeople including information on the investment climate, immigration and residency, exchange control, business regulations and licensing, real estate, banking and finance, tourism, insurance and the Bahamas Development Bank. There are a number of useful appendices and examples of various application forms needed to do business in the country. There are also lists of accounting firms, law firms, and banks and trust companies. In some ways this is a more useful publication for the businessperson than the *Bahamas handbook and businessman's annual* (q.v.).

553 **Labour force and income distribution, 1973.**
Bahamas. Department of Statistics. Nassau: Department of Statistics, 1974. 210p.
This is the first of a two-part report detailing the results of the first National Household Sample Survey conducted by the Department of Statistics in late 1973. It gives information on employment and unemployment in the Bahamas. There are seventy-seven tables of data and fifteen graphs. The work also includes the survey enumerator's handbook, the administrative planning guide, the supervisor's manual and the enumerator's training manual. Part two of the report is entitled *Household expenditure in the Bahamas, 1973* (q.v.).

554 **Industrialization of the Bahamas.**
John H. Bounds. *Revista Geográfica*, no. 77 (Dec. 1972), p. 95–113.
Bounds discusses the growth of industry and economic development in the Bahamas primarily from the end of the Second World War.

555 **Annual shipping statistics report.**
Bahamas. Department of Statistics. Nassau: Department of Statistics, 1969– . annual.
Provides statistics on maritime traffic between the Bahamas and foreign countries. The data tables present information on net tonnage and the number of vessels, crew members and passengers into and out of the Bahamas.

556 **External trade statistics report.**
Bahamas. Department of Statistics. Nassau: Department of Statistics, 1969– . annual.

This work contains statistics for the quantity and value of imports and exports to and from the Bahamas. Each edition provides values of total trade, trade balances, values of imports and exports of selected commodities and countries of origin and consignment, and is comprised chiefly of tables.

557 **Report of the commission appointed to enquire into disturbances in the Bahamas which took place in June 1942.**
Bahamas. The commission . Nassau: Nassau Guardian, 1942. 59p.

In 1942, the British Government and the Government of the United States came to an agreement to build two airfields on the island of New Providence. Bahamian labourers were to be paid four shillings a day while American workers received far more. Hundreds of Bahamian labourers objected to this and on June 1, twelve days after work began, they converged on Bay Street and demanded more money. Satisfaction was not forthcoming and a riot ensued in which two Bahamians were killed, six wounded, eighty arrested and sixty-seven convicted. This fascinating report details the background and the disturbance itself. The commissioners include their findings and recommendations concerning the behaviour of the police, wages and employment, labour legislation, taxation and Bahamian voting practices.

Specific industries

558 **Casinos and banking: organized crime in the Bahamas.**
Alan A. Block, Frank R. Scarpitti. *Deviant Behavior*, vol. 7, no. 4 (1986), p. 301–12.

Examines the complex relationships among gambling casinos, offshore banks and professional criminals. The authors trace the process of bringing casinos and banks together to serve underworld interests and show how US organized crime used them to penetrate the Bahamas. The article also outlines the development of Freeport.

559 **Bahamian sailing craft: notes, sketches, and observations on a vanishing breed of workboats.**
William R. Johnson. Fort Lauderdale, Florida: Benjamin, 1983. 4th ed. 49p. map.

A fascinating description and history of Bahamian sailing craft. The author discusses the smack boat or bowsprit sloop which is the most common Bahamian boat, the dinghy, the gaff-rigged smack boat, the bare-head smack boat and the sponge schooner. There is also a section on boatbuilding. The work is well illustrated with pen-and-ink drawings.

560 **The boat-building industry of the Bahamas.**
Bahamas. Department of Archives. Nassau: Department of Archives, 1981. 46p.
Boat-building has always been an industry in the Bahamas, though it flourished between 1836 and 1860 to satisfy local demand for wrecking and for cargo vessels to service the salt industry. This period was followed by a decline between 1860 and 1890 which was then followed by an economic boom, requiring more boats to transport tomatoes, sponges and pineapples abroad. A second decline between 1930 and 1950 was followed by a revival of the boat-building industry to meet the demand for pleasure boats. This booklet contains black-and-white photographs of documents exhibited in the Post Office Building, 9–28 February 1981, which traced the development of the industry.

561 **The salt industry of the Bahamas.**
Bahamas. Public Records Office. Nassau: Public Records Office, 1980. 36p.
The salt industry has been a viable part of the economy of the Bahamas since the seventeenth century, as this small book testifies. Although a decline was experienced in the industry between 1870 and 1910, by the mid-twentieth century the production of salt was once again a major industry in the Bahamas. The exhibits photographed for this book were displayed at the Senate Building, 11 February–1 March, 1980.

562 **Some aspects of shipbuilding in the Bahamas.**
Paul Albury. *Journal of the Bahamas Historical Society*, vol. 1 (Oct. 1979), p. 9–11.
By describing the building of the *Beatrice* (1907–08), which was specifically built for the lumber trade, Albury provides a view of the Bahamian shipbuilding industry. Boat building was a viable industry from 1648 to 1938, when the sponge industry collapsed, thereby reducing the need for ships. The average Bahamian boat lasted for twenty years so that, in effect, each generation rebuilt the Bahamian fleet.

563 **The pineapple industry of the Bahamas.**
Bahamas. Public Records Office. Nassau: Public Records Office, 1977. 36p.
This booklet accompanied an exhibition held at the Art Gallery, Jumbey Village, 14–27 February 1977. It contains black-and-white photographs, with captions, of all of the exhibits, relating to the pineapple industry. It is not known for certain when the fruit was introduced into the Bahamas but mention is made in print as early as 1722. The pineapple industry reached its peak in 1892 and collapsed as a result of competition from Hawaii in the 1920s.

564 **The sponging industry.**
Bahamas. Public Records Office. Nassau: Public Records Office, 1974. 32p.
An exhibition of historical documents was held at the Public Records Office, 18–22 February 1974. This booklet contains black-and-white photographs of all of the exhibits with captions for each. The sponging industry in the Bahamas, which began

around 1843, reached its peak in 1917 but almost disappeared in 1938 as a result of disease. The industry has never quite regained its former stature.

565   **Bahama Islands: report of the commission of inquiry into the operation of the business of casinos in Freeport and in Nassau.**
       Bahamas. The commission. London: HMSO, 1967. 140p.

This commission was formed in 1967 to investigate persons employed in the casino business, legislation regarding casinos and gambling, involvement by members of the government, the accounting practices of the casino companies and any unrecorded payments by them. The report is fascinating and provides a wealth of information on the business of casinos and gambling in the Bahamas and elsewhere. Its various chapters give an introduction to gambling, explain the Bahamian Certificates of Exemption given to companies wishing to establish casinos and describe how casinos operate. The commission subsequently recommended the introduction of the Gaming Act, the establishment of a gambling commission, changes in accounting procedures and changes to the government revenue received from the casinos. These recommendations are included in the report. Leo Rost's *The conch eaters* (q.v.) was based in part on information contained in this item.

566   **Mafia shadow of evil on an island in the sun.**
       Bill Davidson. *Saturday Evening Post*, vol. 240 (25 Feb. 1967), p. 27–37.

Chronicles the introduction of casinos and gambling into the Bahamas and discusses the roles played by Sir Stafford Sands, a cabinet minister in the United Bahamian Party; Wallace Groves, the developer of Freeport; and Meyer Lansky, long associated with the Mafia.

567   **The wrecking system of the Bahama Islands.**
       James Martin Wright. *Political Science Quarterly*, vol. 30 (1915), p. 618–44.

Throughout the nineteenth century wrecking or salving (salvaging) became a very important industry in the Bahamas. By 1870, wrecking accounted for fifty-four per cent of the value of imports in the country. This article describes the wrecking system, which grew out of privateering, in great detail. Wright also enumerates six factors which led to the decline of wrecking: the reduction in the number of wrecks by blockades, during the American Civil War; government-encouraged agricultural projects; the rise of the sponging industry; improvements in the mechanical means of transportation; greater safety precautions in the shipping industry; and better charts and placement of lighthouses.

Agriculture

568   Food in the Bahamas.
Bahamas. Ministry of Agriculture, Fisheries and Local Government.
Nassau: Ministry of Agriculture, Fisheries and Local Government,
1981. 79p.
This collection of articles was published in observance of World Food Day, 16 October
1981. Topics include cooperatives, animal and crop husbandry and agricultural
education. The emphasis is on future development in the Bahamas in the 1980s.

569   Report of the 1978 census of agriculture: final report.
Bahamas. Department of Statistics.   Nassau: Ministry of Agriculture,
Fisheries and Local Government, 1978. 91p.
This was the first census of its kind in the Bahamas. The report provides a wealth of
agricultural information, both in its text and in thirty-five tables.

570   Agriculture and fisheries: the need to produce more food.
Bahamas. Information Services. Public Affairs Department.   Nassau:
Public Affairs Department, 1974. 62p. map. bibliog. (Sector Working
Paper).
One of a series of booklets which began as National Discussion broadcasts, this
discusses government philosophy, present conditions and future needs and developments,
and gives background information in agriculture and fisheries. It was produced for
Bahamian businesspeople, government officials, teachers and students and those in
farming and fishing.

571   Report on agricultural development in the Bahamas.
A.J. Wakefield.   Nassau: Nassau Guardian, 1942. 55p.
Presents short- and long-term recommendations for agriculture in the Bahamas.
Although now out of date, this work may be useful for background information,
especially when used in conjunction with Richardson's *Review of Bahamian economic
conditions and post-war problems* (q.v.).

Postal System

572 Bahamas early mail services and postal markings.
Morris Hoadley Ludington.   Burnt Mills Hills, Maryland: The Author,
1982. 210p. 12 maps.

Part one of this two-part work is a history of the Bahamian postal service up to the mid
1880s and is of general interest. Part two is of interest only to the real specialist. It
provides detailed information on postal markings (cancellation stamps) which should
not be confused with postage stamps. Part two is a thorough revision of *The Bahama
Islands* by Ludington and Raymond (London: Robson Lowe, 1968).

573 The postage stamps and postal history of the Bahamas.
Harold G.D. Gisburn.   London: Stanley Gibbons, 1950. 144p. map.

Presents a very detailed and informative history of the postal system and especially of
postage stamps in the Bahamas. It informs the reader, for example, that the first
Bahamian stamp, with a portrait of Queen Victoria, was issued in 1859, while the first
stamp with a Bahamian scene was issued in 1901. This work is primarily designed for
the philatelist but is also useful to interested laypeople.

Environment

574 Land resources of the Bahamas: a summary.
B.G. Little. Surbiton, England: Land Resources Division, Ministry of
Overseas Development, 1977. 133p. 4 maps. bibliog. (Land Resources
Study, 27).

This discussion of natural resources – climate, biogeography and vegetation, forests,
groundwater, rocks and landforms, soils, limestones and shorelines – also considers the
relationship of the people and the land – population and communication, land use,
land capability and economic activities. The study includes recommendations for
government support, agriculture and forestry, roads and public works and tourism.

575 The pine forests of the Bahamas.
P.W.T. Henry. Surbiton, England: Foreign and Commonwealth
Office, Overseas Development Administration, Land Resources
Division, 1974. 178p. 18 maps. bibliog. (Land Resources Study, 16).

This report describes the environment and the pine forests on Abaco, Grand Bahama,
Andros and New Providence and looks at the historical exploitation of the forests,
particularly in relation to their past volume and financial yields. Henry investigates the
problems of widespread forest mortality in southern Abaco and the effects of past fires
and current licence agreements. He also discusses natural regeneration studies carried
out on Abaco and provides recommendations on forest policy, legislation, reservation
and management, research, staffing and finance.

576 The development plan of New Providence Island and the city of Nassau.
Columbia University. Institute of Urban Environment. Nassau:
Government of the Bahama Islands, 1968. 348p. 15 maps. bibliog.

This project began as a collaboration between the Columbia University School of
Architecture and the United Nations. The Bahamas government became interested
and invited the School to conduct its project on New Providence Island. The resulting
document is divided into four sections: 'Background information', providing an

introduction to the study and historical/regional information; 'Existing conditions and trends', which outlines the social, economic and physical situation; 'Proposed policies and plans', both general and specific for Nassau and the whole island; and 'implementation and control', which indicates how the proposals should be put into effect.

577   **Pine forests of the Bahamas.**
E.W. March.   *Empire Forestry Review*, vol. 28, no. 1 (March 1949), p. 33–37.

An investigation of the 500,000 acres of pine forests on Grand Bahama, Andros and Abaco, in which March provides ecological and botanical descriptions and discusses the timber industry from 1940 to 1945.

Statistics

578 A collection of statistics on women in the Bahamas, 1979–1985.
Bahamas. Department of Statistics.   Nassau: Department of Statistics,
1987. 109p.

A previous volume appeared in 1982, of the same title, except covering 1970–82, also
produced by the Department of Statistics (184p.). This volume contains updated and
expanded information and consists of sixty-four data tables only; there is neither
interpretation nor any commentary. Statistics are given for population, fertility, health
and public safety, labour force and income and education.

579 Social statistics report, 1985.
Bahamas. Department of Statistics.   Nassau: Department of Statistics,
1987. 67p.

This collection of statistics is divided into five sections focusing on population, health
and nutrition, education, public order and safety and social welfare. The report
includes forty-three tables and nine graphs. Many of the statistics go as far back as
1901, providing good comparison tables of figures for the twentieth century.

580 The Bahamas in figures.
Bahamas. Department of Statistics.   Nassau: Department of Statistics,
1980– . annual.

This small booklet is intended for quick reference and is a consolidation of major social
and economic indicators. Each annual provides information for a six-year period.

581 Statistical abstract.
Bahamas. Department of Statistics.   Nassau: Department of Statistics,
1969– . annual.

The purpose of the *Statistical abstract* is to gather together statistical information on the
Bahamas in one volume, for easy reference. Contents include climate, vital statistics,
population and migration, tourism, external trade, building and construction, public

utilities, transportation, communications, health, crime, education, agriculture, forestry, fisheries, banking, finance, insurance, politics, labour, retail prices and income. A related publication from the Department of Statistics (1971– .), entitled *Quarterly statistical summary*, provides similar information.

582 **Vital statistics report.**
 Bahamas. Department of Statistics.   Nassau: Department of Statistics, 1967– . annual.
Prepared from the records of the Registrar General's Department, this report provides data on births, deaths, marriages and divorces. It also contains an historical summary for five years as well as an analysis of demographic and vital statistics trends for the current year.

Education

583 **The Methodist contribution to education in the Bahamas circa 1790–1975.**
Colbert V. Williams.   Gloucester, England: A. Sutton, 1982. 256p. map. bibliog.

The Methodist contribution to education in the Bahamas began around 1790 with the establishment of the first independent school for Negroes in the Colony. Williams observes that the Methodist contribution has continued unbroken from that time and has been effective and successful, and that the Methodist presence was socially necessary for the integration of blacks and whites, both being taught together in Methodist schools. Furthermore, he urges that government education must continue to be supplemented by independent bodies but that the Methodist Church should make contingency plans to withdraw from formal education and emphasize informal education, should this become politically necessary. This book, originally Williams' PhD thesis, is well researched and well documented.

584 **Educational change in the islands: an assessment of Bahamian trends.**
Robert E. Hendricks, Paul R. Redlhammer.   *Journal of Negro Education*, vol. 49, no. 1 (winter 1980), p. 85–90.

Examines the Bahamian government's attempts since 1973 to reorient Bahamian education away from the élitist notions fostered by colonization and toward an educational system stressing socially useful skills. Up to the time of writing, however, little had been accomplished in the classroom.

585 **Educational development in an archipelagic nation: report of a review team invited by the Government of the Commonwealth of the Bahamas.**
James A. Maraj.   Nassau: Ministry of Education and Culture, 1974. 172p.

This document, commonly called the Maraj Report, outlines the findings and recommendations of an Educational Mission to the Bahamas in 1974 funded by the

Commonwealth Secretariat through the Commonwealth Fund for Technical Co-operation. The team members were charged with reviewing progress on the implementation of the White Paper on Education, *Focus on the future* . . . (q.v.), and recommending plans for its full implementation. They were also responsible for reviewing the organization of the Ministry of Education and Culture and recommending plans for any necessary changes. They finally recommended a programme of external assistance to supplement local manpower and financial resources to meet educational needs. The review team made 121 recommendations which continue to affect educational development in the Bahamas.

586 **Focus on the future: white paper on education.**
Bahamas. Ministry of Education. Nassau: Ministry of Education, 1972. 57p.
This White Paper outlines the Bahamian Government's basic policies for the development of education. It is a useful background paper providing discussion of pre-school, primary and secondary education; independent schools; and the College of the Bahamas.

587 **Report on education in the Bahamas.**
Harold Houghton. London: Colonial Office, 1958. 36p.
This document, commonly referred to as the Houghton Report, is one of two major reports on education in the Bahamas. The other is the Maraj Report (q.v.). Houghton was asked to enquire into and report upon the organization of education in the Bahamas and to offer suggestions for improvements. He found that there was little enthusiasm or demand for education, that the poorer citizens felt resentful and frustrated as regards education and that educational principles were being obscured by personal considerations within the administration. This very critical report offers thirty-three recommendations, most of which were implemented in the 1960s.

Languages and Dialects

General

588 Black English as a Creole: some Bahamian evidence.
Alison Watt Shilling.   Kingston, Jamaica: School of Education,
University of the West Indies for the Society for Caribbean Linguistics,
1984. 16p. map. bibliog. (Society for Caribbean Linguistics. Occasional
Paper, no. 18).
This monograph shows how Bahamian speech can be classed as a creole and is a link
between the Black English of the United States mainland and other various Caribbean
creoles.

589 On the relationship of Gullah and Bahamian.
John A. Holm.   *American Speech*, vol. 58, no. 4 (winter 1983),
p. 303–18.
Holm provides historical and linguistic evidence to support the conclusion that
Bahamian English and Gullah, a South Carolina Sea Islands creole, are closely related,
sharing an immediate ancestor in the eighteenth century creole spoken in the
American South.

590 African features in white Bahamian English.
John A. Holm.   *English World-Wide*, vol. 1, no. 1 (1980), p. 45–65.
Holm presents data indicating that the informal speech of white Bahamians contains
features, ultimately African in origin, reflecting their long contact with speakers of a
creolized variety of English.

591 Smoky Joe says: a volume in Bahamian dialect.
Eugene A.P. Dupuch.   Nassau: Nassau Daily Tribune, 1936. 130p.
Eugene Dupuch began writing his column, 'Smoky Joe says', in the *Nassau Daily*

Tribune (q.v.) in 1934. This volume is a collection of forty articles from the first year; they are topical in nature and each is preceded by a preface introducing the subject. As the subtitle indicates, each article is written in dialect, providing a clue to the rhythms and lilt of Bahamian speech as well as offering a comment on the colony's society of the 1930s. In his preface, Dupuch indicates that there will be annual volumes but none appear to have been produced. A glossary is appended listing colloquial expressions, names with which non-Bahamians may be unfamiliar and words whose pronunciations are confusingly distorted. This is a fascinating book and extremely funny when read with the proper Bahamian accent.

Dictionaries

592 **Dictionary of Bahamian English.**
John A. Holm, Alison Watt Shilling.   Cold Spring, New York: Lexik House, 1982. 228p. 5 maps. bibliog.

Over the centuries, Bahamian English has been influenced by Europe and its colonies and West Africa as well as by Caribbean creole dialects and the Black English of the United States. This work is the first comprehensive study of the words Bahamians use when speaking informally. The introduction traces the development of Bahamian English in its social and historical context. There are over 5,500 entries for words and expressions used in the Bahamas which are not generally found in the current standard English of the UK and the US. Each entry gives a definition and indicates where in the Bahamas it may be found. Entries are based on research among speakers rather than on strictly literary sources. This is a standard reference work and an important contribution to creole culture studies.

Literature

Anthologies

593 Climbing clouds: stories and poems from the Bahamas.
Edited by Telcine Turner.   London: Macmillan Caribbean, 1989. 96p.
This companion publication to *Once below a time* . . . (q.v.) is suitable for ten to fourteen year olds.

594 Once below a time: Bahamian stories.
Edited by Telcine Turner.   London: Macmillan Caribbean, 1989. 80p.
An illustrated collection of sixteen short stories, the interest and language levels of which are suitable for seven to ten year olds. Thirteen of the stories were written by students of the College of the Bahamas and are of Bahamian lore and myths. The remaining three are old Bahamian stories retold by the editor. As well as selecting the stories, Turner has provided notes and questions for the classroom teacher.

595 Bahamian anthology.
College of the Bahamas, introduced by Marcella Taylor.   London: Macmillan Caribbean, 1983. 172p.
This collection of Bahamian creative writing compiled by a committee of lecturers from the College of the Bahamas, includes twelve prose pieces, forty-six poems and three plays by thirty Bahamian authors. It is the first published work to present a collection of writings from the Bahamas. Although none of the pieces is dated, they are all from the 1970s. The critical introduction provided by Taylor, college professor and Bahamian writer, is useful.

596 A book of Bahamian verse.
Compiled by Jack Culmer.   London: The Author, 1948. 2nd ed. 41p.
For the most part, the twenty poems collected in this volume are odes to Nassau written in the late-nineteenth and early-twentieth centuries. The authors, few of whom

are Bahamian, are the Canadian nature poet Bliss Carman (1861–1929); Henry Christopher Christie; Pennington Haile (ca. 1903–82); Richard Kent; the British poet and essayist Richard Le Gallienne (1866–1947); Julia Warner Michael; Margaret Joyce Scott; and Iris Tree (1897–1968). No biographical information is given about any of these authors. The collection was first published in 1930.

Individual writers

597 Bahama fever.
Lolita Armbrister.   Los Angeles: Holloway House, 1982. 197p.
This semi-autobiographical novel was written by a former 'Miss Bahamas'.

598 Bahamas in poetry.
Raymond Waldin Brown.   Nassau: The Author, [n.d.]. [n.p.]. map.
A truly 'home-grown' collection of poems which, while not great literature, show the pride one Bahamian takes in his country.

599 Bahamas in poetry and poems of other lands.
Raymond Waldin Brown.   Nassau: The Author, [n.d.]. 167p.
The 138 poems in this collection are similar in style to Brown's earlier work, *Bahamas in poetry* (q.v.).

600 Expressing myself.
James Julius Catalyn.   Nassau: Nassau Guardian, 1979. 51p.
A collection of forty-five poems by the Bahamian playwright, actor, producer, director and comic.

601 Laughin' at wesef: skits.
James Julius Catalyn.   Nassau: Nassau Guardian, 1986. 118p.
This collection of twenty-five 'skits' written for two, three and four characters catches the essence of Bahamian life and dialogue. The 'skits' were written and first performed between 1974 and 1983, and are extremely popular.

602 Blackbeard or the pirates of the isles, a romance of the Bahamas.
Henry Christopher Christie.   London: Press Printers, 1925. 159p.
This heroic style poem, originally titled *The pirate of the west*, romanticizes the pirate Blackbeard (Edward Teach) and the legends of the Lucayan Indians. It was first published serially in the now defunct Nassau newspaper, *The Watchman* (1901–06).

603 Island breezes: a collection of poems and short stories.
Stanley Sidney Collie.   Nassau: Stratford, 1985. 41p.
These seventeen poems and four stories were written and published by Collie for Bahamian youth, to encourage them to take pride in their culture.

604 **Tomorrow is today's dream.**
Basil Cooper.   Nassau: Bahama Life, 1971. 144p.
This novel chronicles two mixed marriages (black men married to white women) and
the sexual exploits of some black male islanders preying on white female tourists.

605 **The road: poems.**
Robert Elliot Johnson.   Nassau: The Author, 1972. 48p.
These thirty-seven poems present a vivid and candid picture of the Bahamas. The
collection is well known in the Bahamas and is used as a school textbook.

606 **Seapath and other stories.**
William R. Johnson.   Nassau: The Author, 1980. 53p.
Comprises seven stories, dealing with fishermen and the sea, which originally appeared
in *Skipper Magazine* between 1963 and 1967.

607 **Two Bahamian novels.**
Denny Johnston.   Marsh Harbour, Bahamas: Little Harbour, 1982.
175p. 153p.
Neither of these two novels has been published separately. *The Abaco conspiracy* is an
adventure story of plotting and revenge; *Fugitive in the Bahamas* tells the tale of an
English accountant, who mysteriously leaves home and flees to the Bahamas, followed
by detectives from Scotland Yard.

608 **Bahamian jottings: poems and prose: with photographs and**
    reminiscences of old Nassau.
Wilhelmina Kemp Johnstone.   Nassau: Brice, 1973. 192p.
Presents a collection of ninety-nine poems, twelve prose pieces and sixty poorly
reproduced photographs. Poems by Johnstone (1900– .) are pleasant enough; her
pieces in prose, mostly stories of her youth, are fascinating.

609 **Refracted thought.**
Dennis J. Knowles.   Boynton Beach, Florida: Star, 1976. 125p.
This is a collection of fifty-three poems.

610 **Poems with a point.**
C.H. Lightbourn.   Nassau: The Author, [n.d.]. 45p.
These fifty-one poems by Lightbourn, a white Bahamian, reflect his personal
philosophy of life.

611 **At summer's end: south poems.**
Percival A. Miller.   Ardmore, Pennsylvania: Dorrance, 1980. 66p.
These forty-six poems were designed to be read aloud.

612 **Island boy.**
Eric Minns.   Nassau: Lauric; Pickering, Ontario: Lauric, 1981. 214p. map.

John, a Bahamian living in Toronto, finds that he must return to the islands and, although torn between Canada and the Bahamas, realizes he must stay in his homeland to be happy. Minns scatters Bahamian facts, history, scenes and songs throughout the novel ⊣ though not always successfully.

613 **Naked moon.**
Rupert Missick.   New York: Graham, 1970. 30p.

Offers a collection of twenty-seven simple and somewhat unfocused poems.

614 **The magic tree house.**
Francis Peter Noronha.   New York: Vantage, 1986. 42p.

This is the story of two children growing up in the village of Fox Hill on the island of New Providence. On Discovery Day holiday, the second Monday in October, they take a fantasy trip to a number of exotic places, both real and imaginary.

615 **Sonnets of the Bahamas, with notes.**
George J.H. Northcroft.   Nassau: Nassau Guardian, 1899. 51p.

Twenty sonnets written 'to present in a poetical form the more prominent features of Bahamian history, to describe the chief characteristics of the larger islands and to display some sketches of our colonial life' (Preface).

616 **Poetry for all occasions, Bahamian style.**
Wilfred Hannah Pinder.   Nassau: The Author, [n.d.]. 75p.

A collection of seventy-six poems of love and friendship, patriotism and inspiration.

617 **Thoughts in black and white: a collection of poetry.**
Patrick Rahming.   Nassau: The Author, 1986. 85p.

This collection of fifty-five poems has self-exploration as its theme.

618 **Bahamas: in a white coming on.**
Dennis Ryan.   Ardmore, Pennsylvania: Dorrance, 1981. 48p.

A majority of the forty poems collected in this volume offer descriptions of the Bahamas and of the sea. Some of these poems first appeared in *Poem* (Huntsville, Alabama: Huntsville Literary Association, Nov. 1967– . three times yearly), *The Alfred Review* (Alfred, New York: Alfred University, annual) and *The Poet* (Mishawaka, Indiana: Fine Arts Society).

619 **The night of the lionhead.**
Ashley Saunders.   Ardmore, Pennsylvania: Dorrance, 1979. 67p.

These seventeen poems and ten pieces of prose are all written in Bahamian dialect. Unfortunately, Bahamian dialect is a spoken language and often loses its impact in print. Saunders is not as successful at writing in dialect as Susan Wallace and James Catalyn, whose works feature elsewhere in this bibliography. Opposite each page,

Saunders has provided a 'translation' in standard English, which ıs not totally necessary.

620   Searching for Atlantis.
Ashley Saunders.   Ardmore, Pennsylvania: Dorrance, 1980. 26p.

The majority of these twenty-four poems explore the possibility that the island of Bimini is the site of the lost continent of Atlantis. Saunders was born on Bimini.

621   The sun makes it red.
Ashley Saunders.   Philadelphia: Dorrance, 1977. 35p.

Presents thirty-three somewhat trite poems, simple in style and reflecting the themes of life and love.

622   Voyage into the sunset.
Ashley Saunders.   Philadelphia: Dorrance, 1976. 28p.

Twenty-eight love poems, rather sentimental in tone.

623   Them: a play in one act.
Winston V. Saunders.   Nassau: The Author, 1982. 45p.

This celebrated Bahamian play deals with the intense neurosis suffered by many blacks who, under white minority government rule, 'passed' as whites. With the coming of black majority rule, they are forced to decide whether they will continue to 'pass' or to identify with the other blacks.

624   Reflections of the sun and soil.
Noella Smith.   Ardmore, Pennsylvania: Dorrance, 1979. 52p.

A collection of forty-five poems, many of which deal with nature and family life. The author hopes that 'these poems will appeal to primary level students'.

625   Acts: a poem.
Obediah Michael Smith.   Nassau: The Author, 1983. 56p.

An interminable fifty-six-page poem.

626   Bicentennial blues.
Obediah Michael Smith.   Nassau: The Author, 1978. 2nd ed. 48p.

These twenty-nine rather pessimistic poems were first published in 1977.

627   43 poems.
Obediah Michael Smith.   Nassau: The Author, 1979. 56p.

The poems are divided into three sections: 'Sunshine' presents seventeen poems, some with Bahamian settings; the thirteen poems in 'April twelfth' focus on non-fictional writers and painters; the remaining poems in 'Exposed flesh' are general in nature.

628 **Fruits from Africa.**
Obediah Michael Smith.   Nassau: The Author and the Nassau
Guardian, 1988. [n.p.].
A collection of poems reflecting the essential elements of daily Bahamian life.

629 **Ice cubes.**
Obediah Michael Smith.   Nassau: The Author, 1982. 31p.
Each of the forty-four poems is essentially a short thought. 'Crisp', for example, asserts
that '. . .Each poem I write / Is a fortune / Cooky'.

630 **The upturned turtles: a Bahamian story.**
Lilla Sarling.   Sunbury-on-Thames, England: Nelson Caribbean, 1979.
63p. (Tamarind Books).
A story of the Bahamas which is suitable for children.

631 **Song of the surreys.**
Telcine Turner.   London: Macmillan Caribbean, 1977. 59p.
These twenty-nine poems and three riddles have been written to appeal to primary and
junior school children. The poems are based on material learned in science, religious
knowledge, social studies and art, and aim to help children to perceive the relationship
between different aspects of knowledge. They have Bahamian themes to which
children can relate and the life and warmth of the Caribbean comes through strongly.
There are also notes for the teacher, including hints on the teaching of poetry.

632 **Woman take two.**
Telcine Turner.   New York: Vantage, 1987. 93p.
The theme of this three-act play is the disgust, felt by many Bahamians, with the
widespread nature of sexual profligacy. Turner also deals with extra-marital affairs and
incest.

633 **Back home: an original anthology.**
Susan J. Wallace.   London: Collins, 1975. 96p.
This anthology contains three stories, three plays and seven poems, all by Wallace, the
Bahamian author. All of the pieces are written for junior secondary level students and
the anthology can be used as a school text. The author has provided questions and
activities after each piece to facilitate its use in the curriculum.

634 **Bahamian scene.**
Susan J. Wallace.   Philadelphia: Dorrance, 1970. 64p.
Wallace records Bahamian peculiarities and the uniqueness of Bahamian life. Eighteen
of the thirty poems are written in dialect, a device Wallace uses very well.

635 **Island echoes.**
Susan J. Wallace.   London: Macmillan, 1973. 77p.
These thirty-seven poems are divided into three sections. 'The prologue' historically
describes the discovery of the islands and shows the daring and perseverance of the

explorers. 'Travel' tells of various modes of transport and of life in the islands, and highlights aspects of the Bahamian life style. 'Seasons' presents a realistic account of Bahamian customs at Christmas time, during the school terms and on summer holidays. In these poems Wallace avoids dialect, which she uses extensively in her *Bahamian scene* (q.v.).

636 Lyrics of life and love.
Dorral J. Weech. Ardmore, Pennsylvania: Dorrance, 1979. 26p.
(Contemporary Poets of Dorrance Series).
A collection of twenty-six poems which are written in a casual, 'easy-going' style and exhibit a great deal of garden imagery.

637 Four native plays for stage and radio.
Mackey Williams. Nassau: The Author, 1979. [n.p.].
Represented here are the stage plays, 'Prison break' and 'The candidate' and the radio dramas, 'The case of the missing dog' and 'Daddy, please come home', which won a certificate of distinction at the 1977 National Festival of Arts and Crafts.

638 Poems: a toast to you.
Mackey Williams. Freeport, Bahamas: The Author, 1982. 21p.
Forty-one poems which reflect life in the Bahamas.

Foreign literature set in the Bahamas

639 Jingo, wild horse of Abaco.
Jocelyn Arundel. New York: Whittlesey House, 1959. 137p.
Jenny and her friend, Tim, discover a beautiful chestnut mare among a herd of wild horses on the island of Abaco and determine to catch and train it and make it their own. After a summer of patience and hard work, success seems within their grasp when Jingo is captured and spirited away by a fisherman intent on selling the horse. This book for eight to twelve year olds is well written with vivid settings and includes fine pencil sketches.

640 Bahama crisis.
Desmond Bagley. London: Collins, 1980. 250p.
Thomas Mangan is a wealthy white Bahamian hotelier and descendant of Loyalists who fled to the Bahamas following the American Revolution. He encounters murder, kidnapping and arson in his struggle to save the Bahamian tourist industry from the criminal element. This is a spellbinding tale and a realistic picture of life in the Bahamas.

Literature. Foreign literature set in the Bahamas

641 **The secret in the wall.**
Jean Bothwell. London; New York: Abelard-Schuman, 1971. 173p.
In this novel for children, a girl and her brother, recently settled in Nassau, join their friends in a search for buried Spanish treasure.

642 **Boy wanted.**
Ruth Fenisong. New York: Harper & Row, 1964. 148p.
Ten year old Ron lives in Nassau, the victim of a heartless 'money-grubbing' pair called Uncle and Aunt, who will not let him go to school. 'Adopted' long ago to be of use to them, he does not know his last name or how he happens to be with these cruel people. Ron escapes from them to Piper's Cay where other people befriend him and see that he has schooling. Engrossing and well-plotted, fresh and original, this book is for ten to twelve year olds and makes good use of local idiom and the colourful setting.

643 **Thunderball.**
Ian Fleming. London: Cape; New York: Viking, 1961. 248p.
James Bond, the British Secret Service agent, contends with an international crime organization (S.P.E.C.T.R.E.) which threatens destruction using stolen atomic bombs. This is a good, tough, straightforward thriller set in the Bahamas.

644 **Bahamas murder case.**
Leslie Ford. New York: Scribner; London: Collins, 1952. 188p.
When a 'suicide' case haunts the victim's daughter, a trip to the Bahamas, eleven years later, provides a clue to solving the mystery. This novel contains large sections of stream of consciousness writing and little advantage is taken of the unusual setting. Leslie Ford is a pseudonym for Zenith Jones Brown.

645 **Dolly and the doctor bird.**
Dorothy Halliday. London: Cassell, 1971. 250p.
A young doctor accompanies her ailing father to Nassau, where she gets a job at the local hospital and unwittingly becomes involved with espionage: enter Johnson Johnson and his yacht *Dolly*. This is a vivid and stylish novel, enhanced by the lush tropical setting and a bizarre set of characters. Dorothy Halliday is a pseudonym for Dorothy Dunnett. In the United States this novel was published under the title, *Match for a murderer* (Vantage, 1982).

646 **The naked island.**
Basil Heatter. New York: Trident, 1968. 191p.
A Miami charter boat skipper responds to a call for help from an 'old flame' on Grand Bahama Island and finds himself immersed in a complex web of intrigue involving the Mafia and their links to gambling in the island's casinos. Heatter uses veiled references to the life and death of Sir Harry Oakes to add spice to his plot.

647 **Islands in the stream.**
Ernest Hemingway. New York: Scribner, 1970. 466p.
This posthumous and faintly autobiographical novel was written by Hemingway while in residence at Alice Town, Bimini. It presents a man's reflections on his two marriages and his children. The work is divided into three parts. Part one, 'Bimini', takes place

on the island in the mid 1930s and, among other things, contains one of the best descriptions of deep-sea fishing ever written. A 1976 film of the same name, shot in Hawaii, was based on this work.

648 **Bahamian ballads.**
Dorothy Kernochan. Nassau: The Author, 1951. 31p.
Written by a non-Bahamian, these twenty-one pastoral poems extol the virtues of the Bahamas.

649 **Pieces of eight.**
Richard LeGallienne. New York: Peter Smith, 1932. 333p.
A visitor to Nassau comes into possession of a yellowed manuscript from a long-dead pirate. A hunt for treasure is pursued, despite various difficulties encountered. This novel, originally published in London (Collins: 1918) is less bloodthirsty and more poetical than most books of this nature.

650 **Stars on the sea.**
F. Van Wyck Mason. Philadelphia: Lippincott, 1940.
This novel, which is part of a saga on the American Revolution, describes privateering in the early days of the American Revolution. It is set in Newport, Rhode Island, South Carolina and the Bahamas.

651 **The Amyot crime.**
Christopher Nicole. London: Cassell, 1974. 240p.
The fictional Amyot family from Amyot's Cay, a small island twenty miles north-east of Nassau, build their fortune on wrecking, augmented by gun-running and bootlegging. This story of the nineteenth and twentieth century Amyot family was first published in 1965.

652 **Amyot's Cay**
Christopher Nicole. London: Cassell, 1974. 256p.
This work details the early history of the fictional Amyot family. The story, which begins with Catherine Amyot (1695–1783) was first published in 1964.

653 **Blood Amyot.**
Christopher Nicole. London: Cassell, 1974. 256p.
This instalment of the Amyot family's story was first published by Jarrolds in 1964. It is the story of the family during the eighteenth and nineteenth centuries.

654 **Pi Gal.**
Valerie King Page. New York: Dodd, Mead, 1970. 127p.
A young boy finds new meaning and adventure in his life when the search for his lost dog leads him to two white men searching for sunken treasure off Cat Island in the Bahamas. Page, an American living and teaching on Cat Island, won the Edith Busby Award for this novel. The award is given for creative literature aimed at six to sixteen year old readers.

655 **Holiday with a vengeance.**
Ritchie Perry.   Boston, Massachusetts: Houghton Mifflin, 1975. 188p.
(Midnight Novel of Suspense).
A highly competent British thriller in which a 'drinking and wenching' secret agent is
sent to the Bahamas, thinly disguised as an exotic Caribbean island, to rescue the
British consul, kidnapped by the island's monstrous dictator. Involved in all this are
members of the Central Intelligence Agency and a group of counter-revolutionaries led
by a Cuban guerrilla captain. First published in 1974 (London: Collins).

656 **The conch eaters.**
Leo Rost.   Los Angeles: Wollstonecraft, 1973. 266p.
This entertaining and competently written novel traces the efforts of the rich,
politically oriented character, Sandy Beeches, to bring legalized gambling to his native
Bahamian island. Rost does not simply use the Bahamas as a colourful background but
incorporates the atmosphere of the country into his novel.

657 **Pilgrims in Paradise.**
Frank G. Slaughter.   Garden City, New York: Doubleday, 1960.
319p.
The adventures of Puritans from England who settled on Eleuthera in the Bahamas are
explored in this volume.

658 **An affair of honor.**
Robert Wilder.   New York: Putnam, 1969. 383p.
The colony is reflected in the parallel lives of two Bahamians. Max Hertog, a white
Bahamian, exhibits an insatiable greed for wealth and power; a black Bahamian, Royal
Keating, is ambitious to establish a black government.

659 **Wind from the Carolinas.**
Robert Wilder.   New York: Putnam, 1964. 635p.
In this multi-generation novel, Wilder traces the story of the fictional Loyalist
Cameron family from the 1790s, when the family flees the United States for the
Bahamas, to the 1920s when they engage in running liquor from the islands to the
mainland. This is one of the best fictional accounts of Bahamian history available.

The Arts

Visual arts

660 **Randolph Johnston: Cellini meets Crusoe.**
Anne Fadiman. *Life*, vol. 9 (June 1986), p. 21–22, 26.
Presents a profile of sculptor Randolph Johnston who lives on Little Harbour Island in the Abaco chain.

661 **Paint by Mr. Amos Ferguson.**
Amos Ferguson. Hartford, Connecticut: Wadsworth Atheneum, 1984. 64p.
This is a beautiful catalogue of an exhibition held at the Wadsworth Atheneum in the spring of 1985. Ferguson, who primarily uses sign paint on masonite, produces bold, colourful paintings of Bahamian scenes and stories from the Bible. He is one of the more prolific and well known Bahamian painters. The catalogue includes forty-eight well-reproduced colour plates and a more personal and intriguing text than many art exhibition catalogues.

662 **Survive, man! or perish: sculptural metaphors to command allegiance to life, resistance to race suicide, with The art of survival: a critique of the survivalist art and philosophy of Randolph W. Johnston.**
Denny Johnston, edited by Melinda Talkington. Marsh Harbour, Bahamas: Little Harbour, 1980. 114p.
The work and philosophy of the sculptor Randolph Johnston are presented. Thirty-nine pieces of work produced between 1922 and 1979 are described and illustrated with black-and-white photographs. 'The art of survival' is an interview between Randolph Johnston and his son, Denny.

663 **Artist on his island: a study in self-reliance.**
Randolph Wardell Johnston.   Park Ridge, New Jersey: Noyes, 1975.
186p. map.

Johnston, a sculptor, left his home in Massachusetts in 1951 and, with his family,
moved to the Bahamas where he built a home on Great Abaco Island. This is his diary
of life in the Bahamas as an artist from 1951 to 1974. It is a fascinating and well-
narrated adventure.

Music

664 **7 hit songs of Nassau and the Bahamas.**
Eric Minns.   Nassau: Minns Productions, 1979. 24p.

The seven songs referred to in the title are all by Eric Minns. Three of them, 'Fox-hill
gal', 'Island boy' and 'You can take the man out of the island' are well known, award
winning Bahamian songs written to a calypso beat. The music and lyrics are given for
each song, and are also given for the Bahamian national anthem, 'March On,
Bahamaland', written in 1969 by Timothy Gibson.

665 **In the days of yesterday and in the days of today: an overview of
Bahamian folkmusic.**
Basil C. Hedrick, Jeanette E. Stephens.   Carbondale, Illinois:
University Museum, Southern Illinois University, 1976. 63p. bibliog.
(University Museum Studies, 8).

This study shows that Bahamian folk music, a blending of traditions descending from
British and African styles, developed primarily between 1783 and the 1930s. Since
then, the influence of tourism has led to a deterioration of the original musical
tradition. The authors discuss both religious and secular music and make a brief
mention of Junkanoo. The lyrics of eleven songs, including the national anthem, are
given but the music for these songs is not included. The bibliography is accompanied
by a discography.

666 **The Bahamas song book and our national anthem: for voices in
harmony.**
Compiled and arranged by Irving Burgie.   Hollis, New York: Caribe
Music Corp., 1972. 8p. map.

This booklet, a special independence issue, includes the words and music for four
songs popular in the Bahamas. The first song, 'Island in the sun' was written in 1956 by
Irving Burgie for the 20th Century Fox film of the same name. The other three songs,
'Michael row the boat', 'All my trials' and 'Sloop John B' are all traditional Bahamian
songs though the first two have erroneously been referred to at times as American
Black spirituals. The song book also includes the words and music for the national
anthem of the Bahamas.

Festivals – Junkanoo

667 **Junkanoo.**
Bahamas. Public Records Office.   Nassau: Public Records Office, 1978. 45p.
This booklet accompanied an exhibition held at the Art Gallery, Jumbey Village, 13 February–3 March 1978 on Junkanoo, a uniquely Bahamian festival celebrated both on Boxing Day and New Year's Day in the early hours of the morning. This festival appeared in Jamaica in the eighteenth century and was celebrated in the Bahamas as early as 1801. Its origins are uncertain but it does resemble the John Canoe, a festival said to have been celebrated by West African slaves. Captioned black-and-white photographs of all the exhibits are included in the piece.

668 **Junkanoo jamboree.**
G. Ralph Kiel.   *American Magazine*, vol. 152 (Dec. 1951), p. 98–100.
This short article vividly describes the sights and sounds of the Junkanoo festival.

669 **The John Canoe festival: a New World Africanism.**
Ira De Augustine Reid.   *Phylon*, vol. 3, no. 4 (1942), p. 349–70.
Outlines the origins of and the influences on the John Canoe or Junkanoo festival throughout the Caribbean and the southern United States, where it reached its peak of importance between 1880 and 1890. Although the festival is not strictly Bahamian, the three photographs accompanying this article are all of the Bahamian festival. There is an extensive bibliography.

670 **John Kuners.**
Dougald MacMillan.   *Journal of American Folk-Lore*, vol. 39, no. 151 (Jan./March 1926), p. 53–57.
An investigation of the John Kuners (Canoe) festival in the southern United States. MacMillan includes lyrics of songs from these festivals and shows the link between the American John Kuners festivals and the Bahamian Junkanoo. He also includes a description of a Bahamian Junkanoo from the mid 1920s.

Architecture

671 **Pleasures of Villa Contenta: the Bahamian residence of Sir Bernard Ashley.**
Christopher T. Buckley.   *Architectural Digest*, vol. 45, no. 8 (Aug. 1988), p. 114–19.
Examines a Georgian colonial home built in Lyford Cay, New Providence Island in 1960. It is distinctly British and reminiscent of the colonial period. The photographs enhance this article.

672 **Architecture: Thomas H. Beeby.**
Ross Miller. *Architectural Digest*, vol. 40, no. 1 (Jan. 1983),
p. 84–89, 136, 138.

Miller describes Beeby's design for a home on Harbour Island. The design incorporates many Bahamian forms including the indigenous island colours of pink and white, the built-up stucco detailing and the simplified Georgian style. The photographs are a highlight of the article.

673 **Architecture: Frank Dimster.**
Joseph Giovanni. *Architectural Digest*, vol. 39, no. 9 (Sept. 1982),
p. 156–63.

Giovanni examines two homes designed in the International Style by Frank Dimster and built in Freeport, Grand Bahama. The accompanying photographs are quite beautiful.

Food and Drink

674 **True, true Bahamian recipes.**
De'Ynza Burrows.   Nassau: King Conch International Publications,
1979. 103p.
Contains 169 recipes, many of which use the meat of the conch, a Bahamian staple, as
a main ingredient.

675 **Bahamian cookery: Cindy's treasures.**
Cindy Williams.   Nassau: Napco Printing Service, 1976. 62p.
Williams has provided in this volume 117 recipes typical of food served in the
Bahamas.

676 **The Abaco cook book, from a Bahamian Out Island.**
Fran Woolley.   Brattleboro, Vermont: Durrell, 1974. 144p.
A collection of 245 recipes, including some for wild plants found in the Bahamas.

677 **Bahamian cook book: recipes by ladies of Nassau.**
Helen Burns Higgs.   Nassau: The Author, 1970. 11th ed. 155p.
A collection of 424 recipes, originally published as *Lady Brown's Bahamian cook
book: recipes by the ladies of Nassau.*

Libraries and Archives

Libraries

678 **A note on the Bahamian Society for the Diffusion of Useful Knowledge.**
Paul Gordon Boultbee. *Journal of Caribbean History*, vol. 15 (1981), p. 56–58.

Describes the founding and the objectives of the Bahamian Society for the Diffusion of Useful Knowledge. The society, established in Nassau in 1835, was organized after the model of the original Society founded by Henry Brougham in 1825. The Bahamian Society was very active for two years and then formed the Nassau Public Library Reading Room and Museum which essentially replaced the society.

679 **The Nassau Public Library – a Victorian prelude.**
Paul Gordon Boultbee. *Journal of the Bahamas Historical Society*, vol. 1 (Oct. 1979), p. 3–8.

Outlines the development of the Nassau Public Library during the nineteenth century. The library was founded in 1837, following the union of the Bahamian Society for the Diffusion of Useful Knowledge and an unnamed reading society. The Nassau Public Library Act was passed in 1847 and this led to three libraries being established, in Dunmore Town, Harbour Island (1854), Matthew Town, Inagua (1855) and New Plymouth, Abaco (1862).

680 **Library development in New Province [i.e., Providence] (Bahamas).**
Paul Gordon Boultbee. *Library History Review*, vol. 2, no. 2 (June 1978), p. 1–12.

Describes the development of libraries on New Providence Island from the first circulating library in 1804 to the founding of the Nassau Public Library in 1837. The author also traces library development in the twentieth century, covering the establishment of the Grant's Town Library, for the use of the black population, in 1930, and the Southern Public Library, which replaced the burned down Grant's Town

Library, in 1951. He also describes the Eastern (1958), Fox Hill (1970) and Coconut Grove (1974) Public Libraries.

681 **Library service in the Bahamas.**
Paul Gordon Boultbee. *International Library Review*, vol. 10 (April 1978), p. 151–54.
Describes public and school library services and emphasizes the need for cooperation and resource sharing. The author points out that the library service suffers from a combined lack of funds, definite government policy and qualified personnel.

682 **Guide to libraries and archives in Central America and the West Indies, Panama, Bermuda, and British Guiana, supplemented with information on private libraries, bookbinding, bookselling and printing.**
Arthur Eric Gropp.   New Orleans, Louisiana: Middle American Research Institute, the Tulane University of Louisiana, 1941. 721p. map. bibliog. (Tulane University of Louisiana. Middle American Research Institute. Middle American Research Series. Publication 10).
In 1938, Gropp spent twelve days in the Bahamas visiting libraries (public, private and rental), archives, booksellers and printers as part of the Middle American Research Institute's survey of libraries and archives in Central America, the West Indies and Bermuda. Although now quite out of date, his section on the Bahamas (p. 153–75) gives a good overview of the post-war situation in the country. This work also allows for comparison between the Bahamas and what were then other British colonies in the Caribbean.

683 **The libraries of Bermuda, the Bahamas, the British West Indies, British Guiana, British Honduras, Puerto Rico, and the American Virgin Islands: a report to the Carnegie Corporation of New York.**
Ernest A. Savage.   London: Library Association, 1934. 102p.
Like Gropp, Savage spent a short time in the Bahamas during an extended tour of libraries in the Caribbean. The section on the Bahamas (p. 66-71) provides information on the Nassau and Grant's Town Public Libraries, both on the Island of New Providence, and fourteen libraries in the Out Islands. The book also includes Savage's recommendations for an improved library service throughout the Caribbean and, though now out of date, it is useful for research purposes.

Archives

684 **Supplement to the Guide to the records of the Commonwealth of the Bahamas.**
Bahamas. Public Records Office. Archives Section.   Nassau: Public Records Office. Archives Section, 1980. 55p.
Updates the 1973 *Guide to the records of the Bahamas* (q.v.). This supplement lists

records and archival materials deposited since the publication of the first volume, along with materials from new ministries established since 1973. It does not list any Bahamian records found in foreign repositories as did the original and there is no index.

685   **The first ten years, 1969–1979: history of the Bahamian archives.**
Bahamas. Public Records Office.   Nassau: Public Records Office, 1979. 17p.

This booklet was published by the Public Records Office to mark International Archives Weeks celebrated throughout the world at the national and regional levels between 1 October and 15 December 1979. It outlines the background and development of the Bahamian Archives or Public Records Office.

686   **The establishment of the Public Records Office of the Bahamas.**
Edward A. Carson.   *Journal of the Society of Archivists*, vol. 5, no. 1 (1974), p. 31–37.

Carson assisted in establishing the Public Records Office of the Bahamas in 1971. This article describes the selection of the site, the preparation of enabling legislation, the construction of the building, the physical movement of the records, the assembling of an archive system and the drafting of the *Guide to the records of the Bahamas* (q.v.).

687   **Guide to the records of the Bahamas.**
D. Gail Saunders, Edward A. Carson.   Nassau: Government Printing Department, 1973. [138p.] map.

This guide is the first and most important published key to the collections of the Public Records Office of the Bahamas. The body of the guide (p. 1–109) lists the collections from government ministries and departments, public corporations, Family (Out) Island records, government and private schools, churches, private associations and businesses. The location for records not housed in the Public Records Office is given. It also includes a list of the locations of Bahamian records in eighteen repositories in England, the United States, Bermuda and Spain. There is an index (p. 110–38). In 1980 this guide was updated by the *Supplement to the Guide to the records of the Commonwealth of the Bahamas* (q.v.).

Mass Media

Journalism

688   **A salute to friend and foe: my battles, sieges, and fortunes.**
Sir Alfred Etienne Jerome Dupuch.   Nassau: Tribune, 1982. 208p.

This autobiography, written in Sir Etienne's own self-indulgent and inimitable style, is designed to complement his *Tribune story* (q.v). The work covers his marriage and his experiences in the First World War, and includes a collection of his thoughts on individuals who have had an influence on his life. Whatever didn't appear in *Tribune story* appears here. As Sir Etienne is almost a Bahamian 'institution', neither this work nor *Tribune story* can be ignored.

689   **Tribune story.**
Sir Alfred Etienne Jerome Dupuch.   London: Benn, 1967. 162p.

Probably one of the only books written specifically about an individual English-speaking Caribbean newspaper, this work is based on a series of articles in the *Nassau Daily Tribune* (q.v.). Sir Etienne emphasizes the growth of the paper, founded by his father in 1903, his championship of the 'coloured people' (Sir Etienne's own words) of the Bahamas and his devotion to the Commonwealth. Sir Etienne has played a major role in the country for decades, either as a player or as a reporter and commentator. Both this work and *A salute to friend and foe* . . . (q.v.) provide useful and interesting views of Bahamian politics and society in the twentieth century.

Newspapers

690 **The Bahamas Index: 1986– .**
Steve Dodge.   Decatur, Illinois: White Sound, 1987– . annual.

Each annual issue indexes several thousand newspaper articles of political, economic or socio-cultural significance published in the *Nassau Guardian* (q.v.) and the *Nassau Daily Tribune* (q.v.). The entries, each of which includes an abstract, are listed under the categories of government and politics, economic conditions and trends, social conditions and trends, culture, popular culture, arts and sciences, transportation and communication, law and the courts, environment, and international relations and foreign policy. Articles are also listed by region and ·there is a section for personal names. This is the first newspaper index for any Caribbean nation and it is a significant contribution to the access of Bahamian information.

691 **Nassau Daily Tribune.**
Nassau: Nassau Daily Tribune, 1903– . daily.

The *Nassau Daily Tribune* was founded in 1903 by Leon Dupuch. It is still published and edited by the Dupuch family. The best source for information about this newspaper is Sir Etienne Dupuch's *Tribune story* (q.v.).

692 **Nassau Guardian.**
Nassau: Nassau Guardian, 1844– . daily.

For over one hundred years the *Nassau Guardian* was owned and operated by the Moseley family, but in 1948 it was sold to the United Bahamian Party. It has since been purchased by the Perry chain of newspapers based in the United States.

Periodicals

693 **Journal of the Bahamas Historical Society.**
Bahamas Historical Society. Nassau: Bahamas Historical Society,
1979– . annual.
Provides brief historical articles and biographical sketches and a section reporting on
ongoing research. This is the only periodical reporting on historical scholarship in the
Bahamas.

694 **Bahamas Dateline: Business, Investment, Real Estate.**
Washington, DC: Bahamas Dateline, 1976– . monthly.
This newsletter, produced for non-residents of the Bahamas, reviews current news
events and provides up-to-date information on business, investments and real estate.
For the most part, it is critical of the government.

695 **Bahamian Review.**
Nassau: Cartwright Publications, 1952– . monthly.
The magazine's stated policy, as expressed in vol. 1, no. 1, is 'to provide. . .a magazine
which presents a timely, lively and interesting conception of life in these lovely isles'.
Each issue features chatty articles, short news features and articles on Bahamian
personalities. Most changes since 1952 have been purely cosmetic. The *Bahamian
Review* is the only major Bahamian magazine.

Directories

696 **Annual directory.**
Bahamas Chamber of Commerce.   Nassau: Bahamas Chamber of
Commerce, 1960– . annual.
Provides several lists and directories including Chamber of Commerce membership,
diplomatic and consular lists, and commercial and manufacturing directories. It also
gives information about business and finance in the Bahamas.

697 **Personalities Caribbean: the international guide to who's who in the
West Indies, Bahamas, Bermuda, 1965– .**
Kingston, Jamaica: Personalities, 1965– . biennial.
A straightforward 'who's who' which is revised every two years. The majority of
entries for the Bahamas come from politics, government and business, though there
are also entries for individuals from law, religion, medicine, journalism, banking and
education.

Bibliographies

698 **A bibliography of Bahamian prehistory.**
Julian Granberry. Nassau: Bahamas Archaeological Team, 1988.
2nd ed. 14p.
First published in 1982, this bibliography lists 103 unannotated items on archaeology and anthropology, the Lucayans, Columbus and the Loyalists. The list includes monographs and journal articles. It is planned that the bibliography will be updated at five-year intervals.

699 **Bahamian reference collection: bibliography.**
Compiled by Paul Gordon Boultbee. Nassau: College of the
Bahamas, 1981. 2nd ed. 57p.
This bibliography lists items which are housed at the College of the Bahamas' Oakes Field Library. The collection, which numbered 494 items in 1981, was begun in 1979 and has been expanded considerably since this bibliography was prepared. It includes monographs, journals and individual journal articles, government documents, maps and miscellaneous ephemera, as well as author and subject indexes. The first edition was published in 1980.

700 **An annotated ethnographic bibliography of the Bahama Islands.**
Alan G. LaFlamme. *Behaviour Science Research*, vol. 11, no. 1
(1976), p. 57–66.
This bibliography was compiled to acquaint the potential researcher with ethnographic literature pertaining to the Bahamas. It includes seventeen books, thirty-six journal articles, four dissertations and one long-playing record.

Bibliographies

701 **Bibliography of the natural history of the Bahama Islands.**
William T. Gillis, Roger Byrne, Wyman Harrison.   Washington, DC: Smithsonian Institution, 1975. 123p. map. (Atoll Research Bulletin, 191).
Lists nearly 1,650 citations alphabetically by author within twenty-two subject divisions including biology, climate and meteorology, geology, geography and soil science. There are no indexes.

702 **Bahamas bibliography: a list of citations for scientific, engineering and historical articles pertaining to the Bahama Islands.**
Carol Fang, Wyman Harrison.   Gloucester Point, Virginia: Virginia Institute of Marine Science, 1972. 42p. (Special Scientific Report, no. 56).
This bibliography grew out of the demand from marine geologists, biologists and physical oceanographers engaged in studies of the beaches, fishes and inlet currents in the Bahama Islands. The 606 entries are divided into four sections. The archaeology, anthropology, history section lists scholarly books and articles and general sources not cited by Craton in his first edition of *A history of the Bahamas* (q.v.). The biological sciences section lists all references in *Biological Abstracts* (Philadelphia: BioSciences Information Service, 1927– . semi-monthly) from 1960 to 1969 inclusive (excluding anthropology). The other two sections list items for the geological sciences and oceanography and engineering. There is no indication as to where these citations come from. Entries are listed alphabetically by author and there is no other index.

703 **Bahamas.**
Compiled by N.W. Posnett, P.M. Reilly.   Surbiton, England: Land Resources Division, 1971. 74p. (Land Resource Bibliography, no.1).
Originally prepared for members of Land Resource Division projects and published on the completion of the project. The 619 entries in this bibliography are almost exclusively journal articles and government documents from the 1960s. There is a concentration on the environmental sciences, agriculture and forestry and a peripheral interest in the economic and cultural background. The bibliography is not annotated.

Index

The index is a single alphabetical sequence of authors (personal and corporate), titles of publications and subjects. Index entries refer both to the main items and to other works mentioned in the notes to each item. Title entries are in italics. Numeration refers to the items as numbered.

A

Abaco 135
 birds 183, 189, 362
 boat-building 359, 361
 Cooper's Town 461
 Crossing Rocks 463
 Elbow Cay 53
 flora 362
 forestry 575, 577
 geology 60
 Green Turtle Cay 420,
  447, 468
  folk-tales 420
 history 257, 320, 357-362
 Hope Town
  history 358
  travel guides 89, 358
 household composition
  464
 independence 355, 359
 libraries 679
 Man-O-War Cay 9
  history 361
 molluscs 218
 Murphy Town 463
 proverbs 414
 shells 362
 statistics 536
 tourism 122
 travel guides 75, 80
 Treasure Cay
  history 360
 Wilson City 357

Abaco conspiracy 607
*Abaco cook book, from a
 Bahamian Out Island*
 676
*Abaco: the history of an
 out island and its cays*
 359
Abacos 75
Accommodation 71-72, 74,
 76-77, 79, 94
Accounting 542
Acklins Island
 birds 184
 Spring Point 233
Acts: a poem 625
*Addington Venables,
 bishop of Nassau: . . .*
 433
Adelaide, New Providence
 history 370
*Admiral of the ocean sea: a
 life of Christopher
 Columbus* 294
Affair of honor 658
Africa
 influences 258, 379, 590
African crossroads 345
Agor, W.H. 543
Agriculture 23, 66, 114,
 253, 343, 345, 523-524,
 526-527, 530, 532, 535,
 540, 549, 568-571, 574
 Arawaks 246

bibliographies 703
 Cat Island 453
 Exuma 365
 Green Turtle Cay,
  Abaco 468
 Loyalist influences 326
 maps 30
 San Salvador 376
 statistics 569
 Watlings Island 389
*Agriculture and fisheries:
 the need to produce
 more food* 570
*Ai-je tue? Le monde est ma
 prison: autobiographie*
 352
Albury, Carl Thomas 427
Albury, H.L. 361
Albury, P. 265, 375, 562
Albury family 361
Alcoholism 449, 460
 Cat Island 453
Algae 36, 139, 141, 162
Allen, D.F. 472
Allen, E.G. 132
Allen, G.M. 204
Allen, R.P. 199
Allen, William 540
Amatucci, K. 140
Ambergris Cays 234
American Civil War
 see United States (Civil
 War)

American Geographical
Society 14
American Loyalists
see Loyalists
American Revolution
see United States
(Revolution)
Amphibians 219
Andros Island 180
Amyot crime 651
Amyot's Cay 652
Andrews, J.E. 47
Andros Island 135
amphibians 180
anthropology 232
archaeology 232
birds 200-201, 206
blue holes 25, 28-29, 64
bush medicine 481
Congo Town 458
coral reefs 176, 179
ecology 180
ethnology 232
fauna 180
fish 180
flora 156
folk-tales 406, 412
forestry 575, 577
geology 41, 43, 48, 56,
61, 63
household composition
462, 467
Lake Forsyth 180
Long Bay Cays 457, 465-
466
love potions 481
obeah 437
reptiles 180
riddles 415
Seminole Negroes
327-328
statistics 536
tourism 122
travel guides 80
Andros Islanders: a study
of the family
organization in the
Bahamas 465
Anemia 138
Anglican Church
history 423, 429-430, 433
Annual directory 696
Annual shipping statistics
report 555

Anson, P.F. 428
Anstis, Thomas 311
Anthologies 593-596, 633
Anthropology
Andros Island 232
bibliographies 698, 702
Bimini 231
Cat Island 453
Antigua 113
Antilles (Greater and
Lesser) 187
Apprenticeship system
378, 388
Arawaks 230, 246-247
San Salvador 227
Arawaks and astronauts:
twenty years on
Eleuthera 363
Archaeology 237-247
Andros Island 232
bibliographies 698, 702
Bimini 231
Cat Island 243
Gordon Hill, Crooked
Island 242
Long Bay, San Salvador
238
marine 171
Palmetto Grove, San
Salvador 244
Pigeon Creek, San
Salvador 239, 283
Archer, B. 121
Archer, C.B. 449
Architecture
domestic 457, 671-673
Loyalist influences 385
Archives 684-687
research 684, 687
Ardastra Gardens 196
Armbrister, H. 414
Armbrister, L. 597
Art 71
Art of survival 662
Arthropods 170
Artist on his island: a study
in self-reliance 663
Arundel, J. 639
Aspects of Bahamian
culture 451
Aspects of slavery 381, 388
Aspects of slavery, part II 380
At summer's end: south
poems 611

Athol Island 181
Atlantic islands as resorts of
health and pleasure 89
Atlas of the
Commonwealth of the
Bahamas 30
Atlases 30-31
Tongue of the Ocean 50
Atolls 52
Attempt to solve the
problem of the first
landing place of
Columbus in the New
World 299
Atwood Cay
first landfall 299

B

Back home: an original
anthology 633
Bacon, E.M. 99
Bacot, J.T.W. 276
Bagley, D. 640
Bahama crisis 640
Bahama fever 597
Bahama flora 151
Bahama harbors: a pilot
book for the Great
Bahama Bank, British
West Indies 88
Bahama Islands 86, 135,
572
Bahama Islands: a
boatman's guide to the
land and the water 84
Bahama Islands
(Constitution) order in
Council, 1963 515, 517
Bahama Islands
(Constitution) order
1969 515
Bahama Islands: in full
colour 12
Bahama Islands: notes on
an early attempt at
colonization 275
Bahama Islands: report of
the commission of
inquiry into the
operation of the
business of casinos in
Freeport and in

Nassau 565

Bahama songs and stories 405, 412, 418

Bahamas 1-2, 11, 14, 22, 703

Bahamas Agricultural and Industrial Corporation 550

Bahamas archaeology project, reports and papers 240

Bahamas between worlds 446

Bahamas bibliography: a list of citations for scientific, engineering and historical articles pertaining to the Bahama Islands 702

Bahamas business guide: a guide to doing business in the Bahamas and the government's economic and financial policies 552

Bahamas Chamber of Commerce 696

Bahamas. Commission appointed to enquire into disturbances in the Bahamas which took place in June 1942 557

Bahamas. Commission of inquiry appointed to inquire into the illegal use of the Bahamas for the transshipment of dangerous drugs for the United States of America 475

Bahamas. Commission of inquiry into the operation of the business of casinos in Freeport and in Nassau 565

Bahamas consolidated index of statutes and subsidiary legislation to . . . 519

Bahamas Council on Alcoholism 449

Bahamas Dateline:

Business, Investment, Real Estate 694

Bahamas. Department of Archives 256, 317, 329, 337, 339, 341, 356, 369, 380, 560

Bahamas. Department of Statistics 390, 393, 536, 547, 553, 555-556, 569, 578-582

Bahamas Development Bank 552

Bahamas. Development Board 373

Bahamas diver's guide 82

Bahamas during the early twentieth century, 1900-1914 339

Bahamas during the Great War 340

Bahamas during the World Wars, 1914-1918 and 1939-1945 341

Bahamas early mail services and postal markings 572

Bahamas: economic report 524

Bahamas: a family of islands 66

Bahamas handbook 19

Bahamas handbook and businessman's annual 4, 16, 552

Bahamas Historical Society 693

Bahamas in figures 580

Bahamas in poetry 598-599

Bahamas in poetry and poems of other lands 599

Bahamas in the late nineteenth century, 1870-1899 337

Bahamas in the mid-nineteenth century, 1850-1869 329

Bahamas: in a white coming on 618

Bahamas independence order 1973 511

Bahamas Index: 1986- 690

Bahamas. Information

Services. Public Affairs Department 570

Bahamas; isles of June 270

Bahamas. Ministry of Agriculture, Fisheries and Local Government 568

Bahamas. Ministry of Education 586

Bahamas. Ministry of Education and Culture 585

Bahamas murder case 644

Bahamas National Trust 188

Bahamas 1983- . 79

Bahamas Platform 20, 46, 57

Bahamas. Prime Minister 514

Bahamas. Public Records Office 261, 263-264, 388, 561, 563-564, 667, 685, 687

Bahamas. Public Records Office. Archives Section 510, 684

Bahamas reference annual 4

Bahamas: a sketch 276

Bahamas: a social studies course for secondary schools 8

Bahamas song book and our national anthem: for voices in harmony 666

Bahamas ten years after independence, 1973-1983 356

Bahamas Timber Company 357

Bahamas War Relief Committee 340

Bahamian American connection 261

Bahamian anthology 595

Bahamian ballads 648

Bahamian cook book: recipes by ladies of Nassau 677

Bahamian cookery: Cindy's treasures 675

Bahamian folk lore 416
Bahamian interlude: being
    an account of life at
    Nassau in the Bahama
    Islands in the
    eighteenth century 115-
    116
Bahamian jottings: poems
    and prose: with
    photographs and
    reminiscences of old
    Nassau 608
Bahamian landscapes: an
    introduction to the
    geography of the
    Bahamas 20
Bahamian lore 409
Bahamian Loyalists and
    their slaves 385
Bahamian proverbs 408
Bahamian reference
    collection:
    bibliography 699
Bahamian Review 695
Bahamian sailing
    craft: . . . 559
Bahamian scene 634-635
Bahamian sexuality 454
Bahamian Society for the
    Diffusion of Useful
    Knowledge 678, 679
Bahamian symbols: the first
    five centuries 262
Bahamianization 498
Bain Town 372
Bain Town, New
    Providence
    history 370, 372, 450
Banker Research Unit 546
Banking 354, 523-524, 527,
    535-548, 552
    and drug trade 470
    and organized crime 558
    Central Bank of the
        Bahamas 548
    Inter-American
        Development Bank
        (IDB) 530
    off-shore 538-540, 546,
        558
Banking in the Bahamas
    538
Baptist Church
    bibliographies 424

history 421, 423-424
Baptists in the Bahamas: an
    historical review 423
Barbados 105, 113
    social insurance 442
Barbour, T. 223
Barratt, P.J.H. 367
Barry, C.J. 427
Bartsch, P. 215
Bats 213
Bay Street Boys 347, 504,
    507-508
Beaches 37
Becher, A.B. 300-302
Belize
    blue holes 28
Bell, H.H.J. 438, 441
Bell, H.M. 270
Benchley, P. 7
Beneath the seas of the
    West Indies:
    Caribbean, Bahamas,
    Florida, Bermuda 171
Benjamin, G.J. 29
Benjamin, S.G.W. 89
Bermuda
    fish 159-161, 165, 171-
        172
    flowers 143
    tourism 121
    travel guides 71-72, 77
Bernard, J.F. 28
Berry Islands
    flora 153
Berryman, J. 8
Best of Pot Luck 501
Bethell, A.T. 271
Bibliographies 698-703
    agriculture 703
    anthropology 698, 702
    archaeology 698, 702
    Baptist Church 424
    biology 701-702
    Christopher Columbus
        698
    climate 701
    coral reefs 177
    culture 703
    economy 703
    engineering 702
    environment 703
    ethnography 700
    forestry 703
    geography 701

geology 44, 701-702
    health 477
    history 702
    Junkanoo 669
    labour 551
    Loyalists 698
    Lucayans 698
    meteorology 701
    music 665
    obeah 439
    oceanography 702
    prehistory 698
    soils 701
    voodoo 439
Bibliography of Bahamian
    prehistory 698
Bibliography of the natural
    history of the Bahama
    Islands 701
Bicentennial blues 626
Bimini
    anthropology 231
    archaeology 231
    birds 194, 197
    coral reefs 173, 177
    geography 149
    health 477
    history 149
    lizards 222
    lobsters 169
    medicinal plants 482
    medicine 482
    Seminole Negroes 328
    sharks 158
    shells 216
    sponges 163
    tourism 122
    travel guides 80
    vegetation 149
Biological Abstracts 702
Biology 125
    bibliographies 701-702
Birds 125-126, 134, 136-
    137, 182-208
    Abaco 183, 189, 362
    Acklins Island 184
    Andros Island 200-201,
        206
    Bimini 194, 197
    boobies 203
    Cat Island 182, 194
    Cay Sal Bank 221
    Crooked Island 184
    egg birds 203

Eleuthera 185
flamingos 188, 196, 198-201, 203, 205
fossils 195, 202
Grand Bahama Island 191
Great Exuma Island 202
Great Inagua Island 183-184, 188-189, 200
Inagua 199
Little Abaco Island 206
Little Inagua Island 184
man-o-war birds 203
Mayaguana Island 184
New Providence 192, 195
parrots 183, 189
San Salvador 190, 194
Watlings Island 190
West Indies 186
Birds of the Bahama Islands . . . 208
Birds of the Bahamas 193
Birds of the Bahamas: New Providence and the Bahama Islands 192
Birds of New Providence and the Bahama Islands 192-193
Birds of the southern Bahamas: an annotated check-list 184
Birds of the West Indies 186
Birnbaum, S. 72
Birnbaum's Caribbean, Bermuda and the Bahamas 72
Black English as a Creole: some Bahamian evidence 588
Black Power movement 500
Blackbeard
see Teach, Edward
Blackbeard or the pirates of the isles, a romance of the Bahamas 602
Bloch, M. 346-347
Block, A.A. 444, 558
Blockade runners of the Confederacy 334
Blockade-running 330-336

Blood Amyot 653
Blount, S. 73
Blue holes 24-29
Andros Island 25, 28-29, 64
Belize 28
British Blue Hole Expeditions 25
British Honduras 28
ecology 27
fauna 24, 26, 29
flora 29
Grand Bahama Island 25
photographs 28
Blue holes of the Bahamas 25
Boat-building 9, 559-560, 562
Abaco 359, 361
Cat Island 453
Boat-building industry of the Bahamas 560
Bocca, G. 349-350
Bohlke, J.E. 174
Bond, J. 187
Bonhote, J.L.J. 206
Bonney, Anne 309-310
Boobies 203
Boodhoo, K.I. 493
Book about the sea gardens of Nassau, Bahamas 181
Book of Bahamian verse 596
Boswell, T.D. 397-399
Botany 138-139
Bothwell, J. 267, 641
Boultbee, P.G. 678-681, 699
Bounds, J.H. 13, 120, 554
Bowden, A. 534
Bowe, R.M.L. 260
Boy wanted 642
Brace, L.J.K. 157
Brassey, A.A. 110
Breder, C.M. 180
Breeding , J. G. 56
Bregenzer, J. 448
British Blue Hole Expeditions 25
British Empire in America 374
British Honduras
blue holes 28
Britton, N.L. 151-153, 155

Brodkorb, P. 195, 202
Brooks, W.K. 236
Brother Amos 421
Brown, M.W. 360
Brown, R.W. 480, 598-599
Brown, W. 321
Brown, Z.J. 644
Bruce, P.H. 115-116
Brudenell-Bruce, P.G.C. 192-193
Bryce, G. 521
Buckley, C.T. 671
Buden, D.W. 182, 184, 221
Buildings
historic 259, 264, 371
public 259, 264
Burgie, I. 666
Burial inscriptions 260, 263
Burial practices
Arawaks 246
Lucayan 226
Burns, Alan Cuthbert 252, 343
Burrows, D. 674
Busby, R.F. 55
Bush medicine 106, 139, 376, 385, 451, 480-485
and obeah 435
Andros Island 481
Cat Island 453
Exuma 483
Long Island 483
Bush medicine in the Bahamas 484
Business 5, 16, 527, 537
and middle class 445
directories 10, 552, 696
Exuma 365
periodicals 694
Butterflies 210
By intervention of Providence 104-105
By sail and wind: the story of the Bahamas 267
Byrne, R. 124, 701

C

Cable Beach
travel guides 95
Cady, D. 81
Caicos Island
first landfall 282

Caicos Islands
  first landfall 289, 291
Caldecott, A. 430
Campbell, D.G. 125
*Camps and cruises of an
  ornithologist* 203
Canella alba 139
Canzoneri, A. 421, 423-424
Capiscum 138
Caribbean 110
  economy 526
  fish 159-162, 164-165,
    171-172
  flowers 143, 146-148
  history 230, 248-250
  relations with the
    Bahamas 499, 532
  relations with the United
    States 528
  tourism 117
  travel guides 69, 72
  trees 148
*Caribbean basin to the year
  2000: demographic,
  economic, and
  resource-use trends in
  seventeen countries* 528
*Caribbean economic
  handbook* 526
*Caribbean reef
  invertebrates and
  plants: . . .* 162
Caribbean year book 10
Carman, B. 596
Carmichael, New
  Providence 402
  history 370
Carrington, V. 502
Carson, E.A. 686-687
Cartoons 501
Cartwright, D. 371
Casinos 565-566
  and organized crime 444,
    558
Cat Island 135
  alcohol consumption 453
  anthropology 453
  archaeology 243
  birds 182, 194
  boat-building 453
  bush medicine 453
  Catholic Church 428
  ecology 219
  family life 453

farming 453
  first landfall 303
  fishing 453
  flora 152
  geology 219
  kinship 453
  landforms 49
  molluscs 219
  poverty 453
  shells 219
  vegetation 124
  women 453
Catalyn, J.J. 600-601, 619
Catesby, Mark 127, 132,
    136-137, 186, 295
*Catesby's birds of colonial
  America* 186
Catholic Church
  Cat Island 428
  history 376, 427
  San Salvador 376
Caves 37
  development 36
Cay Sal Bank
  birds 221
  reptiles 221
*Census of population and
  housing, 1980:
  preliminary review*
  393
Censuses
  1970 393, 396
  1980 391, 393
  methodology 394
Central America
  fish 159
*Central American and West
  Indian archaeology;
  . . .* 246-247
Central Bank of the
  Bahamas 525, 546, 548
*Central Bank of the
  Bahamas: origin,
  functions, activities* 548
Ceramics
  Arawaks 246
  Lucayans 239, 242
Chalmers, George 324
*Changing house types in
  Long Bay Cays: . . .*
  457
Chaplin, C.C.G. 174
Chapman, F.M. 203, 205,
  207

Chibwa, A.K. 398-399
Child care
  Congo Town, Andros
    Island 458
Christ Church Cathedral
  260
*Christ Church Cathedral
  tombstone and
  memorial plaque
  inscriptions* 260
Christie, H.C. 440, 596,
  602
Christmas, R.J. 77
Christmas, W. 77
*Christopher Columbus,
  mariner* 294
Chronologies 1, 11, 14, 497
Chronostratigraphy 38
Church in the West Indies
  430
Churches 259-260, 428
Civics 502
Civics for the Bahamas 502
Class
  Green Turtle Cay,
    Abaco 447
*Classified digest of the
  records of the Society
  for the Propagation of
  the Gospel in Foreign
  Parts, 1701-1892 (with
  much supplementary
  information)* 432
Clavel, M. 417
Cleare, W.T. 413
Clench, W.J. 214, 216-220
Clifford, Bede Edmund
  Hugh 270, 344
Climate 10, 21, 43-44, 107,
  111, 125, 135, 184, 574
  and health 479
  bibliographies 701
  maps 30
Climate of the Bahamas 21
*Climbing clouds: stories
  and poems from the
  Bahamas* 593
Clough, G.C. 126, 211-212
*Coastal landforms of Cat ·
  Island, Bahamas: . . .*
  49
Coats of arms 262
Cocaine crisis 472
Cochran, H. 334

Cockcroft, G.A. 324
Cocoloba 138
Coconut Grove Public
  Library 680
Cohen, S. 82
Colin, P.L. 162
Collection of statistics on
  women in the
  Bahamas, 1979-1985
  578
College of the Bahamas
  595
Collie, S.S. 603
Collinwood, D.W. 5, 446,
  488
Colonial civil servant 343
Columbia University.
  Institute of Urban
  Environment 576
Columbus and his world:
  proceedings of the first
  San Salvador
  Conference 277
Columbus, Christopher
  277, 279, 287, 294, 302
  bibliographies 698
  burial 296
  first landfall
    Atwood Cay 299
    Caicos Island 282
    Caicos Islands 289, 291
    Cat Island 303
    Egg Island 277, 282,
      284-285
    Grand Turk Island
      282, 300, 303
    Royal Island 284-285
    Samana Cay 278-279,
      281, 297, 299
    San Salvador 238, 277,
      283, 286-287, 294
    South Caicos Island
      292-293
    Turks and Caicos
      Islands 277
    Watlings Island 277,
      280 282, 288, 290,
      294-296, 298,
      300-302
  folklore 409
Columbus landfall in
  America and the
  hidden clues in his
  Journal 278

Columbus never came 289
Commerce
  directories 696
  editorial cartoons 501
  Loyalist influences 326
Commonwealth of the
  Bahamas: profile of an
  offshore investment
  centre 546
Communications 10, 87,
  574
  19th century 337
  20th century 339
  Exuma 365
Compleat guide to Nassau
  94
Conception Island
  flora 152
Conch eaters 565, 656
Condent, Captain 311
Conflicts toward liberation
  495
Congo Town, Andros
  Island
  child care 458
Connor, H.A. 185
Constitution 510-518, 520
  1964 517-518
  1969 515-516
  1973 511-512
  development 4, 510
Constitutional development
  of the Bahamas 510
Contemporary international
  relations of the
  Caribbean 532
Contracts
  law 520
Conway, M. 550
Cooking 16
Coombs, O. 500
Cooper, B. 459, 604
Cooper's Town, Abaco
  courtship 461
  household composition
    461
  marriage 461
Coral reefs 32, 36-37, 53,
  57, 64-65, 125, 159,
  162, 164, 168, 170-172,
  177, 181
  Andros Island 56, 176,
    179
  bibliographies 177

Bimini 173
  ecology 159, 168, 171,
    177
  fauna 159, 162, 166, 177
  flora 166
Correll, D.S. 142
Correll, H.B. 142
Cory, C.B. 208
Cost of living 535
Costa Rica
  emigration to 551
Cottman, Evans W. 478
Cotton industry 385
Courtship
  Cooper's Town, Abaco
    461
  Long Bay Cays, Andros
    Island 465-466
Cousteau, J.-Y. 28
Craton, M. 85, 255, 265,
  387, 702
Crime
  law 520
  organized 444, 558
Crocker, J. 533
Cronau, R. 296
Crooked Island
  birds 184
  Gordon Hill 242
  landforms 58
  medicine 478
Crossing Rocks, Abaco
  social values 463
Crowley, D.J. 406-407
Cruising guide to the
  Abacos and northern
  Bahamas 68, 80
Cruising handbook 75
Cruising voyage around the
  world 312
Crusoe's captain: being the
  life of Woodes Rogers,
  seaman, trader,
  colonial governor 307
Crust of the earth: a
  symposium 57
Crustaceans 125, 134, 162
Cuba 104-105
Cubagua 228
Culmer, J. 596
Culture 1-2, 5, 8, 14-15,
  18, 71, 451
  bibliographies 703
  Eleuthera 448

Loyalist influences 318
Curran, H.A. 32
Currency 73, 535
Currents
 see Ocean currents
Curry, R.A. 409
Custom and conflict on a
 Bahamian Out-Island
 443

D

Dalleo, P.T. 254, 258, 379
Davidson, B. 566
Davies, J.B. 209
Davies, J.E. 477
Davis, Howell 311
De Albuquerque, K. 551
De Backer, R. 527
De Booy, T.H.N. 233-234
De Laubenfels, M.W. 178
De Marigny, Marie Alfred
 Fouquereaux 349, 351-
 353
De Vorsey, L. 282
Declaration of commitment
 489
Deep into the blue holes 25
Defries, A.D. 103, 106
DeGeorge, G. 470
Del Lorraine, A. 112
Delancey Town, New
 Providence
 history 370, 450
Demographic and social
 characteristics 391
Demographic aspects of the
 Bahamian population,
 1901-1974 395
Demographic yearbook 392
Demography 22
Development plan of New
 Providence Island and
 the city of Nassau 576
Dialect 591
Dictionaries
 biographical 497, 697
 language 592
Dictionary of Bahamian
 English 592
Dietz, R.S. 46
Diole, P. 28
Diplomatic and consular

affairs 10, 16
directories 696
Directories
 business 10, 696
 commercial 696
 diplomatic 696
 finance 696
 government 16, 497
 manufacturing 696
 politics 497
Discographies 665
Discovery of America and
 the landfall of
 Columbus 296
Discovery of a nation: an
 illustrated history of
 the Bahamas 266
Diver's almanac: guide to
 the Bahamas and
 Caribbean 69
Diving 69, 73, 82-83, 131
Diving and snorkeling
 guide to the Bahamas:
 Nassau and New
 Providence Island 73
Diving guide to the
 Bahamas: including
 Turks and Caicos
 Islands 83
Documents
 historical 257, 271-274,
 325, 356
Dodge, S. 94, 320, 357-
 359, 446, 488, 690
Doing business in the
 Bahamas 542
Dolley, C.S. 157
Dolly and the doctor bird
 645
Dominica 113
 Loyalists 321
Dominican Republic
 emigration to 551
Dominique, M. 401
Doran, E. 58
Doran, M.F. 450
Dowson, W. 434
Drug abuse 460, 472
Drug trade 7, 469-476
 and banking 470
 and industry 550
Drysdale, R. 333
Du Pont, A.F. 131
Duke of Windsor's war:

from Europe to the
 Bahamas, 1939-1945
 346-347
Dundas, Charles Cecil
 Farquharson 345
Dunigan, K. 81
Dunn, O. 282
Dunnett, D. 645
Dupuch, Alfred Etienne
 Jerome 688-689, 691
Dupuch, E. 315
Dupuch, E.A.P. 351, 591
Dupuch, S.P. 85
Durlacher-Wolper, R.G.
 283, 288
Durrell, Z. 362

E

Early settlers of the
 Bahama Islands, with
 a brief account of the
 American Revolution
 . . . 271
East Plana Cay
 fauna 126, 211-212
 vegetation 126
Eastern Burial Ground 263
Eastern Public Library 680
Echinoderms 170, 219
Ecology 54, 63, 123
 Andros Island 180
 blue holes 27
 Caribbean 123
 Cat Island 219
 coral reefs 159, 168, 171,
 177
 Eleuthera 448
 Florida 123
 Hopetown Reef 53
 Little San Salvador 219
Ecology and oceanography
 of the coral-reef tract,
 Abaco Island,
 Bahamas 53
Economic activity and
 income 391
Economic development 13,
 498, 513, 532, 554
Economic history of the
 Bahamas 529
Economics applied to the

Bahamas 531
Economy 523-535
  19th century 329, 333,
    337, 382
  20th century 1, 3, 5, 7-8,
    17, 33, 267, 354, 400,
    500, 523-524, 526-528,
    532, 534, 541
  and tourism 119, 121,
    533
  bibliographies 703
  Caribbean 526, 528
  Green Turtle Cay,
    Abaco 447, 456
  history 529
  Long Bay Cays, Andros
    Island 465
  Loyalist influences 318,
    385
  slave 382
  statistics 391, 524-525,
    536
Editorial cartoons 501
Education 5, 19, 583-587
  19th century 276, 330,
    337
  20th century 339, 425,
    498
  agricultural 568
  and middle class 445
  editorial cartoons 501
  Methodist Church 583
  statistics 391, 396
  vocational 535
Education 391
Educational development
  in an archipelagic
  nation: . . . 585, 587
Edward VIII, King of
  Great Britain
  see Windsor, Duke of
Edwards, B. 253
Edwards, C.L. 405, 412,
  418-420
Edwards, K.L. 528
Egg birds 203
Egg Island
  first landfall 277, 282,
    284-285
Elbow Cay, Abaco 53
Eldridge, J. 483
Elections 491, 557
  1967 496, 504
Electric rays 164

Elements of Bahamian law
  520
Eleuthera 101-102, 135
  birds 185
  culture 448
  ecology 448
  environment 448
  flora 152
  folk-tales 410
  geography 364
  geology 60
  Harbour Island 9
    libraries 679
    statistics 536
    travel guides 89
  history 363-364, 448
  industry 364
  molluscs 214
  proverbs 410-411
  puzzles 410
  riddles 410-411
  Spanish Wells 9
    statistics 536
    travel guides 89
  statistics 536
  toasts 410
  tourism 122
  travel guides 80, 89
  Upper Bogue 9
Eleuthera: the island called
  "Freedom" 364
Eleutherian Adventurers
  304
  fiction 657
Emancipation 425
Emigrants
  Costa Rica 551
  Dominican Republic 551
  Florida 551
  Guatemala 551
  Honduras 551
  Mexico 551
  Miami 403, 549
  Panama 551
  South Carolina 551
Emigration
  19th century 337
Emlen, J.T. 191
Empire at war 340
Employment 535, 557
  statistics 553
Eneas, Cleveland Wilmore
  372, 425
Energy

Caribbean 528
  consumption 528
Engardio, P. 470
Engineering
  bibliographies 702
England, Edward 311
Environment 8, 574-577
  bibliographies 703
  Eleuthera 448
Environmental atlas of the
  Tongue of the Ocean,
  Bahamas 50
Ephemeral islands: a
  natural history of the
  Bahamas 125
Ethnography
  bibliographies 700
Ethnology
  Andros Island 232
Eshbaugh, W.H. 481
Evans, F.C. 22
Ewan, J. 136
Exchange controls 537,
  542, 552
Exports 276, 535, 542
  statistics 556
Expressing myself 600
External trade statistics
  report 556
Exuma
  agriculture 365
  bush medicine 483
  business 365
  communications 365
  fauna 128
  flora 128, 153
  geography 365
  government 365
  Great Exuma Island
    geology 34
    slavery 387
  history 365
  Norman's Cay 469
  parks 128
  statistics 365, 536
  Stocking Island
    geology 34
  tourism 122
  transportation 365
  travel guides 88, 91, 365
Exuma, historical/pictorial
  guide 365

F

Facies anatomy and diagenesis of a Bahamian ooid shoal 41
Faculty of Law Library. University of the West Indies 519
Fadiman, A. 660
Faith that moved the mountain 496
Family 446, 455, 460, 549
  Cat Island 453
  slave 378, 387
Family Island Regatta 91
Family Islands 4, 16
  see also Out Islands
Fang, C. 702
Fanning, David 326
Farley, M.F. 305
Farquharson, C. 389
Fauna 19, 66, 107, 110-111, 114, 123, 125-126, 128, 134-136, 162, 223
  Abaco 183, 189, 218, 362
  Acklins Island 184
  amphibians 180, 219
  Andros Island 180, 200-201, 206
  arthropods 170
  bats 213
  Bimini 158, 194, 197, 216, 222
  birds 125-126, 134, 136-137, 182-208, 221, 362
  blue holes 24, 26, 29
  boobies 203
  butterflies 210
  Caribbean 123
  Cat Island 182, 194, 219
  Cay Sal Bank 221
  coral reefs 159, 162, 166, 177
  Crooked Island 184
  crustaceans 125, 134, 162
  East Plana Cay 126, 211-212
  echinoderms 170, 219
  egg birds 203
  electric rays 164
  Eleuthera 184, 214
  Exuma 128
  fish 114, 125, 159-162,
164-165, 167-168, 171-172, 174, 180-181
  flamingos 188, 196, 198-201, 203, 205
  flatworms 170
  Florida 123
  gastropods 125
  Grand Bahama Island 191, 218
  Great Inagua Island 133, 183-184, 188-189, 200
  herpetology 133
  Hispaniola 215
  Hogsty Reef 52
  hutia 211-213
  Inagua 199
  insects 125, 137-138, 209-210
  jellyfish 164
  Little Abaco Island 206
  Little Inagua Island 184
  Little San Salvador 219
  lizards 126, 222
  lobsters 169
  Long Island 217
  mammals 125, 137, 211-213
  man-o-war birds 203
  marine worms 162
  Mayaguana Island 184, 220
  molluscs 162, 168, 170, 175, 214-220
  New Providence 192
  parrots 183, 189
  polyps 170
  raccoons 213
  reptiles 125, 137, 180, 219, 221-223
  San Salvador 190, 194
  sandflies 209
  sea anemones 162
  sea cucumbers 162
  sea fans 162
  sea urchins 162, 164
  segmented worms 170
  sharks 158
  shells 134, 175, 216, 220, 362
  spiders 125
  sponges 23, 162-163, 178, 181
  starfish 162
  Watlings Island 190
Fawkes, Randol F. 496, 509
Feduccia, A. 186
Fenisong, R. 642
Ferguson, Amos 661
Ferns 139, 142
Fertility 528
  Caribbean 528
  New Providence 392
  slave 378, 387
  statistics 391-392
Field, R.M. 63
Field guide to coral reefs of the Caribbean and Florida: . . . 159
Field guide to the geology of San Salvador 37
Field guide to some carbonate rock environments: Florida Keys and Western Bahamas 42
Field guide to southeastern and Caribbean seashores: . . . 123
Field guide to the vegetation of San Salvador Island, the Bahamas 141
Fielding's Bermuda and the Bahamas 77-78
Fields, M.H. 87
Fifty tropical fruits of Nassau 150
Finance 10, 16, 524, 526, 530, 536-548, 552
  directories 696
Finlay, H.H. 410
First Loyalist settlements in Abaco, Carleton and Marsh's Harbour 320
First ten years, 1969-1979: history of the Bahamian archives 685
Fish 114, 125, 159-162, 164-165, 167-168, 171-172, 174, 181
  Andros Island 180
  Bermuda 159-161, 165, 171-172
  Caribbean 159-162, 164-165, 171-172
  Central America 159
  Florida 159-160, 162,

164-165, 167, 171-172
Gulf of Mexico 165
South America 159
Fisher, R.C. 79
Fisheries 523, 525, 527,
    530, 570
Fishes of the Bahamas 174
*Fishes of the Caribbean
    reefs, the Bahamas
    and Bermuda* 161
Fishing 2, 85, 90, 535
    Cat Island 453
    Green Turtle Cay,
        Abaco 468
    Lucayans 224-225
    San Salvador 376
*Fishing guide to the
    Bahamas: including
    Turks and Caicos
    Islands* 90
Fitz-James, J. 416
Flags 262
Flamingo hunt 198
Flamingos 188, 196, 198-
    201, 203, 205
Flatworms 170
Fleming, I. 643
Flora 19, 66, 107, 110-111,
    123-126, 128, 134-137,
    139, 142-143, 151, 157
    Abaco 362
    Andros Island 156
    Bermuda 143
    Berry Islands 153
    Bimini 149
    blue holes 29
    Caribbean 123, 143, 146-
        148
    Cat Island 124, 152
    Conception Island 152
    coral reefs 166, 181
    East Plana Cay 126
    Eleuthera 152
    Exuma 128, 153
    ferns 139, 142
    Florida 123
    flowers 142-143, 145-148
    fruits 141, 150
    Grand Bahama Island
        153
    grasses 142
    Great Inagua Island 154
    herbs 143
    Little Inagua Island 154

Little San Salvador 152
Long Island 152
Hogsty Reef 52
Nassau 150
New Providence 153,
    155-156
    orchids 143
    palms 139, 142, 144
    Rose Island 153
    San Salvador 140-141
    seagrasses 138-139
    shrubs 143
    sisal 134
    South America 148
    trees 114, 142-144, 148,
        480
    Turks and Caicos Islands
        142
    Watlings Island 152
*Flora of the Bahamian
    archipelago (including
    the Turks and Caicos
    Islands)* 142
*Flora of New Providence
    and Andros . . .* 156
Florida 104
    emigration to 551
    fish 159-160, 162, 164-
        165, 167, 171-172
Florida Keys
    geology 42
    travel guides 75
Flowers 142-143, 145-148
    Bermuda 143
    Caribbean 143, 146-148
    South America 148
Flowers of the Bahamas
    145
*Flowers of the Caribbean,
    the Bahamas, and
    Bermuda* 143
*Flowers of the West Indies:
    Caribbean and
    Bahamas* 147
*Flying the Bahamas: the
    weekend pilot's guide*
    78
Flying guides 68, 78, 81
FNM *see* Free National
    Movement
*Focus on the future: white
    paper on education*
    585-586
Fodor's Bahamas 70, 78, 86

*Fodor's Caribbean and the
    Bahamas* 70
*Fodor's Caribbean,
    Bahamas, and
    Bermuda* 70
Fodor's fun in the Bahamas
    74
*Fodor's guide to the
    Caribbean, Bahamas,
    and Bermuda* 70
*Folk tales of Andros
    Island, Bahamas* 405-
    406, 412
Folklore 2, 107, 404-420
    and legal system 443
    and obeah 436
    Blackbeard 409
    Christopher Columbus
        409
    Eleuthera 410
    hags 417
    Lucayans 409
    proverbs 408, 410, 414,
        480
    puzzles 410
    riddles 404, 410, 415,
        631
    toasts 410
Folk-songs 409, 418, 451
Folk-tales 404, 406-407,
    409, 416, 418-419, 451
    Andros 406, 412
    Eleuthera 410
    Fortune Island 413
    Green Turtle Cay,
        Abaco 420
Food and drink 568, 674-
    677
Food in the Bahamas 568
Forbes, J.R.T. 101-102
Ford, E. 422
Ford, L. 644
Ford, Paul Dean 422
Foreign investment 507,
    523, 537, 542, 552
Foreign relations 5, 354,
    498, 513
    with the Caribbean 499,
        532
    with the United States
        261, 335, 475-476, 493,
        499
Forestry 535, 574-575, 577
    bibliographies 703

Forests 574-575, 577
Fort Charlotte 373
Fort Fincastle 373
Fort Montagu 315, 373
Fort Nassau 314, 373
Fort Winton 373
Fortifications 116, 259, 373
Fortunate Islands, being adventures with the Negro in the Bahamas 103
Fortune Island 413
43 poems 627
Fossils 36-38, 195, 202
  Lucayan 226, 236
Four native plays for stage and radio 637
Fox, G.V. 298-299
Fox Hill, New Providence history 370
Fox Hill Public Library 680
Francis, C. 539, 546
Francis, C.E. 534
Fraser, P.D. 526
Free National Movement (FNM) 489
Freeport, Bahamas: a dream come true 366
Freeport/Lucaya, Grand Bahama Island
  business directories 10
  history 366, 368, 558
  migration 393
  tourism 122
  travel guides 92-93, 368
Freeport/Lucaya, Grand Bahama Island 93
Frick, G.F. 127, 132, 136
From Adam's rib to women's lib 459
From Columbus to Castro: the history of the Caribbean, 1492-1966 249
From sand banks to Treasure Cay 360
Frommer's Dollarwise Guide to Bermuda and the Bahamas, 1986-87- . 71
Fruits 141, 150
  Nassau 150
  see also Pineapple industry

Fruits from Africa 628
Fugitive in the Bahamas 607
Fulk, G. 126
Funnel of gold 306
Fuson, R.H. 277, 279

G

Galapagos Islands 28
  vegetation 124
Gambier, New Providence history 370
Gambling 94, 565-566
  and organized crime 444, 504, 558
Games 480
Gardiner, J. 157
Gardner, R.E. 463
Garrard, J. 145, 147
Garrett, P. 35
Garrett, W.E. 281
Gastropods 125
Gates, A. 74
Gebelein, C.D. 44
General information guide on the economy of the Bahamas 525
Geography 11, 13, 20-31, 54, 96, 107, 184, 267
  Abaco 359
  bibliographies 701
  Bimini 149
  Eleuthera 364
  Exuma 365
  physical 20
Geology 20, 22, 32-65, 111, 125, 134-135, 184, 253
  Abaco 60
  Andros Island 41, 43, 56, 61
  Bahama Platform 20, 46, 57
  bibliographies 44, 701-702
  Cat Island 49, 219
  chronostratigraphy 38
  Eleuthera 60
  Florida Keys 42
  Great Bahama Bank 56, 61-62
  Great Bahama Canyon 45, 47

Great Exuma Island 34
Hogsty Reef 52
Little San Salvador 219
mineralogy 51
New Providence 35, 114
Pleistocene 36, 42, 51, 57
post-Pleistocene 36
Ragged Island 60
San Salvador 36-38
Stocking Island 34
stratigraphy 32, 36-37, 63
structural 63
Tertiary 57
Tongue of the Ocean 45, 47, 55
Geology of Great Exuma Island: . . . 34
Geomorphology 49, 58
Gerace, D.T. 37, 240, 277
Gerace, K. 319
Gibbs, G. 302-03
Gibson, T. 664
Gillis, W.T. 701
Ginsburg, R.N. 40
Giovanni, J. 673
Gisburn, H.G.D. 573
Gnam, R. 183
Goggin, J.M. 232, 327
Goodson, G. 165
Goombay 94
Gordon Hill, Crooked Island 242
Gould, R.T. 295
Gould, S.J. 35
Government 4, 8, 10, 17, 451, 486-509
  19th century 109, 253, 276
  20th century 267, 343, 345
  1920s 19
  and tourism 119
  corruption 473, 550
  directories 16, 497
  Exuma 365
Graham, F. 188
Graham, N.A. 528
Granberry, J. 228, 231, 241-242, 245, 698
Grand Bahama 367
Grand Bahama Island 106
  birds 191

blue holes 25
flora 153
forestry 575, 577
Freeport/Lucaya
    history 366, 368, 558
    tourism 122
    travel guides 92-93,
        368
history 366-368
molluscs 218
travel guides 70, 75, 79-
    80, 92-93
Grand Caicos Island 234
Grand Turk Island
    first landfall 282, 300,
        303
    landforms 58
Grant's Town, New
    Providence
    history 370, 450
Grant's Town Public
    Library 680
Grasses 142
Grau Triana, P. 280
Gravity surveys 60, 63
Great Bahama Bank 33, 40
    geology 56, 59, 61-62
    lobsters 169
    travel guides 88
Great Bahama Canyon 45,
    47
Great Britain. Parliament
    511-512, 515-518
*Great days of piracy in the
    West Indies* 308
Great Exuma Island,
    Exuma
    fossils 202
    geology 34
    slavery 387
Great Inagua Island 133
    see also Inagua
    birds 183-184, 188-189,
        200
    fauna 133
    flora 154
    tourism 122
Green Cay 100, 135
Green Turtle Cay, Abaco
    420
    agriculture 468
    class 447
    economy 447, 456
    fishing 468

folk-tales 420
housing 468
nutrition 468
politics 447, 456
race relations 447, 456
religion 447
sanitation 468
social organization 447
tourism 447, 456
*Green Turtle Cay: an
    island in the Bahamas*
    447
Greenberg, I. 164, 172
Greenberg, J. 164, 172
Grenada
    obeah 441
Gropp, A.E. 682-683
Groundwater 574
Groves, Wallace 366, 566
*Growth of the modern West
    Indies* 250
Gruber, S.H. 158
*Guanahani again: the
    landfall of Columbus
    in 1492* 292-293
Guatemala
    emigration to 551
Guettermann, S.F. 69
*Guide and history of Hope
    Town* 358
*Guide to African villages in
    New Providence* 370
*Guide to libraries and
    archives in Central
    America and the West
    Indies, Panama,
    Bermuda, and British
    Guiana, . . .* 682
*Guide to the records of the
    Bahamas* 684, 687
*Guidebook for modern
    Bahamian platform
    environments* 44
Gulf of Mexico
    fish 165
Gulf Stream 16, 114
Gullah 589

H

Hackett, P. 526
Haile, P. 596
Haiti

voodoo 439
Haitian immigrants 7, 401-
    402
*Haitian problem: illegal
    migration to the
    Bahamas* 402
Halberstein, R.A. 477, 482
Halkitis, M. 21
Halliday, D. 645
Halophytes 139
*Handbook on alcoholism
    in the Bahamas* 449
*Handguide to the coral reef
    fishes of the Caribbean
    and adjacent tropical
    waters including
    Florida, Bermuda and
    the Bahamas* 159-160
Hanna, A.D. 534
Hannau, H.W. 12, 92-93,
    97, 145, 147, 168, 171
Harbour Island, Eleuthera
    9
    libraries 679
    statistics 536
    travel guides 89
Hardie, L.A. 43
Hargreaves, B. 148
Hargreaves, D. 148
Harnanan, I.C. 493
Harris, P.M. 41
Harrison, W. 701-702
Hart, Miss (pseud.) 112
Hartwell, G.W. 90
Hassam, J.T. 275
Hawaii
    vegetation 124
Haweis, S. 181
Hawes, Jerome 428
Hawes, John Cyril
    see Hawes, Jerome
Hayes, N.T. 100
Headquarters, New
    Providence
    history 370
Health 5, 111, 135, 477-479
    and climate 479
    bibliographies 477
    Bimini 477
    mental 460
    slave 378, 386
Heatter, B. 646
Hecht, M.K. 213
Hedrick, B.C. 405, 435, 665

Helweg-Larsen, K. 289, 363

Hemingway, E. 647

Hendricks, R.E. 584

Henry, P.W.T. 575

Herbal medicine and home remedies: a pot pourri in Bahamian culture 480

Herbs 143

Hermit of Cat Island: the life of Fra Jerome Hawes 428

Herpetology 133

Herrnkind, W.F. 169

Higgs, H.B. 98, 484, 677

Highlights in Bahamian history 256

Hines, N.C. 368

His light for an island nation: a missionary account of God's faithfulness to His Word in the Bahama Islands 422

Hispaniola
molluscs 215

Historic forts of Nassau 373

Historic Nassau 371

Historical documents relating to the Bahama Islands 273

Historical geography of the British colonies 23

Historiography 254, 258

History 1-3, 7-8, 10-14, 23, 66, 71, 76, 85-86, 94, 96, 108, 135, 250, 252-253, 255-256, 261-262, 265-268, 270, 451
15th-19th centuries 257, 276
17th century 275, 304
17th-18th centuries 305-312, 374
17th-19th centuries 378, 380, 388
17th-20th centuries 271
18th century 313-318, 320-323, 325-326
18th-19th centuries 319, 324, 384
19th century 327-338, 371, 383, 389
19th-20th centuries 382, 445
20th century 339-356
Abaco 257, 320, 355, 357-362
American Civil War 89, 331-336
American Revolution 313-316
Anglican Church 423, 429-430, 433
apprenticeship system 378, 388
Baptist Church 421, 423-424
bibliographies 702
Bimini 149
Caribbean 230, 248-250
Catholic Church 376, 427-428
chronologies 1, 11, 14, 497
church 260, 428
communications 337, 339
documents 257, 271-274, 325, 356
economy 329, 333, 337, 529
education 276, 330, 337, 339
Eleuthera 363-364, 448
Eleutherian Adventurers 304
emigration 337
Exuma 365
First World War 340-341
Grand Bahama Island 366-368
Hog Island 375
House of Assembly 272
immigration 337
independence 355, 359
industry 329, 337, 339
justice 109
lighthouses 269
Lords Proprietors 275
Loyalists 99, 253, 257, 317-326, 358, 371, 385
Methodist Church 434
Nassau 99, 116, 313-316, 332-335, 369, 371-372, 450
New Providence 276, 304, 313-316, 369-374, 378
obeah 435-436, 439
Paradise Island 375
periodicals 693
police force 338
politics 503
postal system 572-573
prehistory 224-236
prohibition 342, 345
religion 421-424, 427-434
riot (1942) 347-348, 500, 557
San Salvador 376
Second World War 341
slave trade 228
slavery 113, 228, 318, 327, 377-389
social 259, 319, 372
social conditions 337
strike (1958) 500
technology 339
tourism 120, 329
trade 324, 333
voodoo 439
Wesleyan-Methodist Church 431
West Indies 248, 250-253

History and guide to the Bahama islands, . . . 108

History, civil and commercial, of the British West Indies. With a continuation to the present time 253

History of the Bahamas 255, 265, 702

History of the Bahamas House of Assembly 272

History of the British West Indies 252

History of the Isle of Providence 374

Hoffman, C.A. 238, 244

Hog Island 181
see also Paradise Island history 375

Hog Island Battery 373

Hogsty Reef 52

Holiday with a vengeance 655

Holm, J.A. 589-590, 592

Holmes, F. 340
*Homeward bound: a
   history of the Bahamas
   to 1850, with a
   definitive study of
   Abaco in the American
   Loyalist plantation
   period* 257
Honduras
   emigration to 551
Hone, R. 522
Hope Town, Abaco
   history 358
   travel guides 89, 358
Hopetown Reef 53
Hopkins, J.W. 5
Hotels
   historic 259
Houghton, H. 587
Houghton Report 587
House of Assembly 272,
   514
Household composition
   Abaco 464
   Andros Island 462, 467
   Cooper's Town, Abaco
   461
   Long Bay Cays, Andros
   Island 465
*Household expenditure in
   the Bahamas, 1973*
   547, 553
Household income, 1986-
   536
Housing
   Green Turtle Cay,
   Abaco 468
   historic 259, 264
   Long Bay Cays, Andros
   Island 457
   statistics 393
Houts, M. 349
Howard, R.A. 149
Hughes, C.A. 491
Hunte, G. 11
Hurley, R.J. 47
Hutia 211-213
Hydrography 39, 62
Hydrology 32, 44

I

*I could talk old-story good:
   creativity in Bahamian
   folklore* 406
Ice cubes 629
IDB *see* Inter-American
   Development Bank
IDB in the Bahamas 530
Illing, L.V. 59
Immigrants
   Haitians 7, 401-402
   West Indian 400
Immigration 498, 552
   19th century 337, 379
   20th century 354, 400
Imperial Lighthouse
   Service 269
Imports 276, 535
   statistics 556
*In the coral reefs of the
   Caribbean, Bahamas,
   Florida, Bermuda* 168,
   171
*In the days of yesterday
   and in the days of
   today: an overview of
   Bahamian folkmusic*
   665
*In a forgotten colony, being
   some studies in Nassau
   and at Grand Bahama
   during 1916* 106
*In sunny isles; chapters
   treating chiefly of the
   Bahama Islands and
   Cuba* 431
*In the trades, the tropics,
   and the roaring forties*
   110
*In the wake of Columbus:
   islands and
   controversy* 282
Inagua 130
   see also Great Inagua
   Island
   birds 199
   libraries 679
   medicinal plants 485
*Inagua: which is the name
   of a very lonely and
   nearly forgotten island*
   130
Ince, B.A. 532

Income 528
   Caribbean 528
   statistics 396, 536, 553
Independence 6, 355-356,
   513-514
*Independence for the
   Commonwealth of the
   Bahamas* 513-514
Industry 549-567
   19th century 110, 329,
   337
   20th century 1, 10, 13,
   19, 267, 339, 343, 523,
   526-527, 530, 532, 535,
   554
   and drug trade 550
   Eleuthera 364
*Innocent island: Abaco in
   the Bahamas* 362
Insects 125, 137-138, 209-
   210
Insurance 523, 540-541,
   552
   social 442
Inter-American
   Development Bank
   (IDB) 530
Internal migration 397-399
   Puerto Rico 399
*Internal migration in the
   Commonwealth of the
   Bahamas, 1960-1970*
   398
International
   Oceanographic
   Foundation 171
*Introduction to some wild
   flowers of the
   Bahamas and the
   Caribbean* 146
Ireland, J. 544
*Is Massa day dead?: Black
   moods in the
   Caribbean* 500
Isaacs, Kendal 488
Island boy 612
*Island breezes: a collection
   of poems and short
   stories* 603
Island echoes 635
Island Missionary Society
   422
Islands in the stream 647
Islands in the sun 101

Islands of the Bahamas in full colour 12
Isles of summer: or, Nassau and the Bahamas 111
It's a natural fact: obeah in the Bahamas 435
Ives, C. 111

J

Jamaica 105, 113
  Loyalists 321
  obeah 439
  slavery 387
  social insurance 442
  tourism 117
Jellyfish 164
Jingo, wild horse of Abaco 639
Johnson, D.L.S. 503
Johnson, H. 338, 377, 382, 400, 549
Johnson, J.L. 260
Johnson, R.E. 605
Johnson, W.R. 559, 606
Johnston, D. 607, 662
Johnston, Randolph Wardell 660, 662-663
Johnstone, W.K. 608
Jordan, A.T. 508
Jordan, P.B. 480
Journal of the Bahamas Historical Society 693
Journals and other documents on the life and voyages of Christopher Columbus 238
Journey through New Providence 96
Joyce, T.A. 246-247
Judge, J. 278, 281
Judiciary 520
Junkanoo 94, 106, 385, 451, 667-670
  bibliographies 669
Junkanoo 667
Justice
  19th century 109

K

Kaplan, E.H. 123, 159, 165
Karst topography 32, 38
Keegan, W.F. 224-226, 237
Keenan, J. 314
Kelley, J.E. 282
Kent, R. 112, 116, 596
Kepler, C.B. 189
Kernochan, D. 648
Kettell, S. 279
Kiel, G.R. 668
King over the water 346-347
King, W.B. 189
King, W.F.H. 433
King's X: common law and the death of Sir Harry Oakes 349
Kingston Publishers 30
Kinship
  Cat Island 453
Kiwanis Club 425
Klausner, P. 444
Klaw, S. 507
Kline, H. 84
Klingel, G.C. 130, 133
Knowles, D.J. 609
Knowles, L.J. 520
Koopman, K.F. 213
Kornicker, L.S. 54

L

Labour 549-567
  19th century 549
  20th century 549
  bibliographies 551
  legislation 557
  migration 403, 549, 551
  statistics 396, 536, 553
Labour force and income distribution, 1973 547, 553
Labour Party 496
Labour relations 542
Lady Brown's Bahamian cook book: recipes by the ladies of Nassau 677
LaFlamme, A.G. 118, 447, 456, 700
Lake Forsyth, Andros

Island 180
Lake Titicaca 28
Lambert, W. 504
Land bird communities of Grand Bahama Island: the structure and dynamics of an avifauna 191
Land of the pink pearl; or, Recollections of life in the Bahamas 109
Land resources of the Bahamas: a summary 574
Land use 8, 574
  maps 30
Landfall of Columbus on his first voyage to America 301
Landforms 20, 58, 574
  Cat Island 49
  Crooked Island 58
  Grand Turk island 58
Landforms of the southeast Bahamas 58
Landis, R.A. 450
Landscape 20
Langton-Jones, R. 269
Language 10, 588-589, 591
  African influences 590
Lansky, Meyer 566
Last resting place of Columbus 296
Latin American and Caribbean contemporary record 5
Laughin' at wesef: skits 601
Law 520
Law of the sea 493, 520
Lawes, D.N. 79
Laws 519, 521
  slavery 381
Lawson, J. 186
Leasor, J. 353
LeBlanc , R . J. 56
Ledecky-Janecek, E. 213
Lee, C.S. 60
Legacy of the American Revolution to the British West Indies and Bahamas: a chapter out of the history of the American Loyalists 326
Legal system 519-522

and folklore 443
and obeah 443
and politics 443
and religion 443, 452
corruption 475
Mayaguana Island 443,
452
LeGallienne, R. 596, 649
Legislation 519, 522
Lehder, Carlos 469, 473
Leicester, L.A. 286
Lennox, G.W. 143
Lester, G. 431
*Let the church roll on: a
collection of speeches
and writings* 425
Letson, C.A. 405
*Letters from the Bahama
Islands, written in
1823-4* 112
Lewis, G.K. 250
Lewis, V.A. 354
Libraries 678-683
Abaco 679
Harbour Island,
Eleuthera 679
Inagua 679
New Providence 16, 678-
680
*Libraries of Bermuda, the
Bahamas, the British
West Indies, British
Guiana, British
Honduras, Puerto
Rico, and the
American Virgin
Islands: a report to the
Carnegie Corporation
of New York* 683
*Life and death of Sir Harry
Oakes* 349-350
Life in Freeport/Lucaya 92
Lightbourn, C.H. 610
Lighthouses 269
Lignum vitae 16
Lime mud 33, 41
Limestone 33, 57, 574
Lind, A.O. 49
Link, E.A. 290-291
Link, M.C. 290-291
Linley, J.R. 209
*List of documents relating
to the Bahama Islands
in the British Museum*

*and Record Office,
London* 274
Literature
and family life 446
and sexuality 446
anthologies 593-796, 633
novels 597, 604, 607,
612, 614, 630, 639-647,
649-659
plays 595, 623, 632-633,
637
poetry 480, 593, 595-596,
598-600, 602-603, 605,
608-611, 613, 615-622,
624-629, 631, 633-636,
638, 648
prose 595, 608, 619
short stories 593-594,
603, 606, 633
skits 601
Lithification 38
Little, B.D.G. 307
Little, B.G. 574
Little Abaco Island
birds 206
Little Bahama Bank 233
Little Inagua Island
birds 184
flora 154
Little Lake, San Salvador
hydrography 39
sedimentology 39
topography 39
Little San Salvador
ecology 219
flora 152
geology 219
molluscs 219
shells 219
*Living reef: corals and
fishes of Florida, the
Bahamas, Bermuda
and the Caribbean* 172
Lizards 126
Bimini 222
Lloyd, R.M. 48
Lobsters 169
Loftin, R.W. 185-
*Log of Christopher
Columbus* 279
Lomer, G. 83
Long, E.J. 14
Long Bay, San Salvador
238

Long Bay Cays, Andros
Island
courtship 465-466
economy 465
household composition
465
housing 457
Long Island 135
bush medicine 483
flora 152
molluscs 217
Loomis, G. 67
Lords Proprietors 275
Los Coralles
see Hogsty Reef
Love potions 481
Loven, S. 246
Loyalist bi-centennial 317
Loyalists 99, 253, 257, 317-
326, 358, 385
bibliographies 698
fiction 659
in Dominica 321
in Jamaica 321
influences 318, 321, 326,
371, 385
plantations 319
*Loyalists in East Florida,
1774 to 1785: the most
important documents
pertaining thereto* 325
Lucas, C.P. 23, 340
*Lucayan artifacts from the
Bahamas* 233
Lucayans 229, 233-235, 247
bibliographies 698
burial practices 226
ceramics 239, 242
fishing practices 224-225
folklore 409
fossils 226, 236
poetry 602
pottery 239, 243-244
San Salvador 227
slave trade 228
tools 239
Ludington, M.H. 572
Lumbering 357, 360
Lurry-Wright, J.W. 443
see also Wright, J.W.
Lusca 24
Lyons, A.N. 122
Lyons, E. 281
Lyrics of life and love 636

M

McCartney, T.O. 436, 454, 460, 500
McClure, S.A. 481
McCoy, Bill 342
McCulla, P.E. 1
McElroy, J.L. 551
MacIntosh, R.J. 384
McKenna, S. 104-105
McKinnon, D. 113, 253
Maclaury, J.C. 243
MacMillan, D. 670
Magic tree house 614
Magnetometer surveys 60
Major, A. 392, 395
Major, R.H. 300, 302
Malcolm, H.G. 272-274
Malone, V. 358
Malpighiaceae 138
Mammals 125, 137, 211-213
Man with the wart: an Obeah story 440
Man-o-war birds 203
Man-O-War Cay, Abaco 9
history 361
Man-O-War, my island home: a history of an outer Abaco island 361
Manuel, G. 495
Manufacturing 19, 524, 532
directories 696
Manwaring, G.E. 312
Many-splendored fishes of the Atlantic coast including the fishes of the Gulf of Mexico, Florida, Bermuda, the Bahamas and the Caribbean 165
Maps 30-31
agriculture 30
climate 30
land use 30
landforms 58
population 30
Maps of the Bahama Islands 30-31
Maraj, J.A. 585, 587
Maraj Report 585, 587
March, E.W. 577
Marden, L. 281
Mariguana Island

see Mayaguana Island
Marine life 114, 137, 158-181
Marine worms 162
Mark Catesby: the colonial Audubon 127, 132
Marriage
Cooper's Town, Abaco 461
Marshall, D.I. 402
Martel, John 311
Martin, R.A. 166
Martin, T. 6
Mary Read: the pirate wench 310
Mason, F.V.W. 650
Match for a murder 645
Mayaguana Island 233
birds 184
legal system 443, 452
shells 220
Maynard, C.J. 64, 235
Medicinal plants 138, 484
Bimini 477, 482
Exuma 483
Inagua 485
Long Island 483
Medicine
19th century 386, 479
and obeah 436
Bimini 482
Crooked Island 478
Memoir on the topography, weather, and diseases of the Bahama Islands 479
Memoirs of Peter Henry Bruce, Esq., a military officer in the services of Prussia, Russia & Great Britain, . . . 115-116
Mental health 460
Mesa-Lago, C. 442
Meteorology
bibliographies 701
Methodist Church 434
and education 583
Methodist contribution to education in the Bahamas circa 1790-1975 583
Mexico
emigration to 551

Meyer, Prosper 427
Miami
emigration to 403, 549
Miami Herald 351
Michael, J.W. 596
Microbiology 63
Middle class
role 445
Migration 391, 395
internal 397-399
Puerto Rico 399
statistics 396
Migration 391
Miller, J.R. 190
Miller, P.A. 611
Miller, R. 672
Miller, W.H. 304
Milliman, J.D. 52
Mills, T.W. 468
Millspaugh, C.F. 151
Miner, R.W. 179
Mineral resources 528
Caribbean 528
Mineralogy 51
Ministries *see* Bahamas (ministries by name)
Minnis, E.A. 501
Minns, E. 612, 664
Missick, R. 613
Mission to the West India Islands: Dowson's journal for 1810-17 434
Missionaries 422, 431-432
Mitchell, C. 15, 17-18, 196
Mitchell, S. 34
Mock, B.H. 171
Modern Bahamian society 446
Mohl, R.A. 403
Molander, A.B. 277, 282, 284-285
Molluscs 162, 168, 170, 175, 214-220
Abaco 218
Cat Island 219
Eleuthera 214
Grand Bahama Island 218
Hispaniola 215
Little San Salvador 219
Long Island 217
Monetary and financial system of the

Bahamas: growth, structure and operation 541
Moore, J.E. 76
More devil than saint 352
Mores Island 233
Morison, S.E. 238, 290, 294
Morrison, A.J. 114
Mortality
  population 395
  slave 378
Morton, J. 150
Morton, K. 150
Moseley, M. 19
Moulding, M.B. 175
Multer, H.G. 42
Murder of Sir Harry Oakes, Bt. 351
Murdock, J.B. 295, 298
Murphy Town, Abaco
  social values 463
Music 106, 418, 664-666
  bibliographies 665
Musical instruments 114
My political memoirs: a political history of the Bahamas in the 20th century 487
Mysterious island 129

N

Naked island 646
Naked moon 613
Naranjo, R. 471
Nash, G.V. 154
Nassau 96, 101, 104-107, 112, 114-116
  business directories 10
  flamingos 196
  fruits 150
  history 99, 116, 313-316, 332-335, 369, 371-372, 450
  migration 397
  Over-the-Hill district 450
  slums 450
  travel guides 66, 79, 85, 89, 94-95, 97-99
Nassau Daily Tribune 351, 591, 688-691
  indexes 690

Nassau Guardian 501, 506, 690, 692
  indexes 690
Nassau in the Bahamas 97
Nassau Public Library 16, 678-680
Nassau's historic buildings 259
National Audubon Society 188
Nationalist Movement 495
Native trees of the Bahamas 144
Natural history of Carolina, Florida, and the Bahama Islands 127, 136-137, 186
Natural resources 10, 20, 528, 531, 574
  Caribbean 528
Naturalist in the Bahamas: John I. Northrop, October 12, 1861-June 25, 1891; a memorial volume 134
Nelson, R. 65
Nesbitt, Charles Rogers 330
Neuroses in the sun 460
New Bahamian history: Africa's image revisited 254
New Bahamians 490
New beginning 426
New Providence 19, 96, 135
  Adelaide
    history 370
  Bain Town
    history 370, 372
    birds 192
  Carmichael 402
    history 370
  Delancey Town
    history 370
  fertility 392
  flora 153, 155-156
  forestry 575
  fossils 195
  Fox Hill
    history 370
  Gambier
    history 370
  geology 35, 114

Grant's Town
  history 370
Headquarters
  history 370
  history 276, 304, 313-316, 369-374, 378
  libraries 16, 678-680
  migration 393, 397
  pirates 308
  Sandiland's Village
    history 370
  tourism 122
  travel guides 70, 73, 80, 94-99
  urban planning 576
New theory identifying the locale of Columbus' light, landfall and landing 288
New theory on Columbus's voyage through the Bahamas 291
Newell, N.D. 56-57, 61
Newspapers 10, 688-692
  indexes 690
Nicholas, Samuel 314
Nicole, C. 651-653
Night of the lionhead 619
Nightlife 72, 74, 77
1980 census of population and housing: an overview 394
Norman's Cay, Exuma 469
Noronha, F.P. 614
North Caicos Island 234
Northcroft, G.J.H. 107, 615
Northrop, A.R. 156
Northrop, J.I. 134, 156
Notes on Nassau, the capital of the Bahamas 99
Novels 597, 604, 607, 612, 614, 630, 639-647, 649-659
Nutrition
  Green Turtle Cay, Abaco 468

O

Oakes, Harry, Sir 86, 347, 349-353

Obeah 385, 435-441, 451
  and bush medicine 435
  and folklore 436
  and legal system 443
  and medicine 436
  and religion 436
  Andros Island 437
  bibliographies 439
  fiction 440
  Grenada 441
  Jamaica 439
Obeah: witchcraft in the
  West Indies 438, 441
Obregon, M. 277
Ocean canyons 20, 45
Ocean currents 50, 53, 73
Ocean island (Inagua) 130
Ocean Space Center 171
Oceanographic
  Foundation,
  International 171
Oceanography 50
  bibliographies 702
  Hopetown Reef 53
Oceanology 63
Off-shore companies 507,
  527, 538-540, 546
  and organized crime 558
Old Fort 373
Old stories and riddles:
  Bahamiana culturama
  #1 404
Oldmixon, J. 374
Olsen, F. 230
On the Lucayan Indians
  236
On the trail of the Arawaks
  230
Once below a time:
  Bahamian stories 593-
  594
Once was a time, a wery
  good time: an inquiry
  into the folklore of the
  Bahamas 405
Oolites 41, 57
Operculate land mollusks
  of the family
  Annulariidae of the
  Island of Hispaniola
  and the Bahama
  archipelago 215
Orchids 143
Organizations

charitable 4
  civic 4
  social 4
Organized crime 444
  and banking 558
  and gambling 444, 504,
  558, 566
  and politics 444
  and Resorts
  International 444
  and tourism 444
Origins of Tainan culture,
  West Indies 246
Osborn, H.F. 134
Ostracodes 36, 38
Otterbein, C.S. 458
Otterbein, K.F. 437, 457-
  458, 461-462, 465-467
Oulahan, R. 504
Out Island portraits:
  Bahamas, 1946-1956 9
Out Islands 19, 113, 451,
  535, 549
  religion 433
  travel guides 68, 77, 85
  see also Family Islands
Outermost island: an oral
  history of San
  Salvador, the Bahamas
  376
Out-island doctor 478
Over-the-Hill district,
  Nassau 450
Owens-Illinois Company
  360

P

Page, V.K. 654
Paint by Mr. Amos
  Ferguson 661
Painting 661
Palaeontology 184
Paleosoils 36
Palmer, R. 24-27
Palmetto Grove, San
  Salvador 244
Palms 139, 142, 144
Panama
  emigration to 551
Paradise Island
  history 375
  travel guides 95

  see also Hog Island
Paradise Island story 375
Parker, J. 282
Parks
  Exuma 128
Parrots 183, 189
Parry, J.H. 248
Parsons, A. 104
Parsons, E.W.C. 405-406,
  411-412, 415
Pascoe, C.F. 432
Paterson, A. 193
Patterson, J. 144
Paulson, D.R. 194
Peagam, N. 523, 540
Pearl industry 228
Peat, Marwick, Mitchell
  and Company 538
Peek, B. 408
Peffer, R. 68
Peggs, A.D. 268, 312, 389,
  434
Pelican guide to the
  Bahamas 76
Pelzer, J. 332
Pelzer, L. 332
Perez, A.R. 278
Periodicals 10, 693-695
  business 694
  history 693
Perry, R. 655
Personal narration of the
  first voyage of
  Columbus 279
Personalities Caribbean:
  the international guide
  to who's who in the
  West Indies, Bahamas,
  Bermuda, 1965- . 697
Peters, T. 322-323, 335
Peterson, M. 306
Petroglyphs 233
Pfaff, D. 81
Photographs 2, 9, 12, 15, 66
  aerial 82
  blue holes 28
  flowers 145, 147-148
  Freeport/Lucaya 92-93
  Nassau 97
  New Providence 95
  submarine 50, 129, 131,
  168, 171
  trees 148
Photosphere 129

Pi Gal 654
Pictorial Nassau: . . . 95
Pieces of eight 649
Pigeon Creek, San
    Salvador 239, 283
Pilgrims in Paradise 657
Pilkey, O.H. 51
*Pilot's Bahamas aviation
    guide: including the
    Turks and Caicos
    Islands and Haiti* 81
Pinder, W.H. 616
Pindling, Lynden Oscar 3,
    473, 475, 486, 488,
    498, 523, 527, 534, 540
Pine forests of the Bahamas
    575
Pineapple industry 110,
    329, 337, 358, 563
*Pineapple industry of the
    Bahamas* 563
Pirate of the west 602
Pirates 89, 306, 308-309,
    311
*Pirates and buccaneers of
    the Atlantic coast* 309
*Plan for progress and
    prosperity* 505
Plantations 319, 378
    Exuma 387
    Jamaica 387
    Watlings Island 389
Plays 595, 623, 632-633,
    637
PLP
    see Progressive Liberal
    Party
Poems: a toast to you 638
Poems with a point 610
Poetry 480, 593, 595-596,
    598-600, 602-603, 605,
    608-611, 613, 615-622,
    624-629, 631, 633-636,
    638, 648
*Poetry for all occasions,
    Bahamian style* 616
Poldervaart, A. 57
Police force
    19th century 338
    20th century 557
    corruption 475
*Political leadership in the
    Bahamas: interviews
    with the Prime
    Minister of the
    Commonwealth of the
    Bahamas and Leader
    of the Opposition* 488
Politics 451, 486-509
    19th century 324
    20th century 3, 5, 94, 96,
    347, 363, 425, 487-488,
    492, 495-497, 503
    and legal system 443
    and middle class 445
    and organized crime 444
    and race 491
    corruption 473, 475, 504,
    508
    directories 497
    editorial cartoons 501
    Green Turtle Cay,
    Abaco 447, 456
    history 503
    Loyalist influences 318,
    385
    see also Political parties
    by name, e.g.
    Progressive Liberal
    Party; Politicians by
    name, e.g. Pindling,
    L.O.
Polyps 170
Population 10, 390-403,
    535, 574
    census (1970) 393, 396
    census (1980) 391, 393
    distribution 395
    fertility 391-392, 395
    growth 395, 528
    Loyalist influences 326
    maps 30
    migration 391, 395
    mortality 395
    projections 390
    Puerto Rico 399
    slave 378
    statistics 390-391, 536
*Population projections for
    the Bahamas until
    2015* 390
Porter, D. 71
Porter, E. 360
Porter, K.W. 328
Posnett, N.W. 703
*Postage stamps and postal
    history of the Bahamas*
    573
Postal system 572-573
Potter's Cay Battery 373
Pottery
    Lucayans 239, 243-244
Poverty
    Cat Island 453
Power, R.H. 282
Powles, L.D. 109
Prehistory 224-236
    Arawaks 227, 230
    bibliographies 698
    Lucayans 224-229, 233-
    236
Presenting Nassau 98
Prewit-Parker, J. 366
Price, Waterhouse and
    Company 542
Privateers 306
*Proceedings of the first
    symposium on the
    botany of the Bahamas*
    139
*Proceedings of the first
    symposium on the
    geology of the
    Bahamas, March
    23-25, 1982* 38
*Proceedings of the second
    symposium on the
    botany of the Bahamas*
    138
*Proceedings of the second
    symposium on the
    geology of the
    Bahamas, June 16-20,
    1984* 36
*Proceedings of the third
    symposium on the
    geology of the
    Bahamas, June 1986*
    32
*Proconsul: being incidents
    in the life and career of
    the Honourable Sir
    Bede Clifford* 344
Progressive Liberal Party
    (PLP) 487, 492, 495-
    496, 498-499, 503, 505
Progressive Liberal Party.
    Silver Jubilee
    Research Committee
    497
*Progressivism and
    independence: a*

selection from the
writings of L.O.
Pindling, 1969-1978
498
Prose 595, 608, 619
Proverbs 408, 410-411,
414, 480
Providenciales 234
Pryor, R. 45
*Psychologically speaking:
attitudes and cultural
patterns in the
Bahamas* 455
Psychology 455, 460
*Public life of George
Chalmers* 324
Public utilities 10
Public works 574
Puerto Rico
population 399
Puzzles 410
Pye, M. 346-347

Q

Quarterly statistical abstract
581
*Quiet revolution in the
Bahamas* 503

R

Rabley, M.B. 146
*Race and politics in the
Bahamas* 491
Race relations
and politics 491
and tourism 118
Green Turtle Cay,
Abaco 447, 456
Raccoons 213
Ragged Island
geology 60
Rahming, Patrick 617
Rahming, Philip A. 426
Rainey, Froelich G. 242
Rainfall 21
Ramsaran, R.F. 119, 499,
532, 541, 545
Randall, J.E. 128
Rathbun, F.H. 316

Rathbun, John Peck 313,
316
Ray, C. 128
Read, Mary 309-310
Real estate 507, 540, 552
Real McCoy 342
Rea-Salisbury, V. 227
Recaptives 379
Recipes 361, 480, 674-677
Reddy, K.S. 480
Redlhammer, P.R. 584
Redway, J.W. 297
*Reflections of the sun and
soil* 624
Refracted thought 609
*Regional aspects of
carbonate deposition*
56
Reid, I.D.A. 669
Reilly, P.M. 703
*Relic of slavery:
Farquharson's journal
for 1831-32* 389
Religion 4, 10, 19, 106-107,
421-434
and legal system 443,
452
and obeah 436
Anglican Church 423,
429-430, 433
Baptist Church 421, 423-
424
Catholic Church 376,
427-428
Green Turtle Cay,
Abaco 447
Island Missionary
Society 422
Methodist Church 434
Wesleyan-Methodist
Church 431
*Report of the Bahamas
Constitutional
Conference, 1963* 518
*Report of the Bahamas
Constitutional
Conference, 1968* 516
*Report of the Bahamas
Independence
Conference, 1972* 512
*Report of the commission
appointed to enquire
into disturbances in the
Bahamas which took*

place in June 1942 557
*Report of the commission
of inquiry appointed to
inquire into the illegal
use of the Bahamas for
the transshipment of
dangerous drugs for
the United States of
America* 475
*Report of the 1980 census
of population* 391
*Report of the 1970 census
of population* 396
*Report of the 1978 census
of agriculture: final
report* 569
*Report on agricultural
development in the
Bahamas* 571
*Report on education in the
Bahamas* 587
Reptiles 125, 133, 137,
219, 221-223
Andros Island 180
Cay Sal Bank 221
Resorts International
and organized crime 444
Restaurants 71-72, 74, 76-
77, 79, 94
*Review of Bahamian
economic conditions
and post-war problems*
535, 571
Richardson, J.H. 535, 571
Riddles 404, 410-411, 415,
631
Rigby, J.K. 56
Rigg, J.L. 84
Rigg, K. 21
Riley, S. 257
Rindge, F.H. 210
Riot (1942) 347-348, 500,
557
Road: poems 605
Rodgers, W.B. 463-464
Rodriguez, R. 9
Rogers, Woodes 305-308,
310-312
Rolle, Denys 387
Rolle, John 387
Roof of the wind 100
Rose, R. 239
Rose Island
flora 153

Rost, L. 565, 656
Roukema, E. 290
Royal Island
first landfall 284-285
Rucker, J.B. 51
Rum Cay 135, 233
Rum-running 342
Running the blockade: . . .
336
Russell, C.S. 259
Ryan, D. 618

S

Sailing guides 68, 75, 80,
84-85, 87-88
St. Augustine's College
428
St. Augustine's Monastery
428
St. George, A. 355
St. Lucia
tourism 117
St. Matthew's Cemetery
263
*St. Matthew's Cemetery
and the Eastern Burial
Ground* 263
Salinity 39, 53, 62
Salt industry 329, 385, 561
*Salt industry of the
Bahamas* 561
*Salute to friend and foe: my
battles, sieges, and
fortunes* 688-689
Samana Cay
first landfall 278-279,
281, 297, 299
San Salvador
agriculture 376
Arawaks 227
birds 190, 194
Catholic Church 376
first landfall 238, 277,
283, 286-287, 294
fishing 376
geology 36-38
history 376
Little Lake
hydrography 39
sedimentology 39
topography 39
Long Bay 238

Lucayans 227
Palmetto Grove 244
Pigeon Creek 239, 283
vegetation 140-141
*San Salvador: the forgotten
island* 280
Sandflies
and tourism 209
Sandiland's Village, New
Providence
history 370
Sands, Stafford 566
Sanitation 111
Green Turtle Cay,
Abaco 468
Saunders, A. 619-622
Saunders, A.B. 482
Saunders, D.G. 66, 318,
331, 348, 371, 378,
383, 385-386, 445, 687
Saunders, W.V. 623
Savage, E.A. 683
Savishinsky, J.S. 453
Sawyer, W.H. 485
Sayle, William 304
Scaevola 139
Scarpitti, F.R. 558
Schlager, W. 40
Schoener, T.W. 222
Schoepf, J.D. 114
Schreiner, Chrysostom 427
Schwartz, A. 221
Scofield, J. 287
Scott, K. 494
Scott, M.J. 596
Scrivens, Sambo 421
Sculpture 660, 662-663
Sea anemones 162
'Sea Beast' 100
Sea cucumbers 162
Sea fans 162
Sea Gardens 181
Sea urchins 162, 164
Seagrasses 138-139
Sealey, N.E. 20, 117
Seals (symbols) 262
Seapath and other stories
606
Searching for Atlantis 620
Sears, W.H. 229
Secret in the wall 641
*Sedimentation on the
modern carbonate tidal
flats of northwest*

*Andros Island,
Bahamas* 43
Sedimentology 39
Sediments 20, 32-33, 40-41,
43-44, 51, 53-54, 59-
61, 63
distribution 39, 55
Seddon, S.A. 143
Segmented worms 170
Seismic surveys 60
Seitz, D.C. 311
*Select letters of Christopher
Columbus . . .* 300,
302
*Selection of historic
buildings of the
Bahamas* 264
Seminole Negroes
Andros Island 327-328
Bimini 328
*Settlements in New
Providence* 369
*7 hit sings of Nassau and
the Bahamas* 664
Sexuality 446, 454
*Shallow-water sponges of
the western Bahamas*
163
Sharks 158
Shattuck, G.B. 135
Shay, F. 310
Shedden, R.G. 429
Shells 134, 175
Abaco 362
Bimini 216
Cat Island 219
Little San Salvador 219
Mayaguana Island 220
*Shells at our feet: an
introduction to shelling
in the Bahamas* 175
Shepard, F.P. 47
Sherlock, P.M. 248, 251
Shilling, A.W. 588, 592
Shinn, E.A. 33, 48
Shipping
registry 540
statistics 555
Shopping 71-74, 76-77, 79
*Short history of the
Bahamas* 268
*Short history of the West
Indies* 248
Short stories 593-594, 603,

606, 633
Shreve, B. 223
Shrubs 143
Siebert, W.H. 325-326
Silent sentinels 269
Sightseeing 71
Simpich, F. 18
Simpson, Wallis Warfield
  see Windsor, Duchess of
Sisal 106, 134, 337, 358
Sketches of summerland,
  giving some account of
  Nassau and the
  Bahama Islands 107
Skits 601
Slaughter, F.G. 657
Slave trade
  Lucayans 228
Slavery 113, 327, 377-389
  abolition 380
  credit system 377
  emancipation 330, 380,
    388
  family 378, 387
  fertility 378, 387
  Great Exuma Island,
    Exuma 387
  health 378, 386
  Jamaica 387
  laws 381
  Loyalists 318, 326, 385
  Lucayans 228
  mortality 378
  occupations 378, 384
  population 378
  recaptives 379
  resistence 378-379, 383
  runaways 384
  sharecropping system
    382
  truck system 377
  Watlings Island 389
Slavery in the Bahamas,
  1648-1838 378
Slums 450
Smith, A.E. 451
Smith, C. Lavett 62, 176
Smith, Charles R. 313
Smith, E.T. 86
Smith, F.K. 78
Smith, L. 3
Smith, N. 624
Smith, O.M. 625-629
Smith, R.R. 138-141

Smith, S. 21
Smith, W. 262
Smoky Joe says: a volume
  in Bahamian dialect
  591
Snorkeling 73
Snow, E.R. 309
Snyder, N.F.R. 189
Social conditions 5, 125,
  442-468
  19th century 337
  Arawaks 246
  editorial cartoons 501
  Green Turtle Cay,
    Abaco 447
  Loyalist influences 326,
    385
Social development 513
Social insurance 442
  Barbados 442
  Jamaica 442
Social security 535, 542
Social services 10
Social statistics report, 1985
  579
Social values
  Abaco 463
Social welfare 535
Socialism 494
Society for the Propagation
  of the Gospel in
  Foreign Parts 432
Sociology 94, 96
Soils 22, 36, 135, 574
  bibliographies 701
Some aspects of fertility in
  New Providence 392
Song of the surreys 631
Songs 480, 664-666, 670
Sonnets of the Bahamas,
  with notes 615
South America
  fish 159
  flowers 148
  trees 148
South Caicos Island
  first landfall 292-293
South Carolina
  emigration to 551
Southern Public Library
  680
Spangler, L.L. 75
Spanish Wells, Eleuthera 9
  statistics 536

travel guides 89
Spence, Frank 421
Spiders 125
Sponges 23, 162-163, 178,
  181
Sponging 89, 106, 110, 337,
  345, 358, 564
Sponging industry 564
Sports 19, 66, 74, 77, 79
Spring Point, Acklins
  Island 233
Sprunt, Alexander 188
Squires, D.F. 177
Starfish 162
Stark, J.H. 108
Stars on the sea 650
Statistical abstract 581
Statistics 1, 5, 578-582
  agriculture 569
  economy 391, 524, 536
  education 391, 396
  employment 553
  exports 556
  Exuma 365
  fertility 391, 392
  housing 393
  imports 556
  income 396, 536, 553
  labour 396, 536, 553
  migration 396-397
  population 390-391, 393,
    396, 536
  shipping 555
  trade 556
Statute law of the Bahama
  Islands, 1799-1987; in
  force on the 30th June
  1987 521
Statute law of the Bahama
  Islands, 1799-1965 522
Statutes 519, 521
Stearns, R.P. 127, 132
Stephens, J.E. 435, 665
Stephens, W.M. 52, 173
Stevenson, C. St. J. 4
Stevenson, G. 144
Stirling, L. 630
Stocking Island, Exuma
  geology 34
Stokes, F.J. 159-160, 165
Storr, J.F. 53
Story of the Bahamas 265
Story-telling 385
Strangers no more:

anthropological studies of Cat Island, the Bahamas; report of an ethnographic research project conducted in 1977 453
Stratigraphy 32, 36-37
Andros Island 63
Strike (1958) 500
Stromatolites 36
Strong, A.C. 88
Struggle for freedom in the Bahamas 492
Submarine geology of the Tongue of the Ocean, Bahamas 55
Subsidiary legislation of the Bahama Islands, 1799-1965; in force on the 1st August 1965 522
Sullivan, S.O. 229
Sun makes it red 621
Sun 'n sixpence: a guide to Nassau and the Bahama Out Islands 85
Superstitions 2, 436
Supplement to the Guide to the records of the Commonwealth of the Bahamas 684, 687
Survive, man! or perish: sculptural metaphors to command allegience to life, resistence to race suicide, with The art of survival: a critique of the survivalist art and philosophy of Randolph W. Johnston 662
Symonette, Michael A. 266, 490
Symonette, Michael Carrington 423

T

Talkington, M. 662
Taviani, P.E. 277
Tax and investment profile: Bahamas 537

Taxation 527, 532, 537, 541-542, 545, 557
Taylor, Henry Milton 487
Taylor, M. 595
Taylor, T.E. 336
Teach, Edward 309-311
folklore 409
poetry 602
Technology
20th century 339
Teeter, J.W. 36, 39
Temperature 21, 110
water 39, 53, 62
Ten, ten the Bible ten: obeah in the Bahamas 436
Tertullien, J.E. 394
Tertullien, M.C. 404, 455
Them: a play in one act 623
Thompson, A.A. 529
Thompson, J.K. 365
Thorn, P. 546
Thoughts in black and white: a collection of poetry 617
Three adventures: Galapagos, Titicaca, the blue holes 28
Thunderball 643
Tides 24, 26, 43, 50
Toasts 410
Tomorrow is today's dream 604
Tongue of the Ocean 45, 47, 51, 55, 61, 176
atlases 50
Took, I.F. 161
Tools
Lucayans 239
Topographic, hydrographic and sedimentologic setting of Little Lake, San Salvador Island, Bahamas 39
Topography 1, 23, 39, 44, 69
karst 32, 38
Topology 50
Touche Ross International 537
Tour through the British West Indies, in the years 1802 and 1803, giving a particular

account of the Bahama Islands 113
Tourism 7, 10, 16-17, 117-122
19th century 329
20th century 345, 354, 507, 523-524, 526, 528, 530-533, 535, 540, 552, 574
Abaco 122
and organized crime 444
and sandflies 209
Andros 122
Bermuda 121
Bimini 122
Caribbean 117
Eleuthera 122
Exuma 122
Freeport 122
Great Inagua 122
Green Turtle Cay, Abaco 447, 456
history 120
Jamaica 117
New Providence 122
St. Lucia 117
statistics 120
Tourism in the Bahamas and Bermuda: two case studies 121
Tourism in the Caribbean 117
Tours 77, 79
Townsend, P.S. 479
Trade 10, 19, 549-567
19th century 324, 333
20th century 526, 528
statistics 556
Trade unions 498
Trainor, J.M. 330
Transportation 71, 530
Exuma 365
Travel guides 66-99
Abaco 75, 80
accommodation 71-72, 74, 76-77, 79, 94
air travel 67
Andros 80
Bermuda 71-72, 77
Bimini 80
Cable Beach 95
Caribbean 69, 72
currency 73
Eleuthera 80, 89

Exuma 88, 91, 365
Florida Keys 75
Freeport/Lucaya 92-93, 368
Grand Bahama Island 70, 75, 79-80, 92-93
Great Bahama Bank 88
Harbour Island 89
Hope Town 89, 358
Nassau 66, 79, 85, 89, 94-95, 97-99
New Providence 70, 73, 80, 94-99
nightlife 72, 74, 77
Out Islands 68, 77, 85
Paradise Island 95
restaurants 71-72, 74, 76-77, 79, 94
shopping 71-74, 76-77, 79
sightseeing 71
Spanish Wells 89
tours 77, 79
transportation 71
Turks and Caicos Islands 83, 85, 90
Travellers' accounts 100-116
18th century 114-116
19th century 107-113
20th century 100-106
Travels in the Confederation, 1783-1784 114
Treasure Cay, Abaco history 360
Tree, I. 596
Trees 114, 142-144, 148, 480
Trevett, John 313
Tribune story 688-689, 691
Tropical blossoms 148
Tropical marine fishes of southern Florida and the Bahama Islands 167
Tropical marine invertebrates of southern Florida and the Bahama Islands 170
True, true Bahamian recipes 674
Trust companies 538, 552

Truth about Freeport/Lucaya 368
Tryin' to make it: adapting to the Bahamas 448
Turks and Caicos Islands 11, 58
first landfall 277
flora 142
travel guides 83, 85, 90
Turner, T. 593-594, 631-632
Turnquest, H. 502
20,000 leagues under the sea 129
Twenty years under the sea 129
Two Bahamian novels 607

U

Uber die wurzelm der tainischen kultur 246
UBP
see United Bahamian Party
Under the black flag 311
Under the sea with helmet and camera: experiences of an amateur 131
Unicorn in the Bahamas 102
Union status and fertility 391
United Bahamian Party (UBP) 499, 506, 566
United Empire Loyalists
see Loyalists
United States
Civil War 89, 331-336
Prohibition 342, 345
relations with the Bahamas 261, 335, 475-476, 493, 499
relations with the Caribbean 528
Revolution 313-316
fiction 650
United States. Congress. House of Representatives. Committee on Foreign Affairs 476

U.S. narcotics interdiction programs in the Bahamas 476
United States. Naval Oceanographic Office 50
Upon these rocks: Catholics in the Bahamas 427
Upper Bogue, Eleuthera 9
Ups and downs in a West Indian diocese 429
Upturned turtles: a Bahamian story 630
Urban planning 576

V

Van de Water, F.F. 342
Van Der Valk, H.M.H.A. 531
Vane, Charles 311
Vanguard Nationalist and Socialist Party of the Bahamas 492
Vaurie, C. 197
Vegetation 22, 135, 138-157, 184, 574
Bimini 149
Cat Island 124
East Plana Cay 126
Galapagos Islands 124
Hawaii 124
San Salvador 140-141
Vegetation of North Point, San Salvador Island, Bahamas 140
Venables, Addington Robert Peel 433
Venezuela 228
Verhoog, P.H.G. 282, 290-293
Verne, J. 129
Vertebrate fauna and the vegetation of East Plana Cay, Bahama Islands 126
Vital Statistics Report 582
Vocational training 535
Voodoo
bibliographies 439
Haiti 439

Voodoos and obeahs:
phases of West Indian
witchcraft 439
Voyage into the sunset 622

W

Wages 535, 557
Waitzkin, B. 474
Wakefield, A.J. 571
Wallace, S.J. 619, 633-635
Water
chemistry 43
depth 39, 73, 83
physical properties 50
salinity 39, 53, 62
temperature 39, 53, 62
Waterproof guide to corals
and fishes of Florida,
the Bahamas and the
Caribbean 164
Watling Island 135
birds 190
first landfall 277, 280,
282, 288, 290, 294-296,
300-302
flora 152
riddles 411
slavery 389
Waves 50
Weather 43, 68
Weech, D.J. 636
Wesleyan-Methodist
Church 431
West Indian immigrants
400
West Indian Regiment 338

West Indies
birds 186
history 248, 250-253
obeah 441
West Indies 251
West Indies and Caribbean
year book 10
West Plana Cay 126
Westgate, V. 91
Wetmore, A. 202
What the UBP has done for
you 506
White, V. 376
Whitings 33
Whittell, P. 469
Whittier, S. 2
Who killed Sir Harry
Oakes? 353
Who's who in the Bahamas
government, 1953-1978
497
Wiedenmayer, F. 163
Wilder, R. 658-659
Wilensky, J.M. 68, 80
Williams, Cindy 675
Williams, Colbert V. 583
Williams, E. 249
Williams, J.J. 439
Williams, M. 637-638
Williams, P.M. 370, 381
Williams, Prince 421
Williamson, John Ernest
129
Wilson City, Abaco 357
Wind from the Carolinas
659
Winds 21
Windsor, Duchess of 346-
347

Windsor, Duke of 345-347
Winter in paradise 104
Witches and fishes 438
Woman take two 632
Women 459
Cat Island 453
Woodbury, G. 308
Woodes Rogers, privateer
and governor 312
Woolley, F. 676
World Bank 524
Worthy Park, Jamaica 387
Wrecking 89, 114, 276,
329, 358, 567
Wright, James Martin 567
Wright, Jerome Wendell
452
see also Lurry-Wright,
J.W.

Y

Yachtsman's guide to the
Bahamas 68, 84, 87
Yoruba tribe 372
You should know your
government 509
Young, E. 364
Young, R.N. 22

Z

Zahl, P.A. 198, 200-201
Zeiller, W. 167, 170

Map of the Bahamas

This map shows the more important islands, towns and other features.

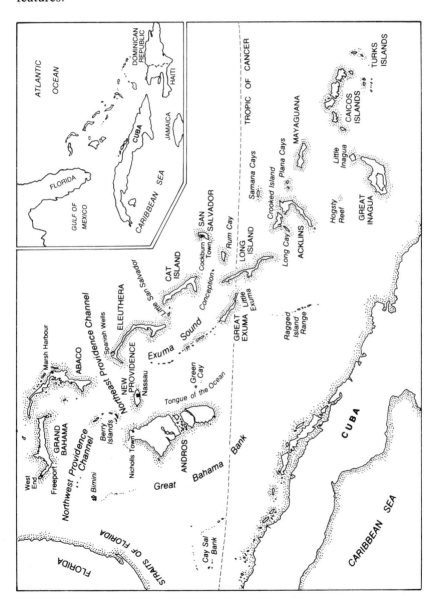